AFTER THE PARIS ATTACKS

Responses in Canada, Europe, and around the Globe

The violent attacks on journalists at *Charlie Hebdo* and shoppers in a Jewish supermarket in Paris in January 2015 raise important questions concerning security, terrorism, and the role of the media in fostering public debate about multiculturalism and freedom of expression.

After the Paris Attacks brings together a group of leading scholars, journalists, and political observers to explore how the world reacted to these events and to examine what opportunities exist for a saner and safer future. This timely, interdisciplinary volume presents perspectives from experts in fields such as law, political science, philosophy, and international relations, as well as from the media, offering penetrating insights into how the world can and should respond to the challenge of recent events.

EDWARD M. IACOBUCCI is the Dean and James M. Tory Professor of Law at the Faculty of Law at the University of Toronto.

STEPHEN J. TOOPE is the Director of the Munk School of Global Affairs at the University of Toronto.

After the Paris Attacks

Responses in Canada, Europe, and around the Globe

EDITED BY EDWARD M. IACOBUCCI AND
STEPHEN J. TOOPE

UNIVERSITY OF TORONTO PRESS
Toronto Buffalo London

© University of Toronto Press 2015
Toronto Buffalo London
www.utppublishing.com
Printed in the U.S.A.

ISBN 978-1-4426-3000-0 (cloth)
ISBN 978-1-4426-3001-7 (paper)

Printed on acid-free paper.

Publication cataloguing information is available from Library and
Archives Canada.

University of Toronto Press acknowledges the financial assistance to its
publishing program of the Canada Council for the Arts and the Ontario
Arts Council, an agency of the Government of Ontario.

**Canada Council   Conseil des Arts
for the Arts   du Canada**

ONTARIO ARTS COUNCIL
CONSEIL DES ARTS DE L'ONTARIO

an Ontario government agency
un organisme du gouvernement de l'Ontario

University of Toronto Press acknowledges the financial support of the
Government of Canada through the Canada Book Fund for its publishing
activities.

Contents

Preface

EDWARD M. IACOBUCCI AND STEPHEN J. TOOPE

This volume reflects the wide-ranging and fascinating contributions of presenters at a one-day conference entitled "After the Paris Attacks: Responses in Canada, Europe, and around the Globe," held on March 9, 2015, at the University of Toronto. A range of questions raised by the attacks in Paris in January 2015 was addressed by a variety of experts, predominantly but not exclusively from the University of Toronto. Presenters were also asked to prepare brief written reflections offering their perspective on some aspect or aspects of the attacks, whether for Canada, France, Europe, or globally. As organizers of this event, we could not have been more impressed by the thought and care that the presenters put into their remarks on the day, and into the chapters of this volume.

Some commentators at the conference and in this volume challenged the premise that the Paris attacks were themselves worthy of special attention. Why not study more devastating attacks either in Europe, such as the murderous rampage of Anders Breivik in Norway, or elsewhere? We leave it to the commentary in this volume to discuss this important question, both explicitly and implicitly. Here we note that there is a second, potentially contestable premise embedded in the structure of the conference. The conference and this volume are intentionally multidisciplinary. We have contributors from law, politics, religious studies, history, sociology, philosophy, and the media. This reflects our view that illumination of the causes and consequences of events like those in Paris requires attention to a wide range of perspectives and disciplines. Understanding the events cannot focus only on politics, or only on religion, for example. Reactions to the events cannot rely solely on law, say, or solely on enhanced security institutions. The attacks raise complex questions, and a wide lens is required for perspective. The collaboration between the Faculty of Law and the Munk School of Global Affairs, University of Toronto, in organizing the conference, and in turn our invitation to colleagues across campus and elsewhere, reflect this emphasis.

We acknowledge that with the conference and this book, we are borrowing the idea of swiftly assembling a range of experts and their writings in a timely volume. Dean (as he then was) Ron Daniels of the Faculty of Law, University of Toronto, admirably conceived of such a combination following the September 11, 2001, attacks in New York City. That event focused on the legal reactions to 9/11 in Canada, specifically focusing on Bill C-36. While the "After Paris" conference and this volume have many important things to say about the latest reaction of Parliament to terror attacks in Bill C-51, this volume was designed to broaden the perspective, shedding light not only on legal responses standing alone, but also on social, political, and cultural responses; moreover, each of these responses is situated within a broader context. We hoped that the event would enrich understanding of any given set of reactions – legal reactions, to take one example – by placing them within a broader landscape. We are gratified that the contributions of the various writers have enabled us to do just that.

Thank you to the teams at the Faculty of Law and at the Munk School of Global Affairs, University of Toronto, for putting the conference together and publicizing it with such skill and on such short order. Thanks to the University of Toronto Press for being willing partners in what is a lightning-quick operation by academic publishing standards. Our organizing committee of Jutta Brunnée, Ron Levi, Arthur Ripstein, and Kent Roach was most helpful in conceptualizing the conference, for which we are grateful. Thanks finally to our presenters and authors for putting such powerful reflections together so quickly. We are fortunate to have worked with such wonderful partners and colleagues.

PART ONE

Religion, Culture, and Pluralism

1 After Paris: Liberalism, Free Speech, Religion, and Immigration in Europe

RANDALL HANSEN

On January 7, 2015, two terrorists, Saïd and Chérif Kouachi, entered the offices of a weekly Parisian satirical magazine, *Charlie Hebdo.* They shot twenty-two people, killing eleven, and during the escape executed a prostrate (Muslim) police officer. The same day, Amedy Coulibaly shot and wounded a thirty-two-year-old jogger, and fatally shot a police officer and a street sweeper. Two days later, Coulibaly entered a kosher supermarket and killed four Jews. French police stormed the building, killing Coulibaly. The Kouachi brothers were killed by similar police action in a separate hostage siege.

As in Madrid in 2004, Amsterdam (following an Islamist's murder of Theo van Gogh) in the same year, London in 2005, and Boston in 2013, academics and commentators rushed to judgment. For Fox News and conservative commentators such as Mark Steyn and Richard Dawkins, the cause is Islam, which is inherently more violent than other religions. For the *Toronto Star, Guardian,* and left-wing commentators such as Haroon Siddiqui, the causes lie in Western Islamophobia and the West's war against Muslims. For many in the middle, alienation and poverty among (particularly Europe's) Muslim communities is the root cause. Finally, for many commentators in this country, the solution to Europe's problems is that Europeans should become a bit more Canadian by fully embracing immigration and multiculturalism.

None of these explanations is satisfactory; indeed, they are all wrong. On the first, violent Muslims are a tiny minority of global Muslims; in Europe, millions of Muslims lead quiet and productive, if often not prosperous, lives. Moreover, if Islam were any predictor of violence or social conflict, Islamist attacks would, in the light of the number of Muslims in Europe, be common. They are, of course, very rare. Deprivation and alienation may motivate some individuals, but they are not a general explanation for extremist violence: the London bombers and van Gogh's murderer were not from especially deprived backgrounds; three of the four were educated at the post-secondary level, and all were relatively affluent. Multiple thwarted Islamist attacks involved middle-class, educated aspiring terrorists. Even if all Islamists were poor, the syllogism to the effect that (a) "most Muslims are poor," (b) "Muslims commit terrorist acts," and therefore (c) "Muslims commit terrorist acts because they are poor" would be no more convincing than claiming that (a) "terrorists are Muslim" and (b) therefore "terrorists engage in terrorism because they are Muslim." Strangely, those who reject the second argument gladly endorse the first, and vice versa.

To the other explanations, increased Islamophobia followed rather than preceded Islamist attacks. The invasion of "Muslim lands" (a strangely Orientalist construction by the political left) also post-dated September 11, 2001, and in the case of Iraq did not involve France, which, along with Germany, bitterly opposed the invasion. Finally, Canadian exhortations are well meant, if rather sanctimonious, but irrelevant: a country that creams off the world's most educated and skilled migrants is in a poor position to lecture other countries on how to cope with their very different migration patterns.

It is often easier to determine what something isn't than what it is – in this case, what does not cause violence rather than what does. My aim here is not to provide a definitive statement on the complex causes of Islamist violence, which are likely varied and specific to the individuals (some of whom may simply be deranged). Rather, I want to use this chapter to outline my views on how Europe should respond to Paris and similar events. It is divided into two broad sections: an empirical overview of immigration in Europe, followed by a more prescriptive section in which I outline several suggestions for managing immigration and diversity in the aftermath of *Charlie Hebdo*.

Immigrants in Europe

Following three waves of migration – colonial and guest-worker from the 1950s to the 1970s, family migration from the 1970s, and asylum-seekers from the 1980s – all European countries have become immigration countries. Measured as a percentage of the population that is foreign born, immigrants make up 5.3 per cent of the German population;

3.9 per cent of the British; and 3.8 per cent of the French (Eurostat 2012). Naturally, these figures do not include the naturalized and citizens by birth, so Germany's historically restrictive citizenship regime artificially increases foreign population.

Looking at the broad sociological sweep, European migrant populations are characterized by two features: a diversity of national, ethnic, and religious backgrounds and an homogeneity of class structures. France's migrant and migrant-descended population is chiefly from North Africa; Germany's chiefly from Turkey, the Balkans, and southern Europe; and Britain's from the West Indies and South Asia. Migrants to Europe are Hindu, Muslim, Christian, and Sikh.

Despite this varied background, the vast majority of immigrants to Europe were unskilled (or, in contemporary politically acceptable language, low-skilled) workers or peasants, and they were incorporated into industrial Europe's working classes: as transport workers in London, textile workers in Lancaster, miners in the Ruhr, and so on. As their family members with a similar class background joined them, and as asylum-seekers were also overwhelmingly low-skilled, all European nations have, in immigration-studies parlance, negatively selected migrants. Canada and Australia, by contrast, have, since the introduction of points systems from the late 1960s, positively selected immigrants, by rewarding education, skills, and relevant work experience.

Similarly, whereas Muslim communities in Europe are predominantly poorly educated and low-skilled, they are in Canada and above all the United States educated and high-earning. The relatively few success stories among immigrant groups in Europe – Indians in the United Kingdom and Germany, Chinese in the United Kingdom, and the Vietnamese in Germany – are found among groups with either high skill sets (Ugandan Asians in the United Kingdom, for instance) and/or the respect for education and a willingness to demand the hard, often gruelling, work from children that is a prerequisite to academic success. Thus, fully 59 per cent of Vietnamese Germans' children go on to selective high schools (*Gymnasien*) (compared with 40 per cent for the population overall), and 70 per cent of Chinese Britons secure five good high school grades (GCSEs) (Peters 2011; BBC 2007). Strikingly, British Chinese results held up regardless of class: poor Chinese students do almost as well as rich ones, whereas poor white British do far worse than their wealthy counterparts (BBC 2014). Naturally, a few individuals from every group, as from every social class, are great successes, but we are speaking of aggregates here.

Against this background of low skills and educational achievements, unemployment among migrants in Europe has been high, relative to the average employment levels. Whereas relative unemployment rates (the ethnic minority unemployment rate divided by the overall unemployment rate) in the United States, Australia, and Canada are close to or less than 1.0 (meaning that immigrants are employed as much as or more than citizens overall), they range from 1.5 in Britain to 2.75 in Switzerland. Although there are no published statistics on the matter, since youth unemployment is extremely high in parts of Europe (France, Italy, Portugal, Greece, and Spain), it is a reasonable assumption that it is as high, and likely higher still, among migrant youth.

The causes of ethnic-minority unemployment are complex. The intuitively obvious factor – racism – certainly plays a role. A recent study in France confirmed, as earlier studies in North America had done, that applicants with Muslim-sounding names are less likely to secure an interview than those with Christian ones (Adida, Laitin, and Valfort 2010). There are, nonetheless, several reasons to doubt that racism is the most important variable accounting for high ethnic-minority unemployment. First, unemployment was far lower when racism was far more severe in the 1950s and 1960s. Second, a racism-based account could not explain why certain groups do very well – Indian Hindus and Muslims – while others – Pakistani Muslims – do poorly, despite sharing the same ethnicity. Presumably racists, if they are able to distinguish them at all, are no fonder of Indians than they are of Pakistanis.

These conditions – large and modestly growing ethnic minority populations, including many Muslims, in Britain, France, and Germany; negatively selective immigration policies in these countries; and relatively high unemployment among ethnic minorities in Europe – obtained before the post-2000 increase in extremist terrorism. Three developments followed the 2001 terrorist attacks on the United States and the 2003 invasion of Iraq. The first was an upsurge in anti-Islamic sentiment, and a mobilization by some political parties and individual politicians around the putative threat posed by Islam to Europe and European values. The second was an attendant upsurge in anti-Semitism across Europe, including physical attacks on Jews. And the third development, which is directly relevant to what happened in Paris in January 2015, is an attack by an unholy alliance of religious extremists and progressive thinkers on the principles of free speech.

Islamophobia is a disputed concept, denied by the political right (or, worse still, justified as a logical response to Muslim behaviour) and exaggerated by the political left. As ever, clarity is found in the numbers. Survey data indeed show that Europeans view Islam with greater hostility than Judaism or Christianity, but this hostility remains confined to a minority of north Europeans (Reitz paper under review). Moreover, other surveys, conducted after 9/11 and the Madrid/London bombings, show very positive attitudes towards Muslims among French and British nationals (though not German or Italian ones) (Hansen 2011; Maxwell and Bleich 2014).

Surveys do not, however, tell the full story, and political discourse constraints have relaxed to the point where politicians will blithely make sweeping comments about Muslims that would not be politically tolerable in the case of Jews. This is seen most clearly in the case of the far right (Geert Wilders in the Netherlands, Marine Le Pen in France), but it is also the case with some mainstream commentators and politicians. The successful "Eurabia" literature both exaggerated the demographic effects of Muslim migration and fertility and constructed Islam as a foreign religion (a construction mystifying to anyone with even an inkling of Habsburg and southeastern European history). And when Thilo Sarrazin, a centrist Social Democratic politician and former finance minister of Berlin, wrote a bestselling book on the subject, he became the darling of the talk-show circuit (though he also received much criticism on it) and made a fortune on the basis of highly derogatory comments about Muslims.

Anti-Semitism in Europe has increased in tandem with Islamophobia. In the Paris attacks, five Jews were killed because they were Jews. For years, national authorities have reported increased anti-Semitic incidents such as the vandalizing of Jewish graveyards and synagogues, and assaults on Jews wearing religious dress. In July 2014, a group of what appeared to be North African men tried to launch what can only be described as a modern pogrom, including an effort to ransack a synagogue, in the Parisian suburb of Sarcelles. The case was not an isolated one: the evidence is not systematic, but Muslims, and above all young Muslim men, appear to be overrepresented among those committing anti-Semitic attacks.

The third development, an assault on free speech principles, has a longer pedigree, and it began with the Rushdie Affair of 1989. The basic events replayed themselves, naturally with some variation, during the Danish cartoon controversy of 2006 and following the *Charlie Hebdo* attack of 2015. In all three instances, artists produced works deemed offensive to Islam by some adherents. Protests, threats (including Iran's support for Rushdie's murder from 1989 to 1998), and violence followed. Secular commentators split into basically two camps: those who offered robust defences of free speech, including the right to offend, and those who argued that, although they in principle supported free speech, artists and intellectuals should avoid offending Muslims.

Where to Go from Here

European policymakers thus face three challenges: rising Islamophobia, rising anti-Semitism, and an assault on free speech. Many would dispute this formulation and see only one or two of them as real problems. Necessarily oversimplifying, the right downplays Islamophobia and emphasizes anti-Semitism and threats to free speech, whereas the left emphasizes Islamophobia while downplaying threats to free speech and, to a lesser degree, anti-Semitism. However, all three are real, and they require a common response: a robust assault on extremism.

In the case of Islamophobia and anti-Semitism, a legal and a rhetorical response is required. In the former, and this is easy part, current legal prohibitions on anti-Jewish and anti-Muslim discrimination should be robustly applied (and should be seen to be applied). In the latter, those who argue that Islam is a foreign import incompatible with European values – far-right politicians, commentators such as Bruce Bawer, Mark Steyn, and Christopher Caldwell – must be challenged vigorously. The arguments are known and well-rehearsed, but they need to be repeated: acts of violence are committed by a tiny minority, and we are too inclined in the case of Muslims to associate such violence with the faith itself or with all its believers. By contrast, when Jews or Christians commit acts of violence, we instinctively regard them as "nuts" who are unrepresentative of their faith.[1]

Few people believe that Christian fundamentalists shouting "God hates fags" or Orthodox Jews attacking Palestinian property and hacking down olive trees speak, respectively, for Christianity and Judaism. When the French socialist government published a bill allowing gay marriage (it eventually passed), the most vehement protests came not from French Muslims but from Roman Catholics, who poured into Paris from the provinces to show, often with homophobic placards, their

---

1 A conversation with Erik Bleich clarified this point.

opposition.[2] Few thought that they spoke for all Christians, or even all Catholics. Finally, following what we know from contact theory, the more interfaith interactions (including, importantly, those between believers and non-believers) that can be fostered, the less prejudice we will see. Against this background, moves by governments in Europe to ban the hijab in schools and the burka on the street, though perhaps grounded in concerns for gender equality with which one can sympathize, have been deeply unhelpful and have further encouraged the view that Islam is unwelcome in Europe.

In the current landscape, there are causes for both optimism and pessimism. In the former, efforts by far-right elements in Saxony to form a pan-European anti-Islamic movement, Patriotic Europeans against the Islamicization of the West (PEGIDA), have fizzled, and within Germany itself the "movement" resulted in what a former chancellor called an "uprising of the decent": counter-demonstrations soon outnumbered PEGIDA in Cologne and Berlin. Where there is contact between different groups – in Muslim/gay neighbourhoods such as Berlin's Kreuzberg – inter-group violence and outward hostility are low. Less optimistically, a majority of Italians (63 per cent), Greeks (53 per cent), Poles (50 per cent), and substantial minorities of Spanish (46 per cent), Germans (33 per cent), French (27 per cent), and British (26 per cent) expressed a "negative opinion of the Muslims who live in their country" (Pew 2014). It is noteworthy in the light of the Parisian attacks that attitudes are best in France, the country with the largest number of Muslims: fully 72 per cent of those surveyed expressed a favourable attitude towards Muslims (versus 64 per cent in Britain, 58 per cent in Germany, and 28 per cent in Italy) (Pew 2014).

The final challenge concerns free speech. In the aftermath of (and the lead up to) the attacks, as in the aftermath of the Rushdie and Danish cartoon affairs, substantial sections of opinion, Islamic and non-Islamic, have held that the publications of caricatures of the Islamic Prophet Muhammad go beyond the viable limits of free speech. This is simply absurd. The right to mock religion, any religion, is so within the bounds of acceptable speech that the fact that there is a debate at all is mystifying. Religious requirements apply to followers of the religion and to

---

2 I owe this observation to Isham Rekiouak, an undergraduate student at the University of Toronto.

no one else; to suggest otherwise is to imply that non-Muslims should internalize Islamic rules. This principle has, however, to apply to everyone: there cannot be restrictions on free speech for one religion and an open season in matters of free speech for another. For this reason, existing blasphemy laws in Germany, the United Kingdom, and (at a local level) in France, are an affront to the principle and understandably encourage the view among some Muslims that Europeans operate a double standard in matters of free speech. In this regard, the arrest by French authorities of a virulently anti-Semitic comedian Dieudonné M'bala M'bala was – however offensive his views – unwise.

And what of offence? To be sure, publishing crude caricatures of the Prophet is disrespectful and offensive. Respect, however, is a matter of choice and cannot be mandated: no one has to respect anyone, and many believe that all religions are unworthy of respect. Pious Muslims certainly do not respect philanderers, men who enjoy the delights of gay saunas, or women who like a drink.[3]

The last point raises a further issue. Islam is a large and highly diverse religion; prohibitions of portrayals of the Prophet apply only to Sunni and not to Shia Muslims, and the most religious among them will take the requirement most seriously. All things being equal, the most conservative and orthodox members of any religion are those who will adopt the most literal and uncompromising (and often selective) views of religious texts: compare attitudes towards the Bible among Church of England followers in north London with Pentecostals in the southern United States. And what this in turn means is that those most demanding of respect and religious accommodation are least likely to extend it towards others such as gays and lesbians. That academics and liberal commentators would align themselves with such an illiberal lot is mystifying.

A deferential approach to religious conservatism is also deeply condescending, above all to moderate Muslims, as it suggests that they are somehow not quite as good as the rest of us and need the sort of "pass" that the liberal academy was unprepared, rightly so, to accord Christian fundamentalists who demanded revisions to the American education curriculum in the 1980s. No less a thinker than the political philosopher Charles Taylor has confidently stated that Muslims cannot understand the distinction between religion and politics (Taylor and Gutman 1994, 62). It is hard to imagine a more patronizing statement.

---

3 A conversation with Christian Joppke clarified this point.

No Culture, Just Cash

Over the last decade, discussions of migration have been discussions of culture and identity, with a particularly bitter debate about Muslim women's religious clothing: the hijab, the burqa, and the niqab. The participants have thrown around accusations of racism, Islamophobia, and misogyny, and all except theologians have declared themselves experts on Islam and its requirements. The debate has been exciting, passionate, and largely pointless, for it has ignored the fundamental problem, which is not culture but cash: the low educational attainments, low earnings, and high structural unemployment among most of Europe's ethnic minorities. The key point here is work: in the absence of work, there is no hope of professional advancement and little hope of personal dignity and autonomy.

There are naturally different ways to move people into work. At the bottom end of the scale, income assistance can be reduced with an eye to nudging people into work. Unsurprisingly, such suggestions provoke the ire of progressive scholars. There are nonetheless good reasons for thinking that badly paid work, above all if it is transitional, is better than no work. But most will agree that maximizing both the number of well-paid jobs and minority access to those jobs should be the primary goal. Achieving this aim is at once simple and extraordinarily difficult. It is simple because there is a consensus that the prerequisite for access to better jobs and higher income (as well as higher labour productivity and overall societal wealth) is education and skills training. Better schools, colleges, and universities, more access to them for minorities, and higher educational achievement will translate into more employment and better earnings. In countries such as Germany and Austria, where much training is organized through apprenticeships supplied by employers, expanded access to these opportunities will deliver the same results. These countries, along with Switzerland, actually have a particular advantage in that they have a still-intact industrial base (unlike the United Kingdom, for instance), and thus job opportunities for skilled workers who would not secure places at universities (and who often have no interest in them).

At the same time, this recipe for success is extraordinarily difficult because training and education are expensive, and governments everywhere are more likely to put funds into social programs that benefit the old (health, pensions) than training and education for the young. In addition, success in education requires extraordinarily hard work, and much of the initiative will have to come from ethnic minorities themselves. The school system can, of course, do much, through concentrated resources on local language training, closing bad schools in poor neighbourhoods, and redistributing students to better schools. It can also provide diversity training to teachers who, out of ignorance, might otherwise stream minority students away from academic programs (there is anecdotal evidence of this sort of dynamic in Germany).

It would be glib to suggest that a short chapter could identify, much less resolve, all these challenges, but the central lesson is clear: the conversation about immigration and integration in Europe must be shifted away from identity, religion, and culture and refocused on education, skills, and work. As I have argued for years to anyone who will listen, immigration works when immigrants work.

REFERENCES

Adida, Claire, David Laitin, and Marie-Anne Valfort. 2010. *Les Français musulmans sont-ils discriminés dans leur propre pays ? Une étude expérimentale sur le marché du travail Paris*. Paris: French-American Foundation and Sciences Po.

BBC. 2007. "Black Pupils' Attainment Improves," November 27, http://news .bbc.co.uk/2/hi/uk_news/education/7114772.stm.

Eurostat. 2012. "Foreign Citizens and Foreign-Born Population," July 11 (2011 data).

Hansen, Randall. 2011. "The Two Faces of Liberalism: Islam in Contemporary Europe." *Journal of Ethnic and Migration Studies* 37 (6), 881–97.

Maxwell, Rahsaan, and Erik Bleich. 2014. "What Makes Muslims Feel French." *Social Forces* 93 (1), 155–79.

Peters, Freia. 2011. "Die besten deutschen Schüler stammen aus Vietnam." *Die Welt*, February 6.

Pew Research Center. 2014. "Global Attitudes and Trends," May 12, 2014, http://www.pewglobal.org/2014/05/12/chapter-4-views-of-roma-muslims-jews/.

Reitz, Jeffrey. (Paper under review). "National Models and Public Receptivity to Immigrants in Europe and North America: France, Canada and Quebec in Comparative Perspective."

Taylor, Charles, and Amy Gutman. 1994. *Multiculturalism and the Politics of Recognition*. Princeton: Princeton University Press.

2 Free Speech and Civility in Pluralist Societies

SIMONE CHAMBERS

The Paris attacks have raised many troubling questions and produced much soul-searching. In the immediate aftermath of the massacre, there was a powerful reaction of solidarity with the murdered cartoonists in France and across Europe and North America that was captured by the slogan "Je suis Charlie." But in the days that followed and as analysis and debate replaced shock and anger, a counter-slogan began to appear in the blogosphere and in editorials and commentary: "Je ne suis pas Charlie." Some have seen the divide between these groups as an argument about free speech. But it seems to me that this is not what the debate is about. "Je suis Charlie" certainly defended the right to freedom of speech. "Je ne suis pas Charlie" did not challenge this right but rather defended the value of civility. Free speech and civility do not have to be at odds, or at least this is what I will argue in this short chapter.

A right to free speech is the appropriate principle to defend in the face of anti-liberal radical Islamicists. Most French Muslims are not anti-liberal radical Islamists. Civility is the appropriate principle to defend if the goal is an integrated pluralism in which Muslim minorities feel at home, or at least not threatened. Creating the conditions of civility conducive to this type of integrated pluralism does not involve a limitation of free speech. On the contrary, I argue that civility depends on a full exercise of free speech, especially critical speech. The more *Charlie Hebdo* is publicly criticized (not silenced), the less power *Charlie Hebdo*'s images have to offend and alienate. This in turn brings down the incivility register within the public sphere.

Free Speech and Civility

Charlie Hebdo is a controversial publication. Its content came under criticism long before the Paris attacks. Not just criticism, as *Charlie Hebdo* has seen forty-eight court challenges in the past twenty-two years (*Le Monde* 2015; Style 2015). Most of these challenges have been personal defamation cases, but some have been accusations of hate speech in which those bringing the suits have tried to argue that religious insult is a form of hate speech. *Charlie Hebdo* has been successful, for the most part, in arguing that ridiculing religion in a way that offends a certain group is not the same as promoting hatred and contempt for that group. In the course of these trials, and indeed in its public persona, *Charlie Hebdo* admits that it offends. This is not a controversial point. Everyone agrees, including *Charlie Hebdo,* that its form of satire is offensive, rude, and scurrilous. In addition to public criticism about the general low level and tone of its political commentary, *Charlie Hebdo* also has come under criticism for singling out Islam for more persistent ridicule than other religions. One reason cited for this difference is that Muslims are more likely to take offence, and Charlie Hebdo's raison d'être is to shock and offend, or more charitably, to take down "sacred cows."[1] But the legitimate and acceptable public criticism of *Charlie Hebdo* as offensive was taking place alongside illegitimate and unacceptable threats and violence directed at the publication, including a fire bombing in 2011. Under these conditions, some defenders of *Charlie Hebdo*'s right to freedom of speech mistakenly interpreted the public criticism of its ethics as a failure to stand against these threats. But this confuses calls for civility with calls for a limitation on free speech.

Free speech is, first and foremost, a legal concept having to do with rights and infringements. France has quite strict laws against hate speech. So one debate that we might want to have is whether the courts have been correct in generally seeing *Charlie Hebdo* as protected speech and not hate speech. Or we might want to argue that the present hate speech legislation should be expanded to include religious insult. Such a debate would indeed be about free speech. And although some have

---

1 The philosopher Daniel Weinstock argued in a blog post devoted to this issue that the form of *Charlie Hebdo*'s message, shocking and offensive images, is "inextricably tied to its content." They could not say what they wanted to say in "more stolid prose" (Weinstock 2015).

argued for this expansion of hate speech regulation, many more, and certainly the majority of the "Je ne suis pas Charlie" camp that I am familiar with, have not argued for any additional legal limitation upon *Charlie Hebdo*. The debate is not about the *right* to offend, which is largely unquestioned, but about the ethical choice to offend.

Freedom of speech is about the limitation or restriction of speech. Laws can restrict speech, but so can citizens in forms of direct action. "Shouting down" or forcing the cancellation of a public speech are common protest tactics that can be interpreted as silencing and so a limitation on free speech. While it is true that some forms of criticism can "effectively" silence people if the speaker is in a power relationship vis-à-vis the recipient of the criticism, criticism does not necessarily silence and is qualitatively different from legal restriction as well as actual silencing. I develop the role of differential power with regard to civility at the end of this chapter. Now I want to highlight that it is possible to make a clear distinction between free speech as a right that may be violated in various ways, and civil speech as an expectation that speakers may fail to meet in various ways. Jocelyn Maclure, writing in *L'actualité*, echoes the main sentiment in "Je ne suis pas Charlie" when he says, "The publication of the cartoons is legally defensible but ethically deplorable. Just because one has the right to publish something does not mean that one ought to publish it" (Maclure 2015). The ethical principle that Maclure is appealing to is something like civility.

Civility, unlike the freedom of speech, is not about legal limits or infringements. Standards of civility (and every public sphere has such standards) are informal standards of appropriateness that are administered, if you will, through the twin mechanisms of self-restraint and public criticism. Saying that "X ought not to have said Y because it was hurtful or offensive" does not limit X's freedom to say Y; it questions X's judgment in saying Y. Being free to do something is not the same as having good reasons to do something. The group of people who identify with the slogan "Je ne suis pas Charlie" were voicing this ethical point (Modood 2015). They found the content of *Charlie Hebdo* offensive. And although this criticism implies that they believed that if *Charlie Hebdo* had closed its doors the public sphere would not have lost much, this opinion is a far cry from calling for it to be closed.

How do self-restraint and public criticism function as "enforcers" of civility? I argue that criticism is the more powerful mechanism, but we need to talk about self-restraint first. Every time we think better of a rude or hurtful remark and keep it to ourselves, we exercise self-restraint. The clearest examples of such restraint in the *Charlie Hebdo* case are news outlets that chose not to republish the cartoons while covering the story. The media were deeply divided on this issue. The *New York Times* executive editor Dean Baquet commented that it was a very difficult decision, but in the end he chose not to show the cartoons, because "we have a standard that is long held and that serves us well: that there is a line between gratuitous insult and satire. Most of these [cartoons] are gratuitous insult" (Gollom 2015). David Studer, the director for journalistic standards and practices at the CBC, articulated a similar sentiment when he noted in a television interview that, in the past, when the network had chosen not to show these images, they had taken that decision on principle. Why should they throw out their principle after the attack? Indeed, standing up to terrorism is to stand by one's principles. The only reason to show the cartoons now would be if the CBC could not tell the story without the images, but this was not the case (CBC 2015).[2] These are examples of self-restraint. Both Baquet and Studer are claiming that the decision not to publish is based on considered judgments freely undertaken for ethical reasons. It would make no sense to say that the *New York Times* or the CBC limited its own freedom of speech in this case. Nor would it be accurate to say that self-restraint here is a case of self-censure.

But many other news outlets, particularly in the French-speaking world,[3] did publish the cartoons and often implied that not doing so was letting the bad guys win. This criticism of the self-restraint response came in two forms. One questioned the motivation of the self-restraint, wondering whether it was a freely undertaken decision based on principle rather than a prudential decision based on risk assessment. A second argument was that the proper response to this type of terrorist violence is defiance and the bold exercise of exactly the freedom that has been threatened (Chait 2015).

I think everyone would agree that choosing not to publish the cartoons because of fear of violent reprisals is a serious restriction on what we normally think of as freedom of speech. Even the prudential reason of wanting to avoid provocation potentially compromises the idea of

---

2 In an interesting Canadian twist to this story, Studer was responding to innuendos from Radio Canada (which did show the cartoons) that English-language CBC was acting in a cowardly manner.

3 *Le Monde* and *Le Figaro* were notable exceptions.

self-limitations. But unless we want to accuse Baquet and Studer and like-minded editors of bad faith, we must take their word for it that the decision not to publish was taken because they or their news organization thought it was the right decision, not the safe decision. Ethical self-limitation is an exercise of free speech. Furthermore, our public sphere would be completely dysfunctional if there was not quite a lot of this sort of self-restraint undertaken by individuals, associations, and the media. Self-restraint or self-limitation is an indispensable mechanism in maintaining minimum levels of civility. But *Charlie Hebdo* did not, nor does it plan to, exercise self-restraint. Public spheres that honour and protect free speech will always be home to offensive and rude speech. Criticism of this speech – that is, calling it out as offensive and rude – is not likely to result in an ethical epiphany for the creators of publications like *Charlie Hebdo*. Public criticism rarely functions to persuade offenders to self-limit their speech. Instead it functions to diminish the harm done by *Charlie Hebdo* without diminishing *Charlie Hebdo*'s free speech rights. Before I unpack this argument, I need to take a moment and briefly clarify how I am using the term *civility*.

Minimal Civility, Power, and Respect

I use *civility* to identify informal norms of the public sphere that we use to criticize (but not limit) speech that violates standards of appropriateness. These standards vary greatly from one public context to another, as there is no agreed-upon standard of civility, even though we use this term a great deal in our public debates about standards of public debate. I want to address what is minimally required by any standard of civility. A minimal standard of civility is a baseline, not an ideal. As a baseline it is defined in its breach, not in its fulfilment. It is not a high bar of decorum and respectful speech (something that is praiseworthy in many circumstances but not always necessarily to pursue legitimate political aims and goals). *Civility*, as I'm using the term here, is a necessary, but far from sufficient, condition for a minimally functioning public sphere. It involves the speech and action necessary so as not to derail our civil union, exchange, conversation, or enterprise. As such, civility may be compatible with high levels of partisanship, polarization, ideological divide, and impasse. Civility sets the limits on anger and resentment but does not attempt to suppress or replace these things. Civility, in this sense, is not a substantive form of respect or civic friendship; it is a restraint on words for the sake of continuing the conversation.

This view of civility calls for a strategy of avoidance that often involves the self-restraint I discussed above. We seek to avoid doing or saying things that will make future cooperation difficult or impossible. I understand many of the proponents of the "Je ne suis pas Charlie" campaign as saying that *Charlie Hebdo* crossed this civic baseline. The argument often hinges on the relative power position of the targets of *Charlie Hebdo's* ridicule and offence – which is to say offence and insult have different civility registers, depending on the relative power position of the insulter and insulted. Ridiculing Christianity or Catholicism has a different impact from ridiculing Mohammad or Islam. Christianity is the majority religion in France and is not facing the same type of existential threats facing Islam in Western democracies. In addition, for many nominal Christians, ideas of blasphemy and the sacred have been left behind and do not elicit strong emotional responses when challenged. Thus, part of the impact differential has to do with factors internal to Islam.

But more important for the concept of civility I am offering here is the civil status of the group that feels the insult and whether or not that ridicule contributes to a further erosion of civic confidence and standing in society. LSE Professor Tariq Modood challenges an uncritical celebration of *Charlie Hebdo* and notes, "There is a world of difference between satire against the powerful ('speaking truth to power') and against the powerless, where it becomes not just a form of bullying but risks becoming racist" (Modood 2015). Incivility cannot be invested in words or images independent of context. The question is the power of the words to harm. And here I want to suggest that the relevant harm is not personal but political. The crucial question is whether we can identify a potential harm to democratic citizenship. In what ways do words or images contribute to a feeling of insecurity or a sense of being treated as second-class citizens? This is an empirical question to some extent. I have yet to see good data on how French Muslims generally view *Charlie Hebdo*. Most French Muslims are secular, but secularity does not mean that they cannot feel the sting of insult in a particular way. But more interesting than data about French Muslim attitudes towards *Charlie Hebdo* would be data about French Muslims' attitudes towards "Je suis Charlie." One implication of the "Je ne suis pas Charlie" position is that an uncritical lionization of a publication like *Charlie Hebdo* makes Muslims feel insecure. This brings us to the final point.

There is another dimension to the power of words that brings us back to the way public criticism works as an "enforcer" of civility. *Charlie*

Hebdo's offensive speech stays within the limits of acceptable civility to the extent that the public debate has a place for voices arguing that it crosses the line into incivility. This sounds paradoxical. The claim here is that the fact that, say, "Je ne suis pas Charlie" came to the surface is a contextual factor that diminishes the power of *Charlie Hebdo* to harm in the way I have described. Let me explain.

Speech can harm. There is no dispute about that. In free-speech literature the debate is about how to measure that harm, and especially how to measure that harm against the harm of limiting freedom by suppressing speech. One of the interesting dimensions of the harm that can be inflicted by speech is the authority of the speech act. Some offensive things are said in the public sphere, but because they carry no or only weak authority, they fail to offend, even though they are offensive. Sometimes this is because we think to ourselves something like "He is an idiot and no one listens to him anyway." Or the speakers have so discredited themselves that the offence cannot be taken seriously. One could argue that the power of Westboro Baptist Church to offend has been on a steady decline as they become relegated to the ranks of nuts and irrelevant irritants. Diminishing the authority of the speech act diminishes the potential harm that it can do.

There is a large literature on what gives speech acts authority. One theme that runs through this literature is the idea that some speech acts gain a type of default authority simply because they go unchallenged. If we apply this logic to the *Charlie Hebdo* case, we see that assessing *Charlie Hebdo*'s civility register involves assessing the authority with which *Charlie Hebdo* speaks. For example, linking *Charlie Hebdo* to a long and distinguished tradition of raucous satire that goes back to Voltaire and is said to be a defining feature of French republican political culture adds to its authority. It adds to its authority and insinuates that citizens who have a problem with this brand of satire are not part of this central political culture. Challenging this picture, pointing out that *Charlie Hebdo* is a far cry from Voltaire and closer to a Page 3 tabloid, places its authority in question.

There are and have been many voices raised to challenge or block the authority with which *Charlie Hebdo* speaks. "Je ne suis pas Charlie" is one such voice. It came on the scene at a moment when *Charlie Hebdo* was on the brink of becoming a national symbol of liberalism standing against the forces of darkness. "Je ne suis pas Charlie" asks us to take a closer look at *Charlie Hebdo* and think seriously about the implications of celebrating this type of journalism. How we answer this question in a sense is unimportant. What is important is that we live in public spheres where it can be asked. We live in public spheres where we can argue, challenge, and question each other's authority. This is what it means to have and exercise freedom of speech. And to the extent that we do exercise free speech in this way, the offensive speech of *Charlie Hebdo* has less power to offend. Public criticism "enforces" civility, not by forcing speakers to shut up or even restrain themselves. Public criticism "enforces" civility by diminishing the power of offensive speech to offend.

REFERENCES

CBC. 2015. "Why Not Publish Prophet Muhammad Caricatures," January 8, http://www.cbc.ca/player/News/ID/2646669880/.
Chait, Jonathan. 2015. "*Charlie Hebdo* and the Right to Commit Blasphemy." *New York Magazine*, January 7, http://nymag.com/daily/intelligencer/2015/01/charlie-hebdo-and-the-right-to-commit-blasphemy.html.
Gollum, Mark. 2015. "*Charlie Hebdo* Shooting: Debate over Publishing the Muhammad Cartoons." CBC News, January 9, http://www.cbc.ca/news/world/charlie-hebdo-shooting-debate-over-publishing-the-muhammad-cartoons-1.2894097.
Le Monde. 2015. "*Charlie Hebdo*, 22 and de procès en tous genres," January 8, http://www.lemonde.fr/societe/article/2015/01/08/charlie-hebdo-22-ans-de-proces-en-tous-genres_4551824_3224.html.
Maclure, Jocelyn. 2015. "Le droit de *Charlie Hebdo* de critiquer, et le droit de critiquer *Charlie Hebdo*." *L'actualité*, January 26, http://www.lactualite.com/blogues/le-blogue-politique/charlie-hebdo-la-puissance-des-images/.
Modood, Tariq. 2015. "In Remembering the Charlie Hebdo Attack We Must Not Forget the Responsibility That Goes with Free Speech," January 12, http://blogs.lse.ac.uk/europpblog/2015/01/12/in-remembering-the-charlie-hebdo-attack-we-must-not-forget-the-responsibility-that-goes-with-free-speech/.
Stille, Alexander. 2015. "Why French Law Treats Dieudonné and Charlie Hebdo Differently." *New Yorker*, January 15, http://www.newyorker.com/news/news-desk/french-law-treats-dieudonne-charlie-hebdo-differently.
Weinstock, Daniel. 2015. "The (Messy) Ethics of Freedom of Speech," January 26, http://induecourse.ca/the-messy-ethics-of-freedom-of-speech/.

3 The Status of Muslim Minorities Following the Paris Attacks

JEFFREY G. REITZ

Responses to recent attacks in Paris, including at the offices of the satirical weekly *Charlie Hebdo* on January 7, 2015, raise important questions about how Muslim minority communities are affected by such events, not only in France but throughout the Western world. A backlash against Muslim communities, evident since the attacks on the United States on September 11, 2001, occurs any time perpetrators claim a global Islamic agenda. While an obvious concern is the extent to which local Muslim minorities might feel a sense of kinship with the attackers, underlying this is a deeper concern, perhaps more worrying, that the attacks reveal an alien character to Muslim culture, making it either difficult to reconcile with basic Western values of democracy, state religious neutrality, and gender equity, or actually hostile to those values.

Are these concerns well-founded? Are Muslim minorities not integrating into society as well as other immigrant groups, and do their growing numbers represent some kind of threat? Evidence from social research clearly refutes such concerns. Muslim communities in Western countries represent a variety of cultural and national backgrounds. Each such community tends to reflect these different backgrounds as much as or more than a common Muslim identity. Moreover, Muslim experience in the community or the workplace differs little from that of other religious minorities such as Hindus, Sikhs, and others. Their main problems centre on employment opportunity, recognition of qualifications, and discrimination – problems of visible minority immigrants in general, not Muslims specifically.

Although research suggests the processes of integration of Muslim populations into society are determined by ethnic and racial background, not religion, public opinion says otherwise. Accordingly, public discussion of immigrants has shifted from issues of race and ethnicity to religion. Immigrants to Canada from Pakistan, Iran, and other Muslim countries are now referred to simply as "Muslim" and considered as such. The same has happened elsewhere. In France, immigrants once called Arabs or Turks are now just "Muslim." This focus on religion is not just wrong-headed – in many ways, it has actually been counterproductive, leading to policies attempting to repress religious expression, thereby erecting – not tearing down – barriers to integration.

Integration of Muslim Minorities

Canadian concern about Muslims as a group is clear in public opinion data. The 2010 Environics Focus Canada survey asked, "Do you think most Muslims coming to our country today want to adopt Canadian customs and way of life or do you think they want to be distinct from the larger Canadian society?" A majority of respondents (55 per cent) thought Muslims "want to be distinct." Far fewer (28 per cent) thought Muslims want to adopt Canadian customs (Reitz 2011). And, of course, despite widespread support for multiculturalism, Canadians really want immigrants to "adopt Canadian customs" and blend in. Fully 80 per cent agreed that "ethnic groups should blend into Canadian society and not form separate communities," with 51 per cent agreeing "strongly." Two-thirds (68 per cent) said, "There are too many immigrants coming into this country who are not adopting Canadian values," with 40 per cent "strongly" agreeing.

Characterizations of Muslims as preferring to be "distinct" are challenged by Muslims themselves, the vast majority of whom view their co-religionists as wanting to integrate into Canadian society. A 2006 Focus Canada survey interviewed both mainstream and Muslim populations; 57 per cent of the former viewed Muslims as wanting to remain "distinct," but only 23 per cent of the Muslims agreed. By the same token, 55 per cent of Muslims saw their co-religionists as wanting to adopt Canadian customs, but only 25 per cent of other Canadians agreed (Environics Research Institute 2006). Even more tellingly, Muslim-Canadians are as likely as any other Canadians to express pride in their citizenship; in both cases, three in four said they were "very proud" to be Canadian, and all but 6 or 7 per cent at least "somewhat proud."

The most persuasive evidence of Muslim integration comes from large broad-based social surveys, particularly Statistics Canada's 2002 Ethnic Diversity Survey. Based on over 42,000 interviews with mainstream and minority populations across Canada, this survey provides such indicators of social integration as intercultural friendships, participation in voluntary activities in the community, social trust, voting, sense of belonging, and feeling Canadian (Reitz, Breton et al. 2009; Reitz, Phan et al. 2009). It shows all growing religious minorities, such as Muslims, Sikhs, Buddhists, Hindus, are slower to integrate socially because they are racial minorities, not because of their religious commitments and beliefs.

The irrelevance of religion to social integration is revealed in the survey in two ways. First, among visible minorities, those whose religious commitments are strongest – whether Muslim or otherwise and including Christians – do not differ in their social integration in Canada from those whose religion is more peripheral in their lives. Second, when visible minorities are asked about problems such as discrimination, both Muslims and members of other religious groups describe the problems as a result of skin colour or national origin, not religion.

One issue of particular concern is gender equity. Muslims are thought to hold traditional views on the status of women, and these views are perceived as extreme and impervious to change. But do gender issues hinder Muslim integration? Surveys of Muslims suggest many Muslims, including women, feel Canada should accommodate their traditional beliefs about women's rights and roles. Nevertheless, the reality is that given time in Canada, Muslim minorities adopt Canadian beliefs and practices, including on the status of women.

Muslim assimilation of Canadian values on gender equity is powerfully demonstrated in data on labour force participation (Reitz, Phan, and Banerjee 2015). Recently arrived Muslim women follow traditional roles in the family, and relatively few engage in paid work outside the home. In this, they are not so different from recently arrived Hindu or Sikh women, and the census data show low levels of labour force participation of recent immigrant women is more about country of origin than religion: Muslim women from Pakistan, for example, have much lower labour force participation than Muslim women from the Middle East or Europe. Evidence also suggests those who are strongly religious do not differ from those who are less so.

More importantly, Muslim women's labour force participation rises dramatically over time. Group differences fade for those with more than ten years in Canada and completely disappear for their children born in Canada. The bottom line is that assimilation is alive and well for Muslims in Canada, particularly regarding domestic roles for women as shown in paid employment outside the home.

No matter how hard we look, we do not find evidence that Muslim communities in Canada, whether Pakistani, Iranian, Somali, Afghani, or Turk, are becoming isolated in ways reflecting social outlooks fundamentally – or even slightly – different from those of groups from India, Vietnam, China, Jamaica, or Korea. Concerns about inassimilable Muslims are empirically unfounded. All groups face difficulties integrating in society, but the difficulties relate to visible minority status and particularities of national origin, not religion.

An interesting source of information on integration is a large-scale employment audit study conducted by Philip Oreopoulos (2011). In this study, nearly 13,000 résumés were sent to employers in response to advertised jobs. Résumés containing English or British names prompted employer calls for an interview 39 per cent more often than résumés with Chinese, Indian, Pakistani, and Greek names, even when the latter indicated Canadian education and Canadian experience. (Callback rates were far lower for those with minority names whose education or experience came from outside Canada.) The extent of discrimination against Pakistanis – who are mainly Muslims – is about the same as for the other groups. Of course, we can't know if employers realized someone called Ali Saeed, Chaudhry Mohammad, or Fatima Sheikh probably was Muslim, or Samir Sharma, Panav Singh, or Priyanka Kaur probably was not (these are names used on the résumés in Oreopoulos's study). It made no difference to their inclination to pass over such résumés in preference for Greg Johnson, John Martin, or Emily Brown (again names used in the study). This is consistent with other information about the social experience of Muslims in Canada. Their problems arise from their minority status. These are about the same as the problems of other ethnic groups and are not related to religion.

Impact on Muslims of the Focus on Religion

The empirical evidence says one thing; the general public says another, and the public discourse is all about religion. In the wake of the attacks of 9/11 and subsequent events, the religious affiliation of Muslims has come to define them in public opinion. Regardless of their countries of origin, they are now called Muslim. The salience of religion does not hold nearly as much for other immigrants; for example, those from India remain Indian or "South Asian," rather than Hindu.

What has been the effect of this change? Muslims themselves are very aware of the increased salience of religion in their social identity.

Understandably, many are resentful and fearful, seeing it as an invitation for negative attention. Many, of course, have been attacked. Yet the dominance of religion in public discourse has not substantially altered the pattern of social, economic, and political integration of Muslim communities in Western societies. There is little overall impact on national identity, or on friendship patterns, and so on. Most people, including Muslims, operate on a day-to-day basis with friends and co-workers they know and like, not with hostile people. Bad things happen, but at the same time, there are positive signs. Sometimes even a struggle against stigma and exclusion can bring people into a society and into its social and political dynamic. Some Muslims, for example, have engaged with the project of countering anti-Muslim viewpoints; this effort brings them into closer relations with the political process, producing greater integration in society, not less.

The fact that a public discourse of exclusion does not necessarily lead to exclusion is illustrated by a comparison of settings displaying fairly wide variation: France compared to Canada, and Quebec compared to the rest of Canada. In France, the debate over religion in the public sphere as applied to Muslim immigrants has been intense, bans on the headscarf for Muslim women have been extended to the public schools, and the right-wing National Front has made notable political gains based on its anti-immigrant and anti-Muslim policies. In Quebec, politics are more muted, and the proposed Quebec Charter of Values, which would have imposed French-style bans on the wearing of headscarves for public employees, failed because of the defeat of the Parti Québécois government, which proposed it. And in the rest of Canada, while debates have sprung up, for example, over sharia law in Ontario, and majorities favour headscarf bans, public discourse reflects little if any interest in new policy restrictions.

So it's interesting that in comparing Muslim minorities in the three settings, we find little difference in their social integration – more specifically, in experiences of discrimination, in the establishment of social relations with members of other communities, or in feelings of trust in and identification with the larger society (Reitz, Simon, and Laxer 2014). However, in one place there is a clear difference: in France the headscarf policy seems to have backfired. Instead of facilitating integration by making all women alike, it has thrown up yet another barrier. Many Muslim women comply with the regulations, but other highly motivated and Westernized Muslim women choose to withdraw from the labour market and other arenas where headscarves are banned.

In Canada, as mentioned above, the gender differences in labour force participation observed for recently immigrated Muslims (and recently immigrated Hindus and others) fade over time and are virtually eliminated for the Canadian-born generation. In France, Muslim women also assimilate into the labour market, but this assimilation is limited. Even French-born Muslim women maintain a somewhat lower level of participation in the workforce. Detailed analysis of labour force data show that, whereas in Canada, including in Quebec, the odds of a Canadian-born Muslim woman being in the labour force are identical to those of the mainstream population, in France, the odds that a French-born Muslim woman will be in the labour force remain 13 per cent below the mainstream population. Interviews with Muslim women suggest this difference arises in part, if not entirely, because of the restricted employment opportunities for Muslim women who wear the hijab. There is a clear difference in Canada, where the headscarf bans do not exist.

The conclusion is clear: the Muslim community, regardless of national origins, integrates as well in Canadian society as any other visible minority group. Further, policies restricting their religious expression would not be conducive of integration, as French experience with headscarf bans suggests. As Kazemipur argues, the best policy is to "shift our attention from the theological to the social" (Kazemipur 2014). Put otherwise, the prevailing focus on religion diverts attention from those areas of life that actually determine social integration: getting a job, sending children to school, playing a role in community decision-making. We should remove the barriers to integration, not build new ones.

REFERENCES

Environics Research Institute. 2006. *Focus Canada Report 2006–4*. Toronto: Environics Research Institute.

Kazemipur, A. 2014. *The Muslim Question in Canada*. Vancouver: UBC Press.

Oreopoulos, P. 2011. "Why Do Skilled Immigrants Struggle in the Labor Market? A Field Experiment with Thirteen Thousand Résumés." *American Economic Journal: Economic Policy* 3 (4), 148–71.

Reitz, J.G. 2011. "Pro-Immigration Canada: Social and Economic Roots of Popular Views," IRPP Study No. 20. Montreal: Institute for Research on Public Policy.

Reitz, J.G., R. Banerjee, M. Phan, and J. Thompson. 2009. "Race, Religion, and the Social Integration of New Immigrant Minorities in Canada." *International Migration Review* 43 (4), 695–726.

Reitz, J.G., R. Breton, K.K. Dion, and K.L. Dion. 2009. *Multiculturalism and Social Cohesion: Potentials and Challenges of Diversity.* New York: Springer.

Reitz, J.G., M. Phan, and R. Banerjee. 2015. "Gender Equity in Canada's Newly Growing Religious Minorities." *Ethnic and Racial Studies* 38 (5), 681–99.

Reitz, J.G., P. Simon, and E. Laxer. 2014. "Muslims' Social Inclusion and Exclusion in France, Québec and Canada: Does National Context Matter?" Presented at the Eighteenth ISA World Congress of Sociology, Yokohama, Japan, July 15, https://isaconf.confex.com/isaconf/wc2014/webprogram/Paper35459.html.

4 A Tale of Two Massacres: *Charlie Hebdo* and Utoya Island

MOHAMMAD FADEL

On July 22, 2011, Anders Behring Breivik, a self-described Christian crusader, claiming to be a member of a trans-European network called the "Knights Templar," killed seventy-seven people in Norway. The home-made bombs he placed in government buildings in downtown Oslo killed eight, but more crucially, provided him cover to proceed undetected to his main target, a youth camp sponsored by Norway's Labour Party, where he massacred sixty-nine youth using small arms. He was captured alive, and after a public trial, sentenced to life imprisonment.[1] While there was no question of his guilt, there was a significant issue as to whether he was legally responsible for his conduct or whether he suffered from some mental defect that precluded a finding of criminal guilt. The court, however, concluded he was sane (or sufficiently sane) at the time of his conduct to be convicted criminally for his actions. Ironically, however, it was the prosecution that argued for Breivik's insanity, while it was the defence that insisted he was sane, acting out, in their words, "a radical political project" to defend a Christian Europe from the threat of multiculturalism, Islam, and communism (Lewis 2012); indeed, his defence team even argued that a judicial finding of insanity would deprive him of his right to take responsibility for his actions and thereby transform essentially political action into something pathological.

On January 7, 2015, Cherif and Said Kouachi, two brothers, French-born, but of Algerian descent, made their way into the offices of the

---

1 A life sentence in Norway amounts to twenty-one years, subject to possible extension upon a judicial finding that the defendant remains a threat to society.

satirical French magazine *Charlie Hebdo,* killing twelve people, including several of its most famous cartoonists. Another attacker, Amedy Coulibaly, apparently acting in coordination with the Kouachi brothers, attacked a kosher grocery store, taking several customers hostage and killing four. French anti-terrorism police eventually cornered all three suspects and killed all three in a simultaneous raid on January 9. Since the attackers all died, they cannot explain what drove them to kill, but it was quickly assumed that the Kouachi brothers targeted *Charlie Hebdo* in order to retaliate against that magazine's repeated satirical portrayals of the Prophet Muḥammad. As a result of this interpretation of the attackers' motives, the assault quickly became elevated from a crime, or even an ordinary terrorist attack, into a symbolic attack against the French Republic itself. Internationally, the assault against *Charlie Hebdo* was interpreted as an assault against the sacred, if deeply contested, value of free speech. *Charlie Hebdo,* which had been reportedly struggling for many years financially, suddenly become the symbol of a heroic republic standing firm against fascism, with all patriotic citizens required to pledge their allegiance in the fight against this new fascism by reproducing the hashtag #JeSuisCharlie. The French attackers, unlike Breivik, were not understood to be acting for political reasons (or political reasons intelligible in a modern state), but only to vindicate an atavistic theological doctrine regarding the punishment of blasphemy and blasphemers.

The circumstances that produced both massacres were in many ways similar: both Breivik and the Kouachi brothers and Coulibaly believed they were engaged in an existential battle for the soul of humanity, and that their actions, even if illegal, were ultimately justified by the higher logic of this cosmic struggle. They also believed that they were fighting on behalf of their own people at the same time that they were accusing the very people they were defending of having failed to display sufficient vigour in the fight against the cosmic enemy. Transnational communication and ideological networks provided both sets of attackers with the ideological motivation (and perhaps more) to carry out their attacks.

But there were also significant differences, not least in the reaction to the attacks. Breivik's attack was not taken to represent anything other than himself. There were no massive international rallies in support of Breivik's victims, nor did international leaders fly en masse to Oslo to mourn the victims as martyrs to a noble international ideal, like multicultural tolerance, for example. While numerous articles pointed out the role that organized anti-Islam advocacy groups, particularly in the United States, played in supplying Breivik with the ideas he used to fill his 1500-page manifesto, "2083: A European Declaration of Independence," the media were not filled with hand-wringing about radicalization among young white men, nor was there a call to establish systematic surveillance of right-wing websites or intellectual networks, or to shut down their sources of funding.[2]

Needless to say, there was no wave of arrests or preventive detention of right-wing – or perceived right-wing – European extremists in the wake of Breivik's atrocity. In short, despite the magnitude of the killings, it did not produce a sense of crisis, emergency, or self-criticism among liberal European or North American political and cultural elites. Indeed, so localized were the effects of the Utoya Island massacre that it had already disappeared from our collective consciousness by the time that the *Charlie Hebdo* attack took place. Mike Morrel, a former CIA deputy director and acting CBS news "senior security consultant," confidently (but apparently in a state of amnesia) declared on CBS news in the immediate aftermath of the shooting, "This is the worst terrorist attack in Europe since the attacks in London in July of 2005. We haven't lost this many people since that attack" (CBS 2015).

How can we account for the differences in the cultural treatment of the Utoya Island massacre and the *Charlie Hebdo* attack? The University of Toronto's Law School and Munk School, after all, did not convene a symposium called "After Breivik" or the like to consider the aftermath of the Utoya Island massacre. Clearly, politics matter, and from a political perspective, Muslim political violence is profoundly more salient in its effects on the political culture than the political violence of non-Muslims. Indeed, the different reactions to violence committed, or threatened, by Muslims and non-Muslims recently played itself out in Canada, when the justice minister, Peter MacKay, assured Canadians that a plot in Halifax to kill large numbers of Canadians, which the police successfully prevented, was not terrorism because it was just a bunch of "misfits" who were not motivated by "culture." At the same time, and apparently in response to the actions of two individuals with

---

2 The Center for American Progress, however, has prepared a series of reports exposing right-wing networks, their interrelationships, and their private sources of funding, which contributed $57 million to anti-Muslim organizations and ideologues in just 2011 and 2012.

only a very marginal relationship to the Canadian Muslim community, Martin Rouleau, who ran his car into two Canadian soldiers, killing one (CTVNews 2014), and Michael Zihaf-Bibeau, who, acting alone, killed a Canadian soldier at Parliament Hill (Wingrove, Chase, and Curry, 2014) (and perhaps also in response as well to the *Charlie Hebdo* attack), the Canadian government is seeking to pass Bill C-51, which by all accounts represents a potentially grave threat to the civil liberties of Canadians. The salience of politics, and the way political elites choose to respond to acts of mass violence, clearly has substantial consequences. Politics matters not just because the policy choices made in the immediate aftermath of attacks inscribe certain narratives into our collective memories, but also because the policies those decisions bring in their wake continually reaffirm those events as justification, even when, as in the case of the United States, the original precipitating event took place over a decade ago.

When states respond to acts of terrorism exclusively from the perspective of national security, as appears to be the approach of the current Canadian government, they not only create a particularistic – and often exclusionary – national rhetoric in an attempt to justify a muscular national security posture, they introduce new bureaucracies that enjoy levels of funding that exceed any rational evaluation of actual risk. A pair of economists have estimated that post-9/11 expenditures by the United States on security through 2011, for example, can be justified on a cost-benefit basis only if one believes that in their absence, an incident of the magnitude of the 9/11 attacks on the Twin Towers would have occurred yearly, or that an attack on the scale of the 7/7 attacks on the London Underground would have occurred more than thirty times a year (Stewart and Mueller 2011). And like other governmental bureaucracies, the new national security bureaucracies, once established, have institutional interests in the continuity of the policies that justify their budgets. This internal pressure creates perverse incentives to expand the emergency to widen the circle of potential enemies that must be defeated, if only to justify the outsized budgets.

Accountability in this context is twisted: because declaring complete victory over the "enemy" is never an option, the national security bureaucracy faces the constant need to produce a never-ending series of "trophies" to demonstrate their continued relevance to the public. Unsurprisingly, ever more obscure groups, e.g., the notorious "Khorasan Group" (Brennan 2014), seemingly appear out of nowhere as targets for the U.S. drone war, only to disappear, without further explanation, just as quickly. Likewise, the U.S. Department of Justice, in combination with the FBI, continues to pursue dubious sting operations against what are predominantly young, confused, and alienated Muslim males who, although often lacking the means to engage in political violence, are vulnerable to manipulation by a government agent into becoming a part of a bogus terrorist plot. The principal effect is to convince the public that the government is efficient in rooting out the hidden terrorist threat (Greenwald 2015). Indeed, in the years immediately following 9/11, the FBI was under tremendous pressure to find al-Qa'ida "sleeper cells," who were presumed to be hiding in plain sight within the American-Muslim community. It was as though senior administration officials were acting under an algorithm that predicted a certain number of terrorists, given a certain number of Muslims in a particular region, and demanded that the FBI produce suspects in accordance with that algorithm. U.S. federal prosecutors, using the inchoate crime of "material support for terrorism," prosecuted not only the hapless and clueless, but also groups and individuals closely associated with peaceful Palestinian solidarity work (McConnell 2009). The U.S. Supreme Court facilitated this approach because, in a bit of Orwellian interpretation, it accepted the government's interpretation of the term to include even non-lethal, immaterial support for terrorism (Fadel 2010a, 2010b).

This hyper-vigilance targeting Muslim communities in Western democracies is contrasted with the relative nonchalance that governments of liberal democracies have demonstrated towards the problem of right-wing white supremacist groups, even though intelligence data indicate that white supremacists in Canada, for example, have accounted for more terrorist attacks than Muslims (Boutilier 2015). It would nevertheless be surprising if Canadian security agencies don't adopt the same dubious strategies as their American counterparts against Muslim populations in the event that C-51 becomes law.

This disturbing dynamic of the security response to terrorism is amply demonstrated by the arc of the "war on terror" in the United States. Despite official protests to the contrary, U.S. policies adopted after 9/11 clearly targeted Muslim populations in the United States, without any need for particular evidence of actual wrongdoing beyond the fact that they were Muslims, or from Muslim-majority countries. Muslims at large were identified as a vague but a very real and endemic threat to national security. This threat would be permanently resolved only when Muslims adopted a different set of values, when they accepted a "reformed" Islam whose values would be modern and liberal. Crucially, Muslims would also have to blithely accept the current distribution of global economic, political, and military power and the subordinate position of Muslims and Muslim states within it. And, of course, only the national security state can determine whether the needed reformation has proceeded sufficiently to justify dismantling itself.

The great irony, of course, is that even as the most sophisticated and expansive surveillance operation in human history has been deployed against Western Muslims, the FBI failed to prevent either the underwear bomber from boarding a plane to Detroit, despite the fact that his own father went to the U.S. embassy in Nigeria to warn them, or the Boston Marathon bombings from occurring, despite the fact that Russian intelligence warned the United States about one of the attackers. French security services seem to suffer from the same bizarre combination of omniscient surveillance combined with incompetence in processing the data they acquire: all the *Charlie Hebdo* attackers had been under the surveillance of French intelligence, but the security services nevertheless failed to discover the conspiracy before it was too late. Similarly, Canadian security agencies were unable to prevent either of the October 2014 attacks, despite the fact that both attackers were known to the security apparatus.

The need to "convert" Muslims to the right values is openly expressed in a pair of book-length studies by the RAND Corporation published in the wake of 9/11, "Civil Democratic Islam," and "Building Moderate Muslim Networks." The authors of these studies attempted to classify the Muslim public into various *theological* groups along a scale of dangerousness, determined exclusively by perceived levels of religiosity. The authors ranked possible Muslim interlocutors with the government as falling into four broad categories: religious modernists, religious traditionalists, fundamentalists, and secularists. Of possible interlocutors, the fundamentalists were the worst; traditionalists were acceptable, but only if there were no choice but to deal with them, and even then, only to keep them as credible opponents of fundamentalists; modernists were to be promoted as the "face of contemporary Islam"; and, although secularists were to be defended case by case, the authors advised the government to support "secular civic and cultural institutions and programs" (Benard 2003, 47–8).

RAND's policy recommendations were an express call to manipulate the doctrines of a religious tradition in the service of the state's policies, a position that hardly seems consistent with a liberal state's ostensible commitment to neutrality in matters of religion. The report therefore focuses exclusively on intra-Muslim disputes on issues of concern to Western liberals, such as polygamy, Islamic criminal law, women's rights, and the rights of minorities, but is completely silent on any of the political grievances that Muslim political actors use to justify their violence against the United States and its Western allies (PBS Newshour 1996, 1998). Policymakers' incessant focus on the nature of Islamic theological and ethical doctrines without any consideration of politics is emblematic of the prior decision that it is inconceivable that Muslims, as a group, possess the capacity to make collective political claims against the West in general, and the United States in particular. Alternatively, even if they do possess such capacity, those complaints need not be taken seriously, either because they lack merit on their face, or because the claimants are too weak to press their positions.

Everything that we have seen emerge from Paris in the wake of the *Charlie Hebdo* massacre suggests that the French political elite have wholeheartedly embraced the anti-terrorism model developed in the United States; the French have even taken to calling the *Charlie Hebdo* massacre "France's 9/11." The dominance of the security state model in the French state's immediate policy response is manifested in its decision to ramp up both security pressure *and* ideological pressure on the French Muslim community by aggressively prosecuting scores of Muslims and other dissidents for inchoate associational or expressive crimes, such as allegedly expressing sympathy for terrorism. Such is the case of the French comedian Dieudonné M'bala M'bala, who said "Tonight ... I feel like Charlie Coulibaly." Muslims are also encouraged to embrace *laïcité* by abandoning anything that marks them as "Muslim" (*Boston Review* 2015). Some measures are simply absurd, such as the decision of some French municipalities, in the name of *laïcité*, to refuse to make available non-pork options in schools, while others border on fascism, like the arrest of an eight-year-old who allegedly expressed sympathy for the "terrorists" at school. Unsurprisingly, the political class's embrace of the security response has had the all-too-predictable effect of strengthening the French extreme right; the same risk is surfacing in Canada (Hébert 2015).

The incessant demand for Islamic theological reform quickly operationalizes itself into what amounts to a modern inquisition. In such a climate, outward indicators of religiosity, political views, or both, serve as a proxy for dangerousness and therefore justify casting a broad net of surveillance over what otherwise would be viewed as citizens' constitutionally protected activities. Whether intended or not, Muslim populations certainly experience these policies as inquisitions, with the attendant risks of alienation such policies generate (Siddiqui 2015). Security services have justified their pervasive surveillance of Muslim populations by adopting the "conveyor-belt" model of radicalization. According to this model, radicalization begins with what appears to be innocuous steps, such as attending a mosque for daily prayers or protesting American policy in the Middle East, but then, perhaps imperceptibly, the person is moved, as if he or she is on a "conveyor belt," toward increasingly extreme positions until he or she is tempted to use violence against neighbours (Patel 2011).

Once a person or a group is placed in the crucible of an inquisition, however, the target cannot escape unscathed, because it is impossible to prove the bona fides of one's claims. Because it is impossible to verify the sincerity by which Muslims profess their commitment to civic values, they are subjected to practical tests intended to show that they have sufficiently abandoned their religious identities and accepted their subordinate place in the body politic. It is from the perspective of an inquisition that we should understand the social role of *Charlie Hebdo*'s offensive cartoons of the Prophet Muhammad. Far from a daring act of blasphemy (is there anything *less* blasphemous in Western civilization than insulting the Prophet Muhammad?), *Charlie Hebdo*'s cartoons were purely an exercise of social power, in this case, by a secular republican elite who wished to show French Muslims that it could deride them and their most cherished *private* beliefs without that minority having any power to stop them.

The precise goal is to separate "good" Muslims from "bad" ones. But, like the inquisitor who tried in vain to determine the sincerity of those who had been coerced into Catholicism, French republicans can never be certain of Muslims' loyalty: even if the French Muslim expresses restraint, and indeed does not even protest the cartoons, the republican observer suspects that the Muslim's outward restraint could very well mask a hidden resentment of the republican insistence that he abandon his religious sensitivities. Our suspicion of his insincerity means we must continually renew the test to ensure his or her continued fidelity to the republic. The drawing of the offensive cartoons, just like the national security concerns that drive wars outside the state and the draconian security measures internal to it, must therefore continue until we are sure that the Muslims in our midst have given up any pretences that it is possible to be a faithful Muslim and a good citizen of the republic. The inquisition must continue until the faithful Muslim reveals himself to be a bad Muslim by renouncing Islamic garb, halal food, and other markers of difference.

The inquisition(s) to which Muslims are subjected are not limited to France, but can be found in numerous jurisdictions claiming to be liberal. In the United States, the price Muslims must pay for an invitation to the White House to mark the Islamic month of fasting is that they must break their fast with the ambassador of a country, Israel, that the overwhelming majority of Muslims believe was born out of colonialism, is fundamentally racist, and is involved in an ongoing campaign of ethnic cleansing against a largely Muslim population, at the same time as they are being lectured about its unquestionable right of self-defence.[3] All the while, they are expected to maintain a stoic silence and pretend that no insult occurred. Potential immigrants from Muslim-majority countries to the European Union, meanwhile, are expected to demonstrate their internalization of "European" values of gender equality and sexual autonomy by, for example, watching movies of gay couples kissing in public without visible irritation or other expression of objection. European Muslims in general, and French Muslims in particular, cannot reasonably expect the national judiciaries to push back against the politicians. The French judiciary, it is true, resisted popular legislation targeting Islamic garb, but post-9/11 decisions of the European Court of Human Rights have made it abundantly clear that not only can European states regulate Islamic dress in virtually any fashion they see fit, they are also authorized to regulate Islam, including its public dissemination, because Islam itself is viewed as being inconsistent with European public order. With the ECHR endorsing the applicability of the principles of "militant democracy" to Islam and Muslims, it is hard to see any limits to the anti-Muslim measures that might be adopted in Europe (Macklem 2006).[4]

---

3 Indeed many of the U.S. Muslim organizations that sent representatives to that event soon found themselves at the receiving end of vociferous criticism from the United States, and at times, the international Muslim community (Rydhan 2014; al-Khatahtbeh 2014).

4 A very recent decision of Germany's federal constitutional court striking down a state rule prohibiting school teachers from wearing an Islamic head scarf, however, may suggest that this argument should not be generalized to all European states (*World-Post* 2015).

Western governments will no doubt resist my analogy between the tactics of the Spanish Inquisition and post-9/11 security policies in North America and Europe. But it seems indisputable that since 9/11 Muslims have been marked out for special treatment in liberal democracies, whether de facto, as in the United States, or de jure, as in Europe. In some respects this has had its intended effects: to a large extent, established Muslim organizations – to the extent they exist – have virtually ceased playing any role that could be deemed to be critical of Western governments. While the right continues to accuse them of being soft on terrorism, in fact these organizations often fall over each other in their attempts to disassociate themselves and Islam from political violence. The irony, of course, is that the more Muslim leaders in the West denounce political violence in the name of Islam, the more right-wing non-Muslims, on the one hand, accuse them of engaging in *taqiyya* (dissimulation), and the more liberal non-Muslims accuse them of having a "cotton-candy" or "politically correct" view of their religion (Wood 2015). The complete impotence of Western Muslim leadership to resist the national security policies of Western states, despite their eagerness to cooperate with the authorities at all junctures, has had the more serious practical effect of undermining any credibility that these organizations might have in persuading alienated Western Muslims from sympathizing with or engaging in politically motivated violence in the name of Islam.

If the goal of policy is to reduce the risk of politically motivated violence, Norway's treatment of Breivik offers a more hopeful model than the security-state model adopted by the United States following 9/11, and followed by most Western democracies. Instead of using the attack to mark the threshold of a new order, the political system should treat the attack simply as the actions of the individuals responsible for it under ordinary principles of applicable law. This would mean accepting the political legitimacy of Muslim demands, not in the sense that they must be granted, but that they are to be scrutinized using the same criteria that apply to any political demands, not extraordinary criteria that apply only to Muslim demands on the theory that Islam represents an existential threat to liberal democracy. If liberal democracies can recognize extreme right-wing political parties, surely they are capable of withstanding any imagined threat posed by Muslims, who account for only a small segment of their population.

Practically, this demand means that Muslims should be granted the same access to public support of religion that is available to other

European religions but not presently offered to Muslims: if speech restrictions apply to protect other religions, then they must also apply to protect Muslims; if private ordering is permitted to regulate certain aspects of family law generally, then Muslims ought to be allowed to do the same within the same limits that apply generally; if non-Muslims are allowed to express solidarity with non-citizens on the ground of religious affinity, then so too Muslim expressions of solidarity with foreign Muslims ought not to be suspicious. If Muslims are free to criticize Islamic doctrines only, but not liberalism – whether in its ideal form or in its imperfect embodiments – it is implausible, even delusional, to expect Muslims to develop their own principled responses to marginalization, discrimination, imperialism, and other forms of domination that are consistent with democratic civility. Unfortunately, with each new terrorist incident, and each new war, the choices that Western policymakers are offering Muslims are fast-narrowing to either that of Ayan Hirsi Ali or Anwar al-Awlaki. This "with us or against us" approach, however, will lead only to increased religious persecution of Muslims, increased religiously motivated violence, or both.

While rejecting the path of the security state seems like an obvious and easy choice, I am not particularly optimistic that policymakers will show greater wisdom today than they did fourteen years ago. Instead of "militant democracy" that acts against a relatively powerless minority, we need politicians with the courage to act militantly to defend the political centre, which still exists in liberal democracies, even as it has failed to find sufficiently passionate defenders. Unfortunately, I suspect the exact opposite will take place, with more and more politicians engaging in demagogic rhetoric, either out of irrational conviction, or in a vain effort to appease the right. As a result, things will likely become much worse for Western Muslims generally, but especially for European Muslims. Unless we can sincerely say #JeSuisCharlie and #JeSuisAhmad,[5] then more repression, more *Charlie Hebdos*, and more Breiviks await us in the not too distant future.

---

5 #JeSuisAhmad was a hashtag that many French Muslims, and Muslims worldwide, adopted in response to the *Charlie Hebdo* massacre to honour the French-Muslim policeman whom the *Charlie Hebdo* attackers executed after wounding him on the street following the massacres in the office of *Charlie Hebdo*.

REFERENCES

Ali, Wajahat, Eli Clifton, Matthew Duss, Lee Fang, Scott Keyes, and Faiz
   Shakir. 2011. *Fear Inc.: The Roots of the Islamophobia Network in America.*
   Center for American Progress, https://cdn.americanprogress.org/wp-
   content/uploads/issues/2011/08/pdf/islamophobia.pdf.
Benard, Cheryl. 2003. *Civil Democratic Islam: Partners, Resources and Strategies.*
   Santa Monica, CA: RAND, National Security Research Division, http://
   www.rand.org/content/dam/rand/pubs/monograph_reports/2005/
   MR1716.pdf.
Boston Review. 2015. "Forum: After Charlie Hebdo," March 3, http://www
   .bostonreview.net/forum/john-bowen-france-after-charlie-hebdo.
Boutilier, Alex. 2015. "CSIS Highlights White Supremacist Threat Ahead of
   Radical Islam." *Toronto Star*, March 15, http://www.thestar.com/news/
   canada/2015/03/15/csis-highlights-white-supremacist-threat-ahead-of-
   radical-islam.html.
Brennan, Kate. 2014. "Exclusive: U.S. Renews Air Campaign against Khorasan
   Group." *FP: The Cable*, 6 November, http://foreignpolicy.com/2014/11/06/
   exclusive-u-s-renews-air-campaign-against-khorasan-group/.
CBS News. 2015. "French Newspaper Killings Is Worst Terrorist Attack in
   Europe since 2005, CIA Insider Says," January 7, http://www.cbsnews.
   com/videos/french-newspaper-killings-is-worst-terrorist-attack-in-europe-
   since-2005-cia-insider-says/.
The Center for American Progress. 2015. "Fear Inc.: Explore the $57 Million
   Network Fueling Islamophobia in the United States," https://
   islamophobianetwork.com/.
CTVNews. 2014. "Suspect in Attack on 2 Soldiers in Quebec 'Had Become
   Radicalized': PMO," October 20, http://www.ctvnews.ca/canada/suspect-
   in-attack-on-2-soldiers-in-quebec-had-become-radicalized-pmo-1.2062419.
Duss, Matthew, Yasmine Taeb, and Ken Gude. 2015. *Fear, Inc. 2.0.* Washington,
   DC: Center for American Progress, https://cdn.americanprogress.org/wp-
   content/uploads/2015/02/FearInc-report2.11.pdf.
Fadel, Mohammad. 2010a. "The Supreme Court and Material Support for
   Terrorist Organizations." FP: The Middle East Channel, March 10, http://
   foreignpolicy.com/2010/03/10/the-supreme-court-and-material-support-
   for-terrorist-organizations/.
– 2010b. "The Supreme Court's Troubling Decision on 'Material Support.'"
   FP: The Middle East Channel, June 23, http://foreignpolicy.com/2010/
   06/23/the-supreme-courts-troubling-decision-on-material-support/.
Greenwald, Glenn. 2015. "Why Does the FBI Have to Manufacture Its Own

Plots If Terrorism and ISIS Are Such Grave Threats?" The // Intercept, February 26, https://firstlook.org/theintercept/2015/02/26/fbi-manufacture-plots-terrorism-isis-grave-threats/.

Hébert, Chantal. 2015. "Conservatives Risk Trapping Themselves in Own Web of Fear: Hébert." *Toronto Star*, March 10, http://www.thestar.com/news/canada/2015/03/10/conservatives-risk-trapping-themselves-in-own-web-of-fear-hbert.html.

al-Khatahtbeh, Amani. 2014. "Why We Called for a Boycott of the White House Iftar." *Huffington Post*, July 24, http://www.huffingtonpost.com/amani-alkhatahtbeh/boycott-of-the-white-house-iftar_b_5615167.html.

Lewis, Mark. 2012. "At Trial's End, Lawyers Say Norway Killer Not Insane." *New York Times*, June 22, http://www.nytimes.com/2012/06/23/world/europe/oslo-killers-lawyers-say-he-is-sane.html?ref=topics.

Macklem, Patrick. 2006. "Militant Democracy, Legal Pluralism, and the Paradox of Self-Determination." *International Journal of Constitutional Law* 4:488.

McConnell, Scott. 2009. "Holy Land Foundation Trial Reflects Misguided US Policy towards Hamas." Mondoweiss, May 29, http://mondoweiss.net/2009/05/holy-land-foundation-trial.

PBS Newshour. 1996. "Bin Laden's Fatwa," August 23, http://www.pbs.org/newshour/updates/military-july-dec96-fatwa_1996/.

– 1998. "Al Qaeda's Second Fatwa," February 23, http://www.pbs.org/newshour/updates/military-jan-june98-fatwa_1998/.

Patel, Faiza. 2011. "Rethinking Radicalization." Brennan Center for Justice, New York University School of Law, June 14, http://www.brennancenter.org/blog/rethinking-radicalization.

Rydhan, Irfan. 2014. "Ramadan 2014: White House Iftar and Learning to Play the Game." Patheos, July 25, http://www.patheos.com/blogs/altmuslim/2014/07/ramadan-2014-white-house-iftar-and-learning-to-play-the-game/.

Siddiqui, Haroon. 2015. "Harper Senators Hold McCarthyesque Hearings." *Toronto Star*, March 4, http://www.thestar.com/opinion/commentary/2015/03/04/harper-senators-hold-mccarthyesque-hearings-siddiqui.html.

Stewart, Mark, and John Mueller. 2011. "Ten Years and $1 Trillion Later, What Has All Our Security Spending Achieved?" Nieman Watchdog: Questions the Press Should Ask, June 2, http://www.niemanwatchdog.org/index.cfm?fuseaction=ask_this.view&askthisid=00512.

Waslin, Michele. 2012. "DHS's NSEERS Program, While Inactive, Continues to Discriminate." Immigration Impact, June 28, http://immigrationimpact.com/2012/06/28/dhss-nseers-program-while-inactive-continues-to-discriminate/.

Wingrove, Josh, Steven Chase, Bill Curry, and Jill Mahoney. 2014. "Attack on Ottawa: PM Harper Cites Terrorist Motive." *Globe and Mail*, October 22, http://www.theglobeandmail.com/news/national/parliament-shooting/article21217602/?page=all.

Wood, Graeme. 2015. "What ISIS Really Wants." *Atlantic*, March, http://www.theatlantic.com/features/archive/2015/02/what-isis-really-wants/384980/.

WorldPost. 2015. "In Germany, High Court Overturns Headscarf Ban for Teachers," March 13, http://www.huffingtonpost.com/2015/03/13/germany-headscarf-ban_n_6863336.html?ir=World&ncid=fcbklnkushpmg00000014.

5 The (In)Secure Citizen: Islamophobia and the Natives of the Republic after Paris

RUTH MARSHALL

The day after the *Charlie Hebdo* attacks, France's national daily, *Le Monde,* ran a full front-page headline: "The French 9/11." If this comparison seems apt from the perspective of the degree of shock and revulsion these crimes provoked, it is clearly both inadequate and ideologically freighted. On the one hand, three young French citizens from the poorest, most marginalized *banlieues*[1] – seduced as much by the nihilistic cult of violence promoted by the *Daesh* (ISIS) as its radical jihadist version of Salafism – at once amateurish and utterly ruthless in their suicidal determination to commit these spectacular murders. On the other, nineteen Al Qaeda terrorists enacting a well-financed, sophisticated, and coordinated attack that was years in the making and that killed nearly 3,000, and wounded over 6,000.

Two days after the headline, Olivier Roy, France's leading scholar on radical Islam, protested in very same *Le Monde* – *"un peu de tenu et de retenu!"* (a bit of respect and restraint) (Roy 2015). Yet in the immediate aftermath, restraint by the state and the political class, but also many journalists and public intellectuals, was not on the agenda. President François Hollande called for a massive public demonstration in solidarity with the victims and in defence of "national unity" and "the values of the Republic," turning the massive, spontaneous, national up-swelling of grief and revulsion – the "I am Charlie" of solidarity – into an emotionally charged *mot d'ordre* of state. Parties on the far left (New

---

1 Peri-urban ghettos preponderantly populated by those of North African and West African immigrant origin, whose legal status ranges from second-generation citizens to newly landed immigrants or illegals, called *"les sans papiers"* (without papers).

Anti-Capitalist Party) and far right (National Front) refused to participate, the first denouncing a political recuperation of the tragedy by a
government seeking to improve its disastrous public-approval ratings,
the second in order to stage its own rally in the FN-controlled town of
Beaucaire – "alone in defending liberty." The party Indigènes de la
République (PIR) (Natives of the Republic) observed that the great majority of the "postcolonial" Muslim population, especially the under-
class, would be watching the rally on their televisions, their solidarity
with the victims pitted against the deep sense that the *vivre-ensemble* of
democratic national unity did not include them, an impression reinforced by the presence of Israeli President Benjamin Netanyahu at the
head of the cortège, alongside other heads of state whose democratic
bona fides leave much to be desired.

Two days following the largest public demonstration in France since
the end of the Second World War, Premier Manuel Valls announced
to the National Assembly that France was "at war against terrorism,
jihadism, and radical Islam," promising measures in defence of "freedom" and *"laïcité"* as "demanded by the French" through their massive demonstration against "barbarism" (Valls 2015). The occasion was
thus seized to introduce new, draconian anti-terror legislation, further
increasing the state's powers of surveillance and repression – in a state
that had already passed nineteen security and anti-terror laws since
2001. The naming of the "enemy" and the evocation of a "sacred union"
around the war on terror and the defence of "French values" also effectively shut down public criticism, when it did not criminalize the most
provocative forms of refusal to "be Charlie." In the first two weeks following the attacks, over 100 arrests for the crime of "apology for terrorism" were made, using an expedited judicial procedure that led to
the rapid incarceration of dozens of people, the great majority of whom
were French Muslims of immigrant origin. Arrests included the well-
publicized case of the anti-Semitic stand-up comedian Dieudonné for
his "Charlie Coulibaly" Facebook post, but also several people under
the influence of alcohol, or of diminished mental capacity, a fourteen-
year-old boy who was responding to a question on the events posed by
a teacher to his class, and even the police questioning of an eight- and
a nine-year-old for expressions of solidarity with the perpetrators. Restraint was not evident in many citizens either: the Collective against
Islamophobia reported nearly as many Islamophobic attacks (128) in
the two weeks following the events as throughout the whole previous
year (133), and noted a dramatic increase in their degree of violence.

As the first waves of shock passed, protests and warnings about the dangerous path taken by the state began to be heard. The dramatic, repressive over-reach was denounced in a public statement by the French Union of Magistrates, who lamented the quasi-hysterical nature of the repressive response and demanded the state exercise restraint ("Apologie" 2015). In an op-ed piece in *Le Monde,* leftist political philosopher Alain Badiou blasted the state's "unhinged response," arguing that it was precisely the reaction sought by the perpetrators of this "fascist-type crime." He also savagely indexed *Charlie Hebdo*'s lampooning of the Prophet as "no kind of politics": "Nothing more than third-rate cultural racism ... an indulgent 'Western' provocation against not only vast popular masses in Africa, Asia, and the Middle East, but also a very large section of the working population in France itself: the people who empty our bins, wash our plates, man our pneumatic drills, hurriedly clean luxury hotel rooms and the big banks' windows at 4 a.m." (Badiou 2015).

On January 20, a week after his muscular declaration to the National Assembly, Valls threw a *pavé dans la mare* when he announced, during the traditional New Year's wishes to the press, that "there exists in France a territorial, social and ethnic apartheid" (*Le Monde* 2015). Referring to the "wounds" left by riots in the *banlieues* of 2005 (which most analysts see as having been provoked by the repressive "zero-tolerance" policies of Nicolas Sarkozy), Valls evoked the longstanding but "only intermittently discussed" "fractures, tensions ... social misery ... and daily discriminations" against those "who don't have the right name, skin colour, or because they are women." He declared that the problem facing France is not a question of integration – a word that "no longer means anything" – but rather of a "citizenship that needs to be re-founded, reinforced, and re-legitimated."

It would be naive to see in this recognition of France's failure to include its "postcolonial" citizens a denunciation of the form that the national "sacred union" around "French values" was taking, or a call to seriously address the longstanding and systematic political, economic, and social exclusion of those bearing the combined stigma of being poor, young, of North or West African origin, and of the Muslim faith. Read in the light of Valls's impassioned defence of *laïcité,* his identification of the "radical Islamic terrorist enemy" and the state's response, at once repressive and didactic – 1,000 new special "teachers of citizenship" to be trained and set to work in schools, an official state holiday celebrating *laïcité* – it should rather be seen, if not as a "wink to the right" as some observers claimed, then at least as a determination to reinforce, rather than renegotiate, the state's narrow ideological view of *laïcité* as the foundation of republican citizenship and national identity. The Socialist deputy Malek Boutih, erstwhile leader of the influential association SOS Racisme[2] (with which he subsequently broke), captured the spirit of a slide towards a security-preoccupied "state of exception" when he called for a *"mise sous tutelle"* (trusteeship) by the state of the municipality of Grigny. Already notorious as the poorest, most dangerous *banlieue* in the country, Grigny, as home to Ahmedy Coulibaly, was now indexed in the press as a "factory for terrorists." The Communist mayor, Phillip Rio, countered this demand, as well as Boutih's accusations of municipal corruption and collusion with local criminals, by a court action against him and the declaration that Grigny didn't need trusteeship, but simply a minimum of state services: "We aren't begging for anything, we just want the Republic" (König 2015).

Valls's declaration nonetheless fuelled new debates on this "lack of Republic," its causes and consequences. Such debates require a serious reckoning with the ways in which France has failed politically to address its colonial past and to accord de facto the political rights and possibilities of social and economic inclusion that its Muslim citizenry "of immigrant origin" supposedly have de jure. Yet much of the discussion that has ensued has focused less on the contemporary relays of the longstanding structural violence creating and perpetuating this exclusion, and more on the fungibility of Islam in the republic. While French republicanism has always conceived of *laïcité* as a strong version of secularism, beginning in the 1990s, the defence of republican values and French national identity has been waged in the name of an increasingly narrow understanding of *laïcité* – often tantamount to the hatred or rejection of religion in general, and Islam in particular – which, especially since 9/11, has been instrumentalized in the service of state power. Essential to the deployment and legitimation of a new

---

2 SOS Racisme, an anti-racist activist NGO, was founded in 1984, a year after the first March for Equality and against Racism in France, organized by French of North African origin against growing anti-immigrant violence, and became known as Les Potes, especially through its highly successful popular campaign "Touche pas à mon pote" (Hands off my buddy). Close to the Socialist Party, the association, and especially Boutih, have been criticized for espousing an "assimilationist" view of citizenship.

"anti-terrorist" state apparatus has been the semantic shift whereby the defence of democratic "liberty" against "obscurantism" and "barbarism" is enacted through the register of "security." The "free" citizen not only becomes subordinated to the "secure" citizen through the acceptance of what is presented as a necessary trade-off between liberties and security, but democratic freedom and the rights associated with it are redefined according to a meritocratic scale determined in function of degrees of potential threat and harm posed by individuals or groups. Such propensities are typically indexed according to understandings of identity essentialized in terms of race, ethnicity, culture, and/or religion. Insofar as the security apparatus takes juridical form principally as a preventative regime rather than a punitive one, this has the effect of reinvigorating and transforming dominant modes of social distinction in an effort to identify the "dangerous classes." Through a circular, self-affirming logic, those deserving full citizenship rights are those whose full rights had already been determined and secured by the dominant political and social order. The "insecure" citizen, the landed immigrant or *"sans papiers,"* whose subordinate or precarious social, economic, and political status had been structured by this order, is reinscribed not only as "outsider" but also as an existential threat to the Republic. This logic has the supplementary effect of delegitimizing all challenges to the dominant order that seek to address the structural causes of political and economic exclusion or struggle against their manifestations, especially in the form of racism and Islamophobia. This dynamic is patent in the ways in which, since the late 1980s, France has witnessed the concerted political construction of a new domestic enemy: the Muslim "of immigrant origin," who, by virtue of a cultural and religious difference, presents a security risk and threat to public order.

Contemporary Islamophobia in France can be seen as a "colonial continuity," a series of mutations and relays whereby old registers of racist colonial thought stigmatizing the inferiority and unassimilable character of the "Arab" – a racialized and culturally constructed vision of the North African Muslim – have mutated into the class fear and religious hatred of the Muslim youth of the *banlieues* in particular, and a rejection of Islam and suspicion of Muslims in general. The colonialist categories and conceptions that informed and justified excessive colonial violence, from the nineteenth-century "pacification" of colonial Africa to the Algerian war, continue in a new guise; colonial assimilationist policies functioning both as a mode of regulating and controlling "natives'" lives and legitimizing its "civilizing mission" are repatriated and adapted to the "integration" of the growing North African immigrant population.

Yet as the Socialist politician Michel Rocard argued in 1957 on the eve of French decolonization, integration was nothing more than a political myth in the service of state ideology: "The principle of equality before the law, which is the fundamental principle of our constitution, has never been practiced. Equal obligations exist, especially the blood tax, but never equal rights" (Le Cour Grandmaison 2005). Two years later, General de Gaulle clarified the impossibility of this "bird-brained" idea of the French Arab-Muslim citizen:

> After all, we're first and foremost a European people of white race, Greek and Latin culture, and Christian religion. Let's not kid ourselves! Have you gone to see the Muslims? Have you seen them with their turbans and their djellabas? You can see perfectly well that they're not French. Those who support integration are bird-brains, even if they are very learned. Try to integrate oil and vinegar. Shake the bottle. After awhile, they'll separate again. Arabs are Arabs, French are French. Do you really think that the French national body can absorb 10 million Muslims, who tomorrow will be 20 million, and after tomorrow 40? ... My village won't be called Colombey-les-Deux-Églises, but Colombey-les-Deux-Mosquées. (Peyrefitte 1994)

While de Gaulle's views were popularized by the far-right National Front's frankly racist anti-Arab, anti-immigration, and anti-integration nationalism of the 1980s, they were relayed in muted form as state policies under the centre-right governments of the 2000s of Chirac and Nicolas Sarkozy, especially in Sarkozy's repressive policies against illegal immigration and *banlieue* criminality. These policies culminated in the creation in 2007 of the much-denounced Ministry of Immigration, Integration, National Identity, and Co-Development, whose vast brief included the control of immigration, the management of integration, and the defence of national identity. While the controversial ministry was abandoned, and Sarkozy later "regretted" the focus on "national identity," in a striking example of political convergence of right and left, those policies focused on the defence of *laïcité* as fundamental to both republican values and national identity have been continued and extended under the current Socialist regime.

The crucial shift in focus develops over the 1990s, away from an illegitimate anti-Arab-Muslim cultural racism to a more ambiguous and "respectable" anti-Islamic discourse, publicly dramatized around the "headscarf affair" beginning in 1989. Given the widespread acceptance in France of legislation purportedly defending *laïcité*, it is worth recalling the original responses of the *Conseil d'État* in 1989, 1991, and 1992 as it pronounced on the exclusions from school of girls wearing headscarves (hijabs, or even simple bandanas). Referring to fundamental legal texts on individual rights (1789), state *laïcité* (1905), and the secular, obligatory public school (1882), among others, the *Conseil* established that the ban was contrary to the principle of freedom of conscience, which accorded the right to students to express their religious beliefs inside the school as long as academic programs weren't disrupted nor the security of other students threatened.

The emphasis on freedom of conscience was lost to the double arguments of protection of headscarf-wearing girls from "patriarchal oppression" in the name of the republican value of equality, which paradoxically took the form of excluding these same girls from the principle institutions of these values' inculcation, and the "communitarian threat" presented by the purported domestic growth of radical Islamist movements, of which these headscarves were the sign. Hence, since 2004, France has passed increasingly draconian laws regulating the religious attire and symbols of a tiny section of their population; since 2011, wearing a niqab (involving an estimated 2,000 women) in public is a criminal offence punishable by a fine or a course in "citizenship." The invocation of a security risk legitimates a new culture of informal policing, which often takes the form of physical and verbal aggression against vulnerable headscarf or niqab-wearing women. The state's combination of repression and pedagogy functions to control and police its "postcolonial" populations and enforce a normative concept of citizenship that marks them with an a priori suspicion, and a burden of proof almost impossible to satisfy.

These developments at the level of political discourse and state policy from the 1990s onward are themselves inadequate as explanations for the adherence by a very small but growing minority to a radical jihadist violence, dramatically illustrated in the Paris attacks. The other central factor is the resounding political failure of republican political organizations, as well as the range of associations developed in opposition or response to the injustices of the dominant social and political order over the past three decades, to offer a viable form of political organization and expression to those abandoned by the Republic, or an alternative to delinquency and riot, or radical jihadism. One of the reasons for this failure has been the weakness of the organizations themselves, their lack of means, and an often-sordid history of political infighting and ambition. The other, parasitic on this last point, has been the ability of successive governments to turn the leadership of various organizations challenging the status quo into mere clients. Hence under Sarkozy, the attempt to create an institutionalized, moderate, but politically effective French Islam undermined the political autonomy, but also the political legitimacy, of Islamic organizations such as the Union of Islamist Organizations of France (UOIF), with loose ties to the Muslim Brotherhood, which had attempted to develop a political presence in the *banlieues* in the 1990s.

Sarkozy imagined that an institutionalized Islam could provide a rampart against both delinquency and jihadism, and his efforts to co-opt Muslim leaders can be seen as a sort of state communitarianism. Yet the International Crisis Group's excellent analysis of the riots of 2005 revealed that Islamists had no role in fomenting the riots, and no ability to contain them, any more than they were able to counter a small, but real radical jihadist threat. Islamism in France was not only a victim of political domestication, but also of a broader failure of political Islam in the Arab world, and its succession by new forms of radical Salafism, much more individualist and transnational, and certainly not, as the French state continues to imagine, "communitarian." Contemporary forms of Salafism range from a non-violent, pietistic "sheikist" version, perfectly compatible with late capitalist individualism and consumer culture, and a transnational and virtual radically violent "jihadist," anti-Western, and anti-imperialist version, of which Al Qaeda and its various offshoots and imitators are the model (International Crisis Group 2006).

The same failures attended anti-racist militant groups such as SOS Racisme, which came to be seen as a puppet of the Socialist party and a relay for the French meritocratic vision of citizenship captured by the image of the "social escalator," as well as a vision of the republic in which the "dangerous classes" – from nineteenth-century proletarians to twentieth-century immigrants – were seen as a threat. The soft model of "integration" promoted by the Socialists in the 1990s held up as exemplary, and rewarded politically, those who had achieved a middle-class status and had adopted the cultural practices of the middle class. The recognition that integration was especially hard-won – "the escalator was out of order, so I took the stairs" – did not lead to a questioning of the cultural understanding of nationality to which the concept of integration invariably refers, nor to challenging the colonial semantic register of the civilizing mission. When politicians like Malek Boutih declare proudly that they eat the traditional French dish of salted pork with lentils, or that they drink wine, what they are saying is, "Look! We're good French, just like you, just like the 'real French,' the French *'de souche.'*"

Groups rejecting or questioning this ideology of citizenship saw themselves classified as puppets of other sinister, foreign forces: the Muslim Brotherhood and Islamic "obscurantism" in the case of Tariq Ramadan and the UOIF, or proponents of an anti-Semitic, pro-Palestinian communitarianism that provided an apology for radical Islam. This latter charge was made especially against the association-turned-political-party Les Indigènes de la République. Born in 2005 and drawing many of its members from collectives formed against the headscarf legislation, it claimed as its motivation the response to the riots and the upsurge in anti-immigrant Islamophobia. Both through its provocative name and manifesto, this group frontally attacked the "colonial continuity" in the discourses of integration and *laïcité*. Reacting to the accusation that they were pro-hijab, pro-radical Islam, and anti-republican, one of the movement's founders lamented, "Ninety per cent of us were perfect atheists. Once again we had the impression that we were being treated like a foreign body, that the nation wasn't one, whole and indivisible, as the famous discourse has it, but that the French nation was about managing the arrival of immigrants who happened to be Muslim and wanted to wear the veil" (Robine 2006).

A few days after the attacks, in his courageous article in *Le Monde*, Olivier Roy denounced, once again, "the fear of a community that doesn't exist." For the past decade, the careful research done by many analysts of Islam in France has definitively shown that while there is a very small, albeit growing, group of youth attracted to radical jihadist violence, it is neither organized nor communitarian (Roy 2009; Deltombe 2005). While it must be addressed by security measures, the question of delinquency and criminality in the *banlieues*, as well as the imagined "problem" of Islam in France demand *political* solutions. There is no substantive "Muslim" threat to democracy in France, and certainly not in the shape of headscarves, niqabs, halal school meals, or butchers. Even if the great majority of French Muslims do respect Ramadan, few regularly attend mosques, and those in the middle class have habits of consumption and cultural practices, and degrees of religious commitment on par with the rest of the "secular" citizenry. For the poorest and most excluded, a serious program of political, social, and economic inclusion is the only solution, difficult to imagine under the current climate, much less through the project of the "refoundation and re-legitimation" of citizenship-as-*laïcité*. The ongoing misrepresentations and conflations evident in political discourses and relayed in the media have created a new climate of fear and apprehension on both sides, a growing sense of political exclusion and stigmatization among the "postcolonial" middle class. The aftermath of the events has served as a brutal reminder of the limits of their acceptance as full citizens, limits they imagined or hoped their social mobility had overcome. The risk is great that the continuing response to the events will widen the group of insecure citizens, deepen the divide between them and the rest of the nation, and legitimate the growing turn to the far right's anti-democratic nationalism, handing the Republic to the National Front on a platter.

If France's troubled relation to its colonial past and postcolonial Muslim citizens is in many ways unique, the broader agenda of a defence of "Western values" against terrorist Islam is not. Political discourses and policies across Europe, the United States, and now Canada are fulfilling Huntington's ideologically grounded prophecy of a "clash of civilizations" and legitimating a new neo-imperialism and a security-justified hijacking of liberal democracy and the rule of law. The particular forms and internal effects of this trend vary according to the political and historical specificities of each Western democracy, yet France appears to have a symbolic yet paradoxical place in this unfolding drama around the "defence of civilizational values." The *"pays des droits de l'homme"* and the democratic revolution has faced special political difficulties in adjusting its republicanism and concept of national identity to the realities of pluralism, especially the "integration" of its immigrant populations – from its second-generation citizens to its recent arrivals. The Paris attacks are the latest test of an almost fatally foundering vision of a France *"black, blanc, beur,"* whose survival is entirely dependent on the political choices to come. How French politicians, media, intellectuals, and citizens respond in the coming months to the trauma of these events will be telling, not only for the future of French democracy, but for Western democracy as well. The idea that "it will get worse before it gets better" seems less inaccurate than naive as regards the final outcome.

REFERENCES

"Apologie du terrorisme: la justice face à l'urgence." 2015. *Le Monde*, January 22, http://www.lemonde.fr/societe/article/2015/01/22/ apologie-du-terrorisme-la-justice-face-a-l-urgence_4560603_3224 .html#U2KpqZJ3oMIcZxrW.99.

Badiou, Alain. 2015. "Le Rouge et le Tricolore." *Le Monde*, January 27, http://abonnes.lemonde.fr/idees/article/2015/01/27/le-rouge-et-le-tricolore_4564083_3232.html.

Deltombe, Thomas. 2005. *L'Islam imaginaire: La construction médiatique de l'islamophobie en France, 1975–2005*. Paris: La Découverte.

French Government. 2015. "Discours de Manuel Valls à l'Assemblée nationale en hommage aux victimes des attentats," January 13, http://www.gouvernement.fr/partage/3118-seance-speciale-d-hommage-aux-victimes-des-attentats-allocution-de-manuel-valls-premier-ministre.

International Crisis Group. 2006. La France face à ses musulmans: Émeutes, jihadisme et dépolitisation. Rapport Europe de Crisis Group No. 172, March 9.

König, Benjamin. 2015. "À Grigny, on ne quémande rien, on veut la République." *L'Humanité*, February 27, http://www.humanite.fr/grigny-ne-quemande-rien-veut-la-republique-566927.

Le Cour Grandmaison, Olivier. 2005. *Coloniser, exterminer: Sur la guerre et l'État colonial*. Paris: Fayard.

Le Monde. 2015. "Manuel Valls évoque 'un apartheid territorial, social, ethnique' en France." January 20, http://www.lemonde.fr/politique/article/2015/01/20/pour-manuel-valls-il-existe-un-apartheid-territorial-social-ethnique-en-france_4559714_823448.html.

Peyrefitte, Alain. 1994. *C'était de Gaulle*, tome 1. Paris: Fallois/Fayard.

Robine, Jérémy. 2006. "Les 'indigènes de la République': nation et question postcoloniale. Territoires des enfants de l'immigration et rivalité de pouvoir." *Hérodote* 120 (1): 118–48.

Roy, Olivier. 2009. *Secularism Confronts Islam*. Translated by G. Holoch. New York: Columbia University Press.

– 2015. "La peur d'une communauté qui n'existe pas." *Le Monde*, January 9, http://www.lemonde.fr/idees/article/2015/01/09/la-peur-d-une-communaute-qui-n-existe-pas_4552804_3232.html#5MpzblRIoUAu53Eg.99.

Valls, Manuel. 2015. "Discours de Manuel Valls à l'Assemblée nationale en hommage aux victimes des attentats." French Government, January 13, http://www.gouvernement.fr/partage/3118-seance-speciale-d-hommage-aux-victimes-des-attentats-allocution-de-manuel-valls-premier-ministre.

6 Evil as a Noun: Dichotomous Avoidance of Political Analysis

MARK G. TOULOUSE

The ideologies associated with the history of modern terrorism, beginning with the Reign of Terror in Paris, includes such things as anarchism, nationalism, and fascism. When the Jacobins spread terror in 1790s France, no one had difficulty understanding terrorism as a political strategy. Their motivations included the desire to create a united republic, one capable of defeating both internal enemies and an array of hostile forces surrounding France. Jacobins used terror to consolidate their power and intimidate their enemies. After all, terrorism *is* a strategy, a policy of systematic and rational use of irrational violence to reach some particular end. Terrorism has always been a strategy with an aim, nearly always a political aim, perhaps one occasionally wrapped in religious garb, but always serving a political goal nonetheless. When terrorism strikes these days, now seemingly associated only with radical Islamists, a good many political leaders in the West seem unable to fathom it or to analyse it by connecting it to underlying political aims and motivations. Instead, leaders define it as radical religious fanaticism, and many respond in fear, which in fact only lends credence to just how successful the strategies associated with terrorism can be.

Like almost anyone older than seven or eight in 2001, I won't ever forget the horror of 9/11, watching television coverage on a nine-inch television screen in my office in Texas. For me, watching the Twin Towers live on television immediately joined, and surpassed in intensity, a few of the gut-wrenching events I have witnessed through television in my lifetime. These include the 1960s assassinations of the Kennedy brothers and Martin Luther King, and the 1989 *Challenger* and 2003 *Columbia* explosions, the last occurring on the morning of my birthday. I suppose the fact that these items make my list when other devastating occurrences in the world do not, like the different ethnic cleansings that killed tens of thousands of Georgians (campaign of Abkhaz separatists in 1993) and Bosnian Muslims and Bosnian Croats (campaign of Bosnian Serbs from 1992 to 1995), is rather dramatic evidence itself of the pervasive ethnocentrism found in Western media. But, for me, 9/11 somehow stands in a category all by itself.

In the immediate hours following the attack, President George Bush assumed a measured and cautious tone, speaking about an "apparent terrorist attack." By evening, his tone had changed. Broadcasting from the Oval Office, he said, "Today, our nation saw evil" (2001a). He prefaced that comment with a description of America as the "brightest beacon for freedom and opportunity in the world." Borrowing that night subtly from the Bible, John 1, as he would do again in even more dramatic fashion a year later in his anniversary speech from Ellis Island, Bush described America as the light of the world that no one will ever extinguish. In this way, Bush started down a path of rhetorical characterization meant to justify a war on terrorism as a battle of Good against Evil, and Light against Dark. In fact, during a photo opportunity with the prime minister of Japan, Bush (2001b) quipped to reporters, "Make no mistake about it: This is good versus evil." As I have indicated elsewhere, Bush's religiously oriented perspective after 9/11 made sophisticated political analysis seem unnecessary (Toulouse 2006, 96–104).

President Bush's style of religious response to terrorist activity demanded total allegiance from the faithful. No neutrality allowed. As Bush (2001c) told Congress in the wake of 9/11, "Every nation, in every region, now has a decision to make. Either you are with us, or you are with the terrorists." In general, except on two unfortunate occasions, he avoided describing the conflict as a "crusade." It is interesting to note that the last time Bush (2002) used "crusade" as a description of the war on terrorism, he referred to the Canadian Armed Forces who "stand with us in this incredibly important crusade to defend freedom." Those two occasions, nonetheless, startled the Arab world, where the translation came out as "war of the cross."

When Peter Singer (2004, 2), a philosopher and bioethicist at Princeton, analysed Bush's speeches, he discovered that 319 speeches, fully 30 per cent of them, delivered between his inauguration and June 16, 2003, made reference to "evil." Bush used the term primarily as a noun rather than adjective. Evil is a force, not something people do. Though, for Bush, people could themselves be evil, deep within the nature of who and what they are. Bush's use of *evil* in response to terrorism contained profound theological overtones. His use of the term indicated a state of being that stands over against both God and good. Bush believed America's mission naturally included the eradication of evil, including persons who embodied evil. So Osama bin Laden, characterized by Bush and others as "the evil one," had to be eliminated at all costs.

The events in Paris on January 7 have brought a discussion of evil to the forefront once again, in the media and in the political world. Yet there are distinct differences between the rhetoric of President Obama when compared both to President Bush and to Prime Minister Stephen Harper. Obama (2015a) stressed his solidarity with France as he mentioned the "cowardly, evil attacks" against *Charlie Hebdo,* and emphasized the need "to hunt down and bring the perpetrators of this specific act to justice and to roll up the networks that help to advance these kinds of plots." Obama used *evil* as an adjective, defining the actions of the perpetrators as "evil attacks." The day after, Prime Minister Harper (2015a) emphasized instead the connection between Paris and a unified jihadist movement of terror that has "declared war on any country like ourselves that values freedom, openness, and tolerance." In his speech outlining the need to pass new anti-terror legislation for Canada (Bill C-51), Harper (2015b) echoed George Bush's use of *evil* as a noun when he announced, "A great evil has been descending upon our world, an evil which has been growing more and more powerful: violent jihadism." There are considerable differences, theologically, between *evil* as an adjective and *evil* as a noun.

When the current U.S. president condemns evil actions, he leaves open the need to explore and understand the motivations behind the actions. What kind of environment or context led to these activities? In the case of the 9/11 attacks, had President Bush used the adjective instead of the noun, Americans might have spent some time reflecting as a country whether their government, or their people, or the business world itself (symbolized by those working within the towers) did anything, however great or small, that might have contributed to an environment where these kinds of evil activities could have emerged. Were American foreign policies, national economic interests, self-righteous declarations of American superiority, or the egregious imbalance of global wealth and resources connected in any way to motivations stimulating such terrorist acts? In reflecting about such questions, one is not justifying cowardly or evil acts of terrorism. Evil acts, acts of terrorism, are not justifiable in any sense. Rather, one is attempting to understand contexts within which such evil activities likely arise. In important ways, asking these kinds of questions would help countries and their leaders understand a great deal more about the politics and motivations connected with terrorism.

For me, Harper's recent use of *evil* in response to January 7 is eerily reminiscent of George Bush. Canada, indeed the rest of the world, has no need to understand the motivations or politics standing behind terrorist acts when we hear that "a great evil has been descending upon our world." Whether we like it or not, evil has declared war on us. When you can describe the pilots of planes on 9/11 or the gun-wielders in Paris as evil, or identify the great and global evil behind all such attacks, no other questions are necessary. The perpetrators, whoever they are, are no longer human; instead, leaders like Bush and Harper have dehumanized them. They become part and parcel of the "great evil." Unlike human beings, great evil needs no motivations. And good governments can eliminate great evil with impunity. The dehumanization of our enemies leads to places like Abu Ghraib and Guantanamo, where torture seems a natural response. Evil is simply evil and only begets more evil. Standing against evil with all your might is simply good. Evil must be wiped out. Who can oppose that? No changes are required of us except for the fact that we have to take the fight to the evil ones.

That fight leads right to war. Or, on the domestic front, to legislative responses like the Patriot Act and Bill C-51, without worrying about human rights or democratic freedoms that might be trampled along the way. After all, war demands sacrifice. Yet, things are never so simple. If we neglect to ask questions about the politics and motivations behind terrorist activities, we will only continue to create the politics and motivations within which such evil activities will emerge with regular occurrence. Half-baked legislative responses born of fear only contribute to contexts where radicalization becomes more rather than less likely. The contrast between Obama and Bush (and recently, Harper) is stark and illuminating. In the preface to his administration's new *National Security Strategy*, released on February 6, 2015, Obama said,

> Finally, I believe that America leads best when we draw upon our hopes rather than our fears ... That is why I have worked to ensure that America has the capabilities we need to respond to threats abroad, while acting in line with our values – prohibiting the use of torture; embracing constraints on our use of new technologies like drones; and upholding our commitment to privacy and civil liberties ... Moreover, we must recognize that a

smart national security strategy does not rely solely on military power. Indeed, in the long-term, our efforts to work with other countries to counter the ideology and root causes of violent extremism will be more important than our capacity to remove terrorists from the battlefield.

Here, Obama gives at least a nod to the need to counter not only ideologies and fear, but "root causes" as well, and acknowledges that these efforts are more important than neutralizing terrorists.

Media in North America, whether oriented to the right or left, contribute to a simplistic misunderstanding of terrorism. January 7 has not provided much exception to that tendency. Members of the conservative media, particularly in the United States, often turned their interpretation of *Charlie Hebdo* into arguments for additional surveillance of Muslim groups, tougher immigration laws, and racial profiling (Boguhn et al. 2015). Sean Hannity (2015) argued on air with Imam Anjem Choudary and called him an "evil SOB." Bill O'Reilly argued that Americans are in a "holy war" that Obama needs to take more seriously (Saul 2015). Others on the right, like Chris Selley (2015) writing for the *National Post* in Toronto, complained that newspapers should be publishing the offending cartoons, and attacked those to their left, like the *New York Times* and the *Globe and Mail*, for their cowardice in declining to publish them. While most liberal media outlets did not publish the offending cartoons, they equally stressed the sacred importance of journalistic freedom and the right to publish unlimited satire, defined inherently as material that crosses one line of suitability or another. Generally unlike conservative counterparts, those in the liberal media also simultaneously urged readers not to blame Muslims in general for the attacks in Paris. In the end, however, neither the media's right nor left, with but a few exceptions in between, had much interest in pursuing an understanding of the deeper causes for these kinds of terrorist acts.

The prevailing narrative surrounding terrorist acts like those in Paris continues to establish a largely false dichotomy. Explanations always pit the freedom-loving and democratic values of the West against the ruthless and inhumane violence associated with our common enemies. Duncan Thomas (2015) described this "grand, civilizational framing of events" as "intellectually lazy and analytically useless, substituting the surface of the conflict for its substance." He continues, "While Islamist terrorism may express itself in religious and cultural terms, its origin is political – which is to say that it only takes place within current power relations and material conditions, never outside them. In the production of these conditions, the major actors are the very same western states which now with hypocrisy and hubris claim that their 'values' are under attack by a demonic and incomprehensible foe." Thomas's point is not to excuse terrorism, but rather to understand the meaning and motivations associated with the conflict. Terrorism is, in his view, an attempt to visit the West with the "same senseless horror that the west regularly visits upon the 'Third World.' As such, the abhorrent morality of the acts is itself part of an ethical message that Western societies must have the courage to recognise – not in order to absolve the immediate culprits, but to confront the naked horror of a relationship of violence of which our own states are the pre-eminent producers."

Canadians would not be alone in their rejection of Thomas's interpretation. The vast majority of Americans and French vastly prefer dichotomous approaches. Honest analysis, however, of Iraq and Afghanistan as responses to 9/11 and their impact on civilian populations, rationalized by largely dichotomous thinking, should cause us to pause. Demonizing terrorism through loosely applied theological terms does not help address any matter of substance. Terrorists are human beings, complete with a set of complicated motivations. The audio tape of Amedy Coulibaly, the terrorist connected to the events of January 7 who murdered four hostages in a grocery store in Paris two days later, revealed he understood himself as acting in response to the French military killing of innocents in Mali and elsewhere in the Middle East (Hanrahan 2015). Is it accurate to describe his violent acts, and those of brothers Cherif and Said Kouachi at *Charlie Hebdo,* as deranged, explainable only by their connection to irrational religious fanaticism, killing primarily to avenge sacrilegious and racist cartoons? No, it is not.

Whether connected to Al-Qaeda or the Islamic State or both, terrorism nearly always has an endgame. Cherif Kouachi had a long history of connection to terrorism. Writing two days after the attacks, Myriam Francois-Cerrah (2015) offered a credible political explanation in the pages of Britain's *New Statesman* for the brothers' actions. By attacking the offices of *Charlie Hebdo,* she argued, the brothers participated in a broader motive of creating polarization, acting "to deepen already profound rifts in French society and establish an atmosphere ripe for the recruitment of alienated youths." Life for Muslims has been increasingly difficult in France in recent years as the result a variety of publicized clashes of custom and belief. After January 7, "Je suis *Charlie*" only reinforced natural tendencies to respond to terrorism by creating a "with us or against us" bifurcation. As Francois-Cerrah put it, while it is possible "to have little sympathy with a publication which often crossed the line into racism, while having total empathy and solidarity with the individuals murdered," the popular response to January 7 hardly expresses it. Are Muslim values and European values, particularly in this case French values, compatible? The terrorists want everyone, both Muslims and non-Muslims, to believe they are not. The dichotomy advocated by much of our political leadership in the West only serves the terrorists' endgame.

In October 2013, terrorist Michael Zehaf-Bibeau stormed the Canadian Parliament and killed a soldier. Numerous stories have circulated in Canadian media about the successful recruitment of Muslim youth in Canada. Several attacks on Canadian society have been thwarted and these successes well-publicized. These events have had an impact on Canadian sentiments about Islam. On March 10, Prime Minister Harper, speaking in the House of Commons, made his own contribution to the thesis of an incompatible clash of values between Islam and the West by claiming Canadian values cannot abide the niqab, "a practice ... rooted in a culture that is anti-women" (Bryden 2015). Harper's approach has the political advantage of playing favourably for the 80 per cent of Canadians who oppose wearing niqabs while taking the oath of citizenship in Canada. Yet it also has the side effect of feeding Canadian fear by linking niqabs to his vision of "a great evil ... descending," taking us one step closer to connecting everyday Muslims to terrorists. Polls show anti-Muslim sentiment has grown significantly in Canada since 2009.

The Western response to terrorism can be as damaging as the acts of terror creating it, particularly when it divides the world into good and bad. These two recent political moves of the Harper government, in response to niqabs and to the attacks of January 7, contribute to an increasing polarization between Muslims and non-Muslims in Canada. Terrorism continues to do its work across the world in instilling fear. Will our responses make things better or worse? These days it is tougher than it was even a decade ago to be a Muslim both in France and in Canada. Somewhere out there terrorists are probably smiling.

REFERENCES

Boguhn, Alexandrea, Cal Colgan, Olivia Kittel, and Sophia Tesfaye. 2015.
    "How Conservatives Exploited the Charlie Hebdo Terror Attack in
    Paris." Media Matters for America, January 7, http://mediamatters.org/

research/2015/01/07/how-conservatives-exploited-the-charlie-hebdo-t/202043.

Bryden, Joan. 2015. "Harper: Niqabs 'Rooted in a Culture That Is Anti-Women.'" *Huffington Post Canada*, February 10, http://www.huffingtonpost.ca/2015/03/10/harper-calls-muslim-face-_n_6842768.html.

Bush, George W. 2001a. "Address to the Nation on 9/11," September 11, http://www.americanrhetoric.com/speeches/gwbush911addresstothe nation.htm.

– 2001b. "International Campaign against Terror Grows," September 25, http://2001–2009.state.gov/s/ct/rls/rm/2001/5065.htm.

– 2001c. "Transcript of President Bush's Address," September 20, http:// edition.cnn.com/2001/US/09/20/gen.bush.transcript/.

– 2002. "Remarks to the Troops at Elmendorf Air Force Base in Anchorage, Alaska," February 16. In *Public Papers of the Presidents of the United States, Administration of George W. Bush, 2002*, 237. United States Government Publishing Office, http://www.gpo.gov/fdsys/pkg/PPP-2002-book1/pdf/PPP-2002-book1-doc-pg236.pdf.

Francois-Cerrah, Myriam. 2015. "Is the Charlie Hebdo Attack Really a Struggle over European Values?" *New Statesman*, January 9, http://www.newstatesman.com/politics/2015/01/charlie-hebdo-attack-really-struggle-over-european-values.

Hannity, Sean. 2015. "'I Still Think You're an Evil SOB': Hannity Clashes with Radical Imam." Fox News Inside, January 7, http://insider.foxnews.com/2015/01/07/hannity-clashes-radical-imam-anjem-choudary-following-charlie-hebdo-terror-attack.

Hanrahan, Mark. 2015. "New Audio Purportedly Shows Amedy Coulibaly, Paris Hyper Cacher Hostage-Taker, Tried to Justify Action to Captives." *International Business Times*, January 11, http://www.ibtimes.com/new-audio-purportedly-shows-amedy-coulibaly-paris-hyper-cacher-hostage-taker-tried-1779730.

Harper, Stephen. 2015a. "Jihadists 'Declared War' on Those Who Disagree, Stephen Harper Says." CBC News, January 8, http://www.cbc.ca/news/politics/jihadists-declared-war-on-those-who-disagree-stephen-harper-says-1.2894008.

– 2015b. "PM Delivers Remarks in Richmond Hill," January 30, http://pm.gc.ca/eng/video/38139/transcript.

Obama, Barack. 2015a. "Charlie Hebdo: President Obama Condemns 'Cowardly,' 'Evil' Paris Attacks." ABC News, January 7, http:// abcnews.go.com/News/obama-condemns-cowardly-evil-paris-attacks/story?id=28058882.

– 2015b. *National Security Strategy.* https://www.whitehouse.gov/sites/
default/files/docs/2015_national_security_strategy.pdf.

Saul, Heather. 2015. "Fox News Presenter Bill O'Reilly Declares a 'Holy War'
against Isis." *Independent*, February 19, http://www.independent.co.uk/
news/people/fox-news-presenter-bill-oreilly-declares-a-holy-war-against-
isis-during-talking-points-segment-10056236.html.

Selley, Chris. 2015. "Why Canada's Media Won't Show the Charlie Hebdo
Pictures." *National Post*, January 13, http://news.nationalpost.com/2015/
01/13/chris-selley-why-canadas-media-wont-show-the-charlie-hebdo-
pictures/.

Singer, Peter. 2004. *The President of Good and Evil.* New York: Dutton.

Thomas, Duncan. 2015. "Charlie Hebdo and Western Denial." Open Democracy: Free Thinking for the World, January 15, https://www.opendemocracy
.net/arab-awakening/duncan-thomas/charlie-hebdo-and-western-denial-0.

Toulouse, Mark G. 2006. *God in Public: Four Ways American Christianity and
Public Life Relate.* Louisville: Westminster John Knox.

7 The Search for Equal Membership in the Age of Terror

AYELET SHACHAR

"Install a CCTV in every house" reads a recent headline in a U.K. daily newspaper; it captures the after-the-Paris-attacks sentiment that has echoed throughout the world. It also reflects the immediate response of many governments that focuses on introducing ever more robust counterterrorism legislation, with ever greater surveillance powers that license executives to act swiftly at home and abroad. But, especially in France and in many other countries as well, the attacks also invoked a series of deeper reflections on the boundaries of free speech, patterns of social exclusion, and the fraught relations between majorities and minorities in our increasingly diverse societies. My comments contribute to this latter set of investigations. Stepping back from the immediate pressures of emergency responses, I wish to call attention to the importance of how courts and legislatures frame state-religion relations in France, as compared to Canada, and reflect on the weight of the promise of *liberté*, *égalité*, and *fraternité*, for contemporary re-evaluations of citizenship in the age of terror.

On Majorities and Minorities

France is globally renowned for its valorization of the staunch separation of state and religion, epitomized in the quasi-constitutional principle of *laïcité* (or secularism), according to which the republic neither recognizes nor subsidizes any religion. Far less known, however, is the fact that the legal framework governing the *laïcité* principle dates back to the 1905 law that officially separated the church from the state by abolishing the Concordat system that had previously entrenched the social and political influence of the dominant Roman Catholic Church (Laborde 2008, 33). In other words, the principle of *laïcité* was not designed to target or restrict minority cultures or communities, but to tame the public influence of the *majority* religion, Catholicism and its powerful institutional apparatus, in the affairs of the state. As one scholar eloquently observes, whereas in the United States the purpose of separating church and state was to "avoid interference of the government in church matters … [i]n France, it was exactly the reverse: the purpose of separating church and state was to protect the new French [secular] democracy from the Catholic Church" (Vaïsse 2004, 2). As a result, "the custom in France was (and still is) to keep religious faith as a private matter. This tradition is … linked in France to the long battle against the power and public exposure of Catholic faith" (Weil 2004).

Today, more than a hundred years after the enactment of the 1905 law, the same basic framework of an explicit and unapologetic commitment to secularism (or what some have termed "militant secularism") remains vital to the self-perception of the French republic. It not only shapes the interaction of the state with various religious institutions, but also requires *individuals*, when in public, to express themselves as citizens first and foremost, highlighting their shared civic identity while refraining from any "visible," "ostensible," or "sectarian" manifestations of their (private) religious faith. Indeed, the full force of *laïcité* now manifests itself primarily in responses to demands made by members of *minority* communities who seek to express distinctive aspects of their non-dominant religious affiliation.

Examples abound. In 2004, extensive debates surrounding the donning of the hijab (the headscarf worn by some Muslim women) led to the enactment of national legislation banning the display of "conspicuous religious symbols" in public schools. Although couched in neutral terms, the law is widely understood as interdicting the hijab. The seeds for the 2004 law banning the hijab in public schools had been planted fifteen years earlier, in a saga known as *l'affaire foulard* (the scarf affair), which ignited "national and even international political controversy" (Minow 1991, 122). This protracted public confrontation arose when hijab-wearing Muslim girls arrived at their local public school with their heads covered, defying a compromise previously reached between their parents and school officials, according to which the girls would attend their classes "unscarfed." The girls were responding to the punishing either-or choice into which the compromise had forced them: either they might become "cultureless" members of the state by refraining from wearing the hijab, and thus gaining equal entitlement to valued goods such as public education, or else, were they to uphold their "differences" by veiling, their action might be perceived by the majority as opposing national unity and republican values. After refusing to remove their headscarves, the girls were summarily expelled by the school's principal. This situation and its aftermath have placed a tremendously onerous weight on the (covered) heads of girls and women who are, lest we forget, French *and* Muslim, negotiating an inevitably complex set of multiple affiliations in an environment where their bodies and visible markers of identity have become the home-front battleground upon which the anxieties, interests, and identity struggles of both majority and minority members are fought.

In 1989, *l'affaire foulard* reached the *Conseil d'État*, which, at the time, rejected the notion that the hijab itself posed an affront to the principle of *laïcité*. By 2004, the legal reasoning and tone of debate had already shifted, manifesting a much stronger expression of the *majoritarian* argument against the wearing of the hijab that formally relies on the separation doctrine. As legal commentators in France have noted, the new law holds that "*laïcité* makes demands of religious restraint on the part of pupils" (Laborde 2008, 53). What gets lost in this heated debate is the fact that the "religious restraint" demanded by the law is not equally borne by *all* students. It places a disproportionately heavier burden on those whose faith requires *public* expression denoting their "private" religious affiliation; this is the case for believers who wish to wear the Muslim headscarf, the Sikh turban, or the Jewish yarmulke. In this drama, visible religious markers of identity have become symbols of deep political and societal intercommunal tensions and growing distrust among majority and minority communities in France. These controversies have escalated over time, manifesting growing rifts that engender a dangerous narrative of *"nous" et les "autres,"* creating a binary, zero-sum dynamic of "us" vs "them" (Benhabib 2002, 24–6).

In 2010, France became the first country in the world to *criminalize* the wearing of face veils, such as the niqab (a face veil that leaves only the eyes visible) *anywhere* in public – with the exception of houses of worship. The draft of the 2010 law included an explanatory memorandum, which stated, "Even though the phenomenon, at present, remains marginal, the wearing of the full veil is the sectarian manifestation of a rejection of the values of the republic." The law was passed by the National Assembly by an overwhelming majority (335 votes in favour, 1 vote against, and 3 abstentions). The Senate also followed suit with 246 votes in favour and 1 abstention. In drafting the legislation, as part of its fact-finding mission a parliamentary committee had concluded that "the wearing of the full-face veil on national territory" was a recent phenomenon in France, and by the end of 2009, was practised by only about 1,900 women out of France's 4.7-million-strong Muslim population. This is approximately 0.0004 of the relevant population, or a ratio of less than 1 in 2500. Numbers are not everything in legislation, but in the context of heightened political and legal tensions surrounding an "ostentatious" expression of a minority identity that is increasingly perceived as threatening and "foreign," it is hard not to be reminded of William Blackstone's observation that whereas civil injuries are "an infringement ... of the civil rights which belong to individuals ... public wrongs, or crimes ... are a breach and violation of the public rights and duties, due to the whole community" (Blackstone 1765–69 [1825], book 4). The act of defining an expression of particular, more conservative variants of the Islamic faith as a public wrong bears not only a punitive function, but also an *expressivist* meaning: the outrage of the majority community against what it perceives as an offensive repudiation of *laïcité* and other foundational values of the republic. From that vantage point, the person who breaches the criminal code's prohibition against face-veiling acts in violation of the whole community and its "common culture." In this way, the criminal code – and the state machinery that enacts and enforces it – expresses moral condemnation of the *actor* not just the prohibited act.

From the official statist perspective, however, prohibiting such expression of religious minority identity, or "sectarianism," is merely a manifestation of the familiar *laïcité* principle, which resists *any* expression of religiosity as a breach of neutrality and secularism; it is also a necessary measure for promoting social cohesion. However, this framework fails to take context into account – the realization that using the full force of the power of the state to legally prohibit a member of a *minority community* from expressing certain aspects of her religious identity holds additional dimensions of marginalization and exclusion. Equality among citizens is affected by defining her "veiled" presence in public spaces as harmful to others. These other dimensions are camouflaged when the statist discourse claims simply to be applying the separation doctrine, one that developed under very different circumstances in relation to a *dominant* majority's church. To put this last point somewhat differently, what is missing from the official narrative is an account of the *power relations* and *context* in which the encounter between the individual and the state occurs.

Context Matters

So far, the discussion has focused on France. Let us quickly shift gears and venture closer to home, where the Supreme Court of Canada has repeatedly emphasized the importance of a contextual analysis in its constitutional jurisprudence. A textbook example is found in one of Canada's landmark post-Charter religious freedom cases, *Big M*, in which the Supreme Court of Canada struck down the federal Lord's Day Act. In an oft-cited paragraph of that decision, the Court stated, "What may appear good and true to a majoritarian religious group, or to the state acting at their behest, may not ... be imposed upon citizens who take a contrary view. The Charter safeguards religious minorities from the threat of the 'tyranny of the majority'" (Big M, para. 96). This last point is crucial. The majority of Canadians may accept Sunday as the Lord's Day, but this does not represent the perspective of religious minorities in Canada, be they members of the Jewish faith, Sabbatarians, Muslim Canadians, agnostics, or those with no theistic belief. As Justice Dickson said, speaking for the Court, "To the extent that it binds all to a sectarian Christian ideal, the Lord's Day Act works a form of coercion inimical to the spirit of the Charter and the dignity of all non-Christians." The Lord's Day Act, continues the Court, "takes religious values rooted in Christian morality and, using the force of the state, translates them into a positive law binding on believers and non-believers alike." It is at this stage of the analysis that section 27 of the Charter (the multiculturalism provision) is brought into the discussion: "To accept that Parliament retains the right to compel universal observance of the day of rest preferred by one religion [the dominant majority religion] is not consistent with the preservation and enhancement of the multicultural heritage of Canadians." Here, we find concerns about unequal power relations between majorities and minorities imported directly into the judgment. In fact, respecting diversity and fair inclusion through a wide range of measures designed to make it possible for religious and other minorities, if they so wish, to "express their cultural [or religious] particularity and pride without hampering their success in the economic and political institutions of the dominant society" has become a hallmark of Canadian jurisprudence – from *Multani* to *Amselem* – to mention but a few recent Supreme Court decisions. It is now one of the country's most significant intellectual "trademarks," parading through the comparative "traffic" of constitutional ideas migrating across borders (Ryder 2008, 87; Kymlicka 1995; Choudhry 2011; Shachar 2013; Hirschl 2014).

Unlike Canada's explicit commitment to a multicultural model of citizenship, France adheres to a unitary, civic-republican conception of citizenship. Despite this core distinction, both countries are committed to promoting religious freedom and must responsibly address social tensions surrounding the *"nous" et les "autres"* divide that may only deepen and sharpen in the wake of "home-grown" terrorism attacks. Whereas Canada seeks to resolve these dilemmas by adopting a unity-in-diversity approach, France seems to be promoting a unity-in-unity approach. The gist of these competing visions can be illustrated by comparing the judicial pronouncement in *Big M* with an influential public address delivered by President Jacques Chirac after the enactment of the 2004 law banning headscarves and any other visible religious identity markers from state schools in France.

The president's speech opens with a statement that should sound familiar by now: "What is at stake is supporting the principle of secularism, which is one of the pillars of our republic." This is the entrenched *laïcité* and blindness-to-difference framework that we have already encountered. By banning signs of religious affiliation, argued the president, the new law "protects our schools from breaking down along ethnic lines." (Interestingly, categories between religion and ethnicity, origins and convictions are blurred here.) But the most crucial part of the statement is this: "Choosing to ban conspicuous signs of religion in schools is a decision that respects our history, our customs, and our values." Presumably, the reiterated "our" is inscribed as French, civic-republican, and secular. It requires little imagination to fill in the blanks as to what would constitute "their" history, "their" customs, and "their" values.

The message was not lost upon many French Muslims, including those who demonstrated, in France and elsewhere in Europe, against the ban. This, in turn, only contributed to growing fears among those holding a rigid interpretation of the almost sacrosanct principle of *laïcité* in France. Finally, it fuelled the efforts of opportunistic vote-seeking politicians who stoked fear and prejudice in order to strengthen their numbers. In fact, as several commentators have suggested, the fear of the "Other" (*l'autre*) now only exacerbated after the Paris attacks, has been manifested across Europe as part of a "moral panic" that leads more extreme parties claiming to speak on behalf of *majority* communities that seek to protect *their* "endangered" collective identity, engaging, in effect, in Europe's "cultural defence" (Orgad 2009).

Inclusive Promises, Exclusionary Realities

In the space remaining, I wish to turn quickly to the topics of citizenship, the promise of equal opportunity, and the damning reality of social exclusion. To oversimplify, France adheres to a civic-republican model that treats the citizen as a public persona who must be void of any "particularistic" or group-based markers; in other words, it is a blindness-to-differences model that is formally and legally committed to the idea that "individuals have a fundamental interest in living in a polity that treats them as equal citizens, regardless of their particular loyalties, identities, and beliefs." The vision of civic-republican citizenship is more demanding than a mere liberal conception of membership, in that not only does it create rights for the individual vis-à-vis the state, but also certain duties of public-mindedness and participation. As every student of citizenship will know, since the French Revolution – which abolished the monarchical and hierarchical ancien régime – the national motto of France has been *liberté, égalité*, and *fraternité*. The centrality of the values of equality, liberty, and solidarity is frequently cited as a "foundation-stone of our [French] social covenant." It is also a symbol of the victory of republican secular democrats over the royalists and their closely aligned Catholic Church.

Beyond France, it has also proven a tremendously influential "export" throughout the world. Just to provide one example, it was the French republican model, emphasizing the role of the state in "forging" and educating citizens, that has led to the establishment of a national education system back in 1882, introducing the now-familiar, but then radically novel, concept of publicly funded free *laic* education in non-denominational schools. This history also partly explains why it was necessarily in the public school setting, the presumed "cradle of equal citizenship," that the hijab controversy erupted with such intensity, holding up a disconcerting mirror that revealed the tremendous gap between the rhetoric of an egalitarian mixed society where integration reigns, and the much harsher reality of deep and systemic social exclusion experienced by many members of France's Muslim minority, the largest in Europe. These concerns over the lack of integration, or social exclusion, manifest themselves across multiple and overlapping axes, such as under-employment, socioeconomic deprivation, and lack of political representation. While there is room for legitimate debate about the causes and effects of past social policies on these contemporary patterns, as well as the agency of marginalized minorities themselves, targeting these problems *directly* seems more conducive to achieving the declared goals of equality, liberty, and fraternity than adopting "expressivist" laws that sheathe popular anxieties about the discomfort of living side-by-side with veiled Muslim women who are de jure included in the polity, but are de facto ostracized as the quintessential "Other." The tremendous political capital invested in such laws as symbolic manifestations of an idealized "France [that] is never as much itself, faithful to its history, its destiny, its image, than when united around the values of the republic: liberty, equality, fraternity," as the 2010 law explanatory memorandum reads, may end up detracting attention from France's deep and complex inter-communal problems and waylaying the more difficult task of wrestling them head-on.

Alas, if the past is any prediction of the future, there is little reason to assume that we will see such changes occur overnight, or even in the near future. Precisely because so much rides on the symbolic and historical weight associated with the French civic-republican conception of citizenship, it will likely be harder to amend than less successful models. To draw on Albert Hirschman's seminal *Exit, Voice, and Loyalty,* it is frequently the more established, august institutions and nations that, when the old familiar solutions and slogans no longer work, find confronting a new reality harder to address. Change, even when sorely and pressingly needed, may prove a tough remedy to adopt.

While we cannot read the future in tea leaves, it is safe to assume that France will remain France. It will not become America, Canada, Algeria, or "Eurabia," but it will have to develop new pathways for integration that do not require erasing an individual's sense of membership in a minority community. Criminalizing the expression of religious identity may provide false solace for those fearing a "loss of control" over French national identity as they know it (or imagine it to be); but in contrast to its declared intent, such criminalization contributes to greater marginalization rather than integration. The tragic events in Paris may prove a wakeup call, the kind of shock that reveals that tackling militant, violent radicalism and its sponsors, under the rule of law, begs for an urgent response, but one that respects the delicate balance between security and liberty. But, in the long run, it is the deeper patterns that require redress. Any society seeking to remain true to its ideals, standing tall in the face of uncertainty and adversity, must move beyond the mere rhetoric of integration and national unity to confront the realities of social exclusion. The promise of equal citizenship and emancipatory participation must not remain hollow, granted only to those who already belong. There is no time like the present to undertake the task of realizing it for each and every member of the community.

REFERENCES

Benhabib, Seyla. 2002. *The Claims of Culture: Equality and Diversity in the Global Era.* Princeton: Princeton University Press.

Blackstone, William. 1765–69 [1825]. *Blackstone's Commentaries on the Laws of England.* London: Strahon.

Choudhry, Sujit, ed. 2011. *The Migration of Constitutional Ideas.* Cambridge: Cambridge University Press.

Hirschl, Ran. 2014. *Comparative Matters: The Renaissance of Comparative Constitutional Law.* Oxford: Oxford University Press.

Kymlicka, Will. 1995. *Multicultural Citizenship: A Liberal Theory of Minority Rights.* Oxford: Oxford University Press.

Laborde, Cécile. 2008. *Critical Republicanism: The Hijab Controversy and Political Philosophy.* Oxford: Oxford University Press.

Minow, Martha. 1991. "Identities." *Yale Journal of Law & the Humanities* 3:97–130.

Orgad, Liav. 2009. "Cultural Defence of Nations: Cultural Citizenship in France, Germany and the Netherlands," *European Law Journal* 15:719–37.

Ryder, Bruce. 2008. "The Canadian Conception of Equal Religious Citizenship." In *Law and Religious Pluralism in Canada,* ed. Richard Moon. Vancouver: UBC Press.

Shachar, Ayelet. 2013. "Interpretation Sections (27 and 28) of the Canadian Charter." *Supreme Court Law Review* (2nd) 61:147–90.

Vaïsse, Justin. 2004. *Veiled Meaning: The French Law Banning Religious Symbols in Public Schools.* Washington, DC: Brookings Institution.

Weil, Patrick. 2004. *A Nation in Diversity: France, Muslims and the Headscarf.* Open Democracy, http://www.opendemocracy.net.

8 *Charlie Hebdo* and the Politics of Fear: Questions without Answers

ANNA C. KORTEWEG

What Happened in Paris on January 7, 2015?

The facts seem clear, but the story of how and why these two men came to stand in that office, shooting and killing eleven people (and then a twelfth outside) is very much open to interpretation. In what follows, I'm thinking through some of the ways of telling the story of the attacks and outline what each means for how we conceive of the problems reflected back to us as we bear witness to it. In writing this, I'm very mindful of lives lost, deep grief, anger, and a profound bewilderment on how to move forward. At the same time, I am not offering answers but posing questions in an attempt to figure out where to focus our attention as we think through what these attacks mean. Taken together, these questions are a plea for acknowledging the complexities of the issues that these attacks raise and a warning against falling into an unproductive trap of us/them thinking.

Telling the Story

The stories we tell about the murders have a shifting point of view. Sometimes the perpetrators stand central. In the most simplistic account, one fuelled by their own calls that they were avenging the Prophet, Chérif and Saïd Kouachi were young men defending their faith. Infuriated by *Charlie Hebdo*'s cartoons, they attacked the magazine's offices. At other times, the context, including the French state, takes the lead, with extensive explanations on migration patterns to France, France's colonial histories, and the network of global terrorists, where all these forces are expressed through – but not necessarily by – the two brothers, who at times become almost puppets of these conduits of governance.

The story, however told, resonates across the globe. Excited after what seems a quite fruitful high-level meeting on general issues of race and equity on our university campus, I talk to the cab driver driving me to my next appointment. He asks me what I do, and in my exhilaration I tell him the truth – I study the politics of immigrant integration in Western Europe and Canada. Often I don't tell people, because I don't want to hear the expressions of racism and Islamophobia that come my way as an obviously white woman who doesn't seem Muslim (I'm Jewish, but don't fit the stereotype of that religion either).

My cab driver asks me if I have any ideas about Paris, meaning the *Charlie Hebdo* shootings. "Why did they do it?," he asks.

I tell him that no one knows, the shooters are dead, but most likely because they were profoundly offended, offering a clearly simplistic account but one that seems to fit a ten-minute cab ride.

"No," he responds, "why did *they* do this?"

"What do you mean?," I ask, realizing that we seem to be talking at cross purposes.

He says, "Why did they do that to the Prophet, peace be unto him?"

And I realize he wants to know why *Charlie Hebdo* published these deeply hurtful cartoons.

I end up giving him a brief history of *laïcité*, or secularism, in France – arguing that for the French, kicking the Catholic Church out of public affairs, politics, and education, a process that started in the 1800s and that in some sense continues to be negotiated up to this day, meets up with a sense that democracy requires that absolutely nothing should ever be held sacred. *Charlie Hebdo* personified this in cartoons aimed at any and all that were positioned as authorities solely on grounds of belief. The thought that this is what it means to be French, and that these French cartoonists offended Jesus, the pope, and Muhammad in equal measure clearly intrigued the cab driver, who asked, "So Jesus, too? Really? Those French did that too?" And I left the cab feeling that we had had a perfectly Canadian multicultural moment, in which I explained actions of my near-compatriots (only one country to the south over from the Netherlands, where I was born and raised) in an open exchange of ideas with a devoutly Muslim cab driver. Ironically, this speaking from the position of group membership is exactly the kind of multiculturalism that many French abhor (Laborde 2008; Korteweg and Yurdakul 2014). Their republican values stand in opposition to what is labelled "communalism" or political claims-making rooted in identities other than being French.

The first part of the story the cab driver and I recounted places the attackers in the central role. But the cab driver turned his eye on the provocation by *Charlie Hebdo* and, by extension, on a government that allows such blasphemy. This, in turn, led me to tell a story that places France at the centre. Once the brothers and the French state are put into conversation, the story quickly becomes far more complex than one that focuses solely on the actions of the two brothers. From this perspective, we can begin to ask questions of why and how, and begin to look at possible effects.

Stories of Motives

The first stories of motive place the brothers' context central. As much reporting pointed out, Chérif and Saïd Kouachi were born and raised in the poverty and disenfranchisement associated with the French *banlieues* – the suburban towns circling France's major cities in which clusters of dispirited buildings house vast numbers of underemployed women and men. True enough. However, being poor and disenfranchised doesn't explain a turn to terror.

Perhaps the very high rates of imprisonment of French Muslims, with reports citing that French prison inmates are almost 70 per cent Muslim, far worse proportionally than the abysmal U.S. statistics about African-American prisoners, should be part of the explanation. Perhaps the brutality of the brothers' action can be explained by the idea that prisons breed violence, rather than curtail it. Yet, while the situations described in the Fleury-Merogis prison where Chérif Kouachi was an inmate sound like a scene out of horror movie, they does not explain the turn to this particular target.

Or do they? Maybe the brothers understood *Charlie Hebdo* to stand for the highest values of French society, even if the cartoons the magazine produced were at times boorish and juvenile.

Still, why does this become the outlet for the presumed frustrations of poverty and disenfranchisement? Why not a renewed commitment to a revived socialism or some other movement? Journalists writing in the immediate aftermath of the shootings point out that France's prisons fail to provide the large Muslim prison population with spiritual guidance. The absence of prison imams is then linked to the prisons being a "fertile hunting ground for Islamist recruiters" (Alexander 2015). Indeed, increasing the number of imams in prisons becomes a policy project of the French government. However, if we understand imprisonment as directly related to exploitation and exclusion, then addressing poor prison inmates as Muslim seems misguided. In particular, they presume that being Muslim is the most important part of these prisoners' identity. Might it be that the insistence of treating these French citizens as Muslim first, French second, generates a kind of "reactive religiosity," where the resulting religious identity is akin to what some sociologists call "reactive ethnicity," in which claims to ethnic identity are the result of insistent, often negative appellations to group membership as an explanation for lack of success in society?

A different take on the link between religiosity and motives turns to the question of strategy. Rather than seeing the brothers as driven by circumstance, they become men who designed their actions with careful deliberation. Juan Cole (2015), a Michigan University historian, argues in his blog that the goal of the brothers was to "sharpen the contradiction" between French Muslims and non-Muslim French. In particular, Cole focuses on the difficulty of fomenting large-scale rebellion among French Muslims, few of whom are deeply religious, almost all of whom support the French state, with "the vast majority reject[ing] violence" (see also Selby 2014). Cole proposes that the goal was to incite the general French public to commit further acts of violence against its Muslim compatriots. He concludes, "The only effective response to this manipulative strategy … is to resist the impulse to blame an entire group for the actions of a few and to refuse to carry out identity-politics reprisals."

The fact is that French Muslims already experience significant levels of hostility, both state induced, through bans on the headscarf and niqab and the legal right to discriminate against employees wearing a headscarf (see the Baby Loup case), and in random acts of public violence. Yet, as our book on the production of national belonging in headscarf debates shows, French Muslims respond to this by going to court and taking to the streets in protests in which they wear tricolour headscarves and signs that demand freedom, equality, and brotherhood (Korteweg and Yurdakul 2014). What will it take for French Muslims to not only understand themselves but be seen by others as fully French?

Stories of Effects

How to resist, in our accounting of the *Charlie Hebdo* story, the tendency to reinscribe the boundary between Muslim and French, or Muslim and fill in the blank of any nation-state in which Muslims are a minority?

In asking this question, I move from understanding what the Kouachi brothers did to looking at the potential effects of their actions.

The intended effect, depending on whose accounts you read, is to destabilize society and undermine French republicanism. Accounts that focus on destabilization usually situate the actions of the Kouachi brothers in their connection to transnational Islamist movements – Chérif through his prison connections, Saïd in his Yemeni ventures. This would appear to give added weight to the assertion of attempted destabilization, something too weighty to hang onto two people, but much more clearly understandable as the goal of international terrorist networks.

However, turning to similar attacks elsewhere in Europe, ranging from the 2004 murder of Theo van Gogh in my home country to the 7/7 bombings in London ten years ago suggests a retrenchment of state power and a battening down the hatches, in an almost literal sense. Indeed, these attacks don't destabilize societies directly but rather inspire a politics of fear, which in turn leads to securitization, and an ever-deeper infiltration of the state surveillance into everyday life. I was just in London as a tourist, and found my bag being checked by a lovely young person at Westminster Abbey. I wondered what would happen if I pulled out an automatic weapon and started shooting – would she have time to call in help? Would she be able to prevent me from doing harm (and no, this is not a personal fantasy, I've never held a gun of any kind in my life and have no desire to begin now). The point is, does any of this checking and rechecking, emptying bottles at airports, throwing away too-large containers of a favourite shampoo after security checks, the taking off of endless shoes, jackets, searching of purses and bags do much beyond giving us a quite possibly false security? A belief that "we are doing something" rather than asking the questions we need to ask as to why people would feel so disconnected from their communities that they would go into an office and shoot twenve people dead?

And what about the sense that these forms of violence are unique and uniquely attached to Muslims? I grew up in the Netherlands in the 1970s – trying to understand the Baader-Meinhof Gruppe as a nine-year old, being glued to the news as six Dutch Moluccan terrorists held people hostage in a train compartment, with the train standing silent in a field close to my home town. We lived with terror then, but it was "home grown." There were no calls to exile the children of German Protestant ministers (though we all observed that an unusually high number of the German terrorists were). There were not even calls to send the immigrants from the Moluccas back home – we knew that they were children of those who had come to the Netherlands after fighting on the Dutch side in the Indonesian war of independence and their home was the Netherlands (indeed, their actions were informed by a desire for Dutch assistance in establishing an independent Moluccan state). So, why does this current wave of terrorism inspire the kind of line-drawing, these practices and expressions of exclusion, in which we call even third-generation children "immigrants," as if they had just arrived?

And then there is the effect on those who are Jewish. A friend in Britain tells me she does not want to send her children to a Jewish day school in London – afraid they will get attacked because the school is close to a Muslim neighbourhood. Other friends are thinking of giving up their house in France because they worry that their family might be attacked, not because they are gay parents of three children but because they are Jewish and the town one over has a large Muslim population. Even I worry as I walk my children into our local Jewish Community Centre for their programs, and I worry for myself as I go to the gym there and attend my weekly choir rehearsals. What if someone shows up to try and shoot us all, will the guards be able to stop them? And these private worries are politicized and recognized publicly when Prime Minister Netanyahu of Israel utters a call to all European Jews to come home, in an opportunistic bid for more Jews to make *aliyah* (return to Israel). But the question is to what extent are we actually at risk, and to what extent is our fear – and the behaviours that our fear inspires – the real risk we face?

Finally, the demonstrations and the tremendous outpouring of support for France suggest an important immediate effect of solidarity. But who and what are we supporting as people say, "I'm Charlie, I'm Jewish, I'm Ahmed," as they name the French, Jewish, and Muslim victims of the attack? I'm very leery of these large-scale "we all know what was wrong, and what is right" expressions. They lead me back to the question of who gets to be part of the "we" here. And I wonder whether that boundary is too often or too easily one between French and Muslim, thus overlooking the vast numbers of French who are also Muslim?

Concluding Thoughts: Loss in the Time of Terror

My heart aches for the victims, or more precisely, for the victims' families. The victims are no longer with us, and in my cosmology they live on only in the memories of those left behind. Death and loss are part of life, but certain losses are harder to bear than others. I know from experience that loss of a child is one of the worst things that can happen to a parent. I can only imagine what it must be like to lose a child, partner, brother, sister, dear friend to a wilful act of violence. But what killed these people?

One approach in dealing with these losses might be to stick our head in the sand and treat these murders as akin to an accident, in which two deranged young men took up weapons and killed and maimed. However, as the stories and questions above suggest, that's far too easy. These murders are emblematic of tensions that shape Europe and beyond. The clearest expression of this is perhaps in the state burials Israel gave the victims of the related Hyper Cacher supermarket shootings. Why is further politicization the response to their politically motivated deaths? Why not choose to keep the grief private? I suggest it is because we fear loss.

What are some of the losses other than the tragic loss of life that resulted from the attack on *Charlie Hebdo*?

One loss is the loss of a certain innocence, of a sense of security that the world is understandable and manageable, that pain will be inflicted only in expected ways. Yet the idea "we have been violated" that echoes through much newspaper reporting seems to be such an expression of privilege. So many of us are daily afraid of violence, walking on the street, living in our homes, working in our workplaces, as women, Muslims, queers, or other vulnerable persons. Does it take the absence of such daily fear for one to be able to express this kind of righteous indignation at having "our" sense of security taken away? Because sadly, that sense of security is, has become, or perhaps has always been a privilege extended to far too few. Perhaps the outcry at these murders then, is about the loss of *hope* for security.

Another potential loss is the memory that these were French men, that they knew exactly whom to target, not only because they had the opportunity to attack but because they knew, whether consciously or intuitively, that attacking *Charlie Hebdo* would attack deeply the republican values the French hold as inalienable. Only someone French would know that this would hit hard and deep. One woman who witnessed the shooters leave the scene was quoted in the press to say, "They spoke French without an accent." To inflict deep hurts often requires a greater degree of intimacy than we remember.

The focus on *Charlie Hebdo* can also lead us to lose sight of the fact that we live in a world shaped by many forms of violence. A friend asked me if we had heard of the 200 people murdered recently in a village in Assam? And what about the hundreds of women attacked and killed in gendered violence on any given day? What about people living in abject poverty and despair across the globe, suffering economic violence? What, indeed, of people living in places like Gaza and Syria, whose daily lives are unending experiences of trauma and threat. Why is this particular attack so important? In the end, the attack's importance has to lie in the fact that when we ask the right questions about it, they can lead us to think meaningfully through not only our own but also others' violence and terror.

REFERENCES

Alexander, Harriet. 2015. "What's Going Wrong in France's Prisons?" *Telegraph*, January 17, http://www.telegraph.co.uk/news/worldnews/europe/france/11352268/What-is-going-wrong-in-Frances-prisons.html.
Cole, Juan. 2015. "Sharpening Contradictions: Why al-Qaeda Attacked Satirists in Paris." Informed Comment, January 7, http://www.juancole.com/2015/01/sharpening-contradictions-satirists.html.
Korteweg, Anna, and Gökçe Yurdakul. 2014. *The Headscarf Debates: Conflicts of National Belonging.* Standord: Stanford University Press.
Laborde, Cécile. 2008. *Critical Republicanism: The Hijab Controversy and Political Philosophy.* Oxford: Oxford University Press.
Selby, Jennifer A. 2014. "France." In *The Oxford Handbook of European Islam*: 23.

PART TWO

Geopolitical Effects

9 What Does It Mean to Be at War?

ARTHUR RIPSTEIN

My father lived through two world wars, and my mother spent her adolescence and young adulthood in the middle of one. I grew up in a time of relative peace, a time with multiple declarations of war. There was the Cold War, always in the background, and then the war on poverty, the war on crime, and the war on drugs. My children are growing up during what has been described as a war on terror; more recently that idea has acquired a second life with the suggestion that the international jihadist movement has "declared war" on us.

In this brief comment I want to focus on these images of war and raise a caution about them. As someone who regularly shops for kosher groceries, I must first acknowledge, at a personal as well as intellectual level, the genuineness of the fear and the seriousness of the issues that lead to this talk of war, and the importance of security to the possibility of any decent form of human existence. My point is not that these ends do not matter, but rather that we need to think about the means we use to protect them.

War metaphors have been the subject of a variety of criticisms. I want to endorse many of these criticisms, but only to put them to one side. So it has been pointed out that if you are dealing with a gang of criminals, let alone an isolated group of criminals, they should not be dignified with the status of enemy combatants, with its connotations of those courageously fighting for a cause, or elevated to the status of prisoners of war. Under international law, as well as under traditional understandings of the morality of war, it is not a crime to be a soldier in a war. Terrorists do not belong in that category. I also share reservations expressed in the past about the practical effects of framing the problem of global terrorism in the vocabulary of war, particularly the

Bush-era framing of it in terms of the possibility of total victory. Some people have suggested that this way of framing the issue has been not only ineffective but counterproductive, producing the very conditions in which terrorist is most likely develop (Power 2007).

I put these points to one side because I want to focus on some other features of war as the model through which urgent issues are addressed. Talk of war brings with it the thought that the stakes are so high as to outweigh any competing considerations, that, in war, the end justifies the means. I do not think that this is true of war – in both law and morality, there are significant restrictions on how you can fight a war, restrictions that apply even if your opponent ignores them. Terrorism consists in the rejection of these restrictions, specifically in the collapsing of the distinction between combatants and non-combatants, but more generally in the refusal to restrict the means that terrorists use to achieve their ends.

The wars on each of drugs, crime, and poverty were declared as a way of characterizing the urgency – not mere importance – of the result. You go to war only when the situation is intolerable. That is, war is not just an ordinary instrument of public policy; you go to war only to avert something terrible.

With this urgency comes another thought, that the urgency of war makes means acceptable in its conduct that would not otherwise be acceptable. This idea has an element of truth to it: the paradigmatic action in the course of a war is the use of lethal force against enemy combatants. This is not the place to develop an explanation of how this could ever be permissible, let alone how, as the Geneva conventions say, it could be permissible on both sides, regardless of the merits of either side's claims in the war. Whatever the explanation, however, the rules of armed conflict – international humanitarian law – permit things that are otherwise forbidden.

In times of war, urgency permits the state to make demands on its own citizens that would be excessive in peacetime. When you are at war, everybody has to do his or her part. These are not the ordinary sacrifices of political life – paying your taxes, driving at the speed limit and stopping at traffic lights, waiting in line to renew your health card or get a permit to put an addition on your house. Instead, the urgency of a war is supposed to explain why extraordinary sacrifices may be called for. Conscription is the most conspicuous example, because it requires some people to literally put their lives on the line. The urgency of war also brings on a different set of effects – measures that might be considered significant disruptions of ordinary life in peacetime become normal parts of the war effort: you may have to put up with rationing or price controls, black out your windows, or stop engaging in otherwise profitable trade. The more general feature of war that invites declarations of war on other things, like drugs or terror, is this shifting of national priorities, because in war everyone needs to bear extra burdens. Until this problem is solved, other pressing matters must be put on hold.

It is easy to move from these familiar features of war to one of two conclusions: either the terrorist threat is so severe that the comforts of peaceful life must give way to the resolute pursuit of victory, or the threat is overstated, and we should not blow it out of proportion.

I think both of these conclusions are mistaken. I want to reject the choice between them, by rejecting the supposition on which they rest, that in wartime, the urgency of the end justifies giving up on all of the restrictions on the means that we can use. There is a fundamental difference between asking people to bear extra burdens and asking them to give up on their rights. The familiar prohibitions on the use of certain means cannot be treated as unfortunate "collateral damage" justified by the urgency of the ends sought.

I will make this point in a slightly indirect way. Just over twenty years ago, Isaiah Berlin received an honorary degree from the University of Toronto. In his acceptance speech, which was read on his behalf, and recently published under the title "A Message to the 21st Century," Berlin cautioned against the moral dangers of moral certainty. Reflecting back on the horrors of the twentieth century, he attributed them to the certainty that fascist and communist leaders had about the ends for which they mobilized their societies:

> If you are truly convinced that there is some solution to all human problems, that one can conceive an ideal society which men can reach if only they do what is necessary to attain it, then you and your followers must believe that no price can be too high to pay in order to open the gates of such a paradise. Only the stupid and malevolent will resist once certain simple truths are put to them. Those who resist must be persuaded; if they cannot be persuaded, laws must be passed to restrain them; if that does not work, then coercion, if need be violence, will inevitably have to be used – if necessary, terror, slaughter. (Berlin 2014)

Berlin characterized what he saw as the root cause of this difficulty, in the "conviction ... that the central questions of human life, individual or social, have one true answer which can be discovered." In the place of this conviction, he recommends the recognition that "the central values by which most men have lived, in a great many lands at a great many times – these values, almost if not entirely universal, are not always harmonious with each other." This recommendation, he suggests, will lead to caution and intellectual humility, but above all to the recognition that not all values can be consistently realized: "Compromises, trade-offs, arrangements have to be made if the worst is not to happen. So much liberty for so much equality, so much individual self-expression for so much security, so much justice for so much compassion."

It is difficult to disagree with Berlin about the horrors brought on by the certainties of Stalin, Hitler, Mao, and Pol Pot. The terrorist threat that we now confront is driven by a similar certainty. I am less confident, however, in his diagnosis. It is not that I think that the questions of human life have a single answer, patiently waiting to be discovered, and that their discovery will be convincing to anyone with the intelligence to understand it. My misgiving is rather with Berlin's focus on the inconsistency of a number of competing ends, and his concomitant suggestion that the solution, the alternative to fanaticism, must always be compromise and trade-off. Again, the point is not that there aren't a number of competing ends, but that the fundamental problem with dictators, fanatics, and terrorists is not the ends they seek but the means that they use.

The ends pursued by the dictators of the twentieth century were monstrous ends, but the further problem was not simply their intellectual certainty. Rather, it was the active means that they were prepared to use to achieve those ends. The assumption that it is acceptable to use force, starvation, and murder in order to realize some utopian ideal is mistaken, even if the ideal is less monolithic and more consistent with a wider array of human aspirations. It is possible to overlook this when the end being pursued is itself of questionable value or even consistency. As long as you focus on ends, it is easy – too easy – to think that the only questions about means being used is their efficacy.

Many of the other contributors to this volume have asked searching questions about proposed responses to the Paris attacks and other recent events. Many of these concern factual questions of necessity – "Will they be more effective than what we currently have?" – and their potential side effects – "Will they do so much damage in other areas as to not to be worth their cost?" These are all worthwhile questions in assessing any piece of policy response, and they certainly arise for the proposed anti-terror legislation.

Despite the importance of these questions, I want to draw attention to a different issue, one that cannot be usefully expressed in the vocabulary of compromises and trade-offs. I want to suggest that some means are not acceptable, regardless of the ends for which they are being pursued. That is that the problem we confront in the horrors of the twentieth century: how to maintain the line between civilization and barbarism. Those who would send terrorists into our midst to destroy our society are mistaken in the end they pursue, but they would still be terrorists if they did those acts in support of different actions. The means that they use – wantonly killing civilians – is unacceptable, even in the context of war, in which soldiers killing each other can be acceptable.

Canadians are rightly proud of the way our society values freedom, openness, and tolerance. But those are not the ends that we happen to endorse, in the service of which we stand ready to do whatever it takes. Part of what it is to have and value a free society, one in which no person is the vassal of other people or the state, is to accept restrictions on the means that are available even to support our freedoms. To value these good things is to suppose that it is up to each of us to determine our ends, to refuse to use the coercive power of the state to advance one or another specific conception of the good life. To celebrate these values is to accept that certain means – torture, detention without trial, excessive powers of search and seizure – cannot be justified by the benefits that they are expected to bring, even in times of war.

I am not sure that Prime Minister Harper was correct in his claim that "the international jihadist movement has declared war," because I do not know who could have standing to make such a declaration, or on behalf of whom it might have been made. But if war has been declared, it does not follow that we must accept the declaration or accept the characterization of the terms on which what they call war is to be fought. The fact that terrorists recognize no restrictions on the means that they will use does not require that we must accept no restrictions. Nor does it require that we think of our fundamental rights as matters for compromise or trade-off, in the way that price controls or rationing might be in some situations, something to cost out in figuring out just how much privacy or freedom or presumption of innocence we want.

Declaration or not, there are terrorists who stand ready to use violence because of how we think and act, and the ways in which we value freedom, openness, and tolerance. But the only way to value those things – to have them constitute a system of ordered liberty – is to see them not as values we happen to have, different from the values that other societies have. Instead, we must see them as restrictions on the means that our governments can use to achieve important public purposes, even the purpose of defending us against those who recognize no restraints.

REFERENCES

Berlin, Isaiah. 2014. "A Message to the 21st Century." *New York Review of Books,* October 23.
Power, Samantha. 2007. "Our War on Terror." *New York Times,* July 29.

10 After the Paris Attacks: Long Views Backwards and Forwards

RONALD W. PRUESSEN

Historians specialize in "long views" – and they often seek to apply essentially ambidextrous skills along the way. On one hand, they are best known for looking *backwards,* tracing what are almost always the deep roots of present-day issues in order to understand causes or dynamics that go beyond what is discernible in the sound bites and snapshots of the moment. On the other hand, many historians also look *forward*: is there a momentum to the "past," they ask, that may carry us beyond the "present"? As one insightful scholar once put it, the historian's task is two-fold at heart – to both "imagine the past" (with the verb signalling the presence of art as well as science) *and* to "remember the future."

Only weeks after the slaughter at the *Charlie Hebdo* offices and the kosher grocery store in the Porte de Vincennes neighbourhood, what would the historian writing this particular piece say as he looked backwards and forwards? With a sensitivity to the passage of time that comes with the study of history, he would want to recognize that his immediate reactions to the violent deaths have already begun to evolve. On January 7 and for days afterwards, shock, sadness, and anger held full sway, as they did for many thousands of mourners and demonstrators in Paris and around the world. Nor have such emotions disappeared – and there is actually every reason to believe that they will long feel entirely appropriate in the face of such a tragedy. Other thoughts do emerge, however, prompted partially by the responses of other people, partially by that default tendency in historians to search for "long views." If sadness and anger remain, as a result, they are now joined by the sense that such reactions to the horrifying Paris attacks are selective – and the fear that some of the best of them may be temporary.

I

Set against the backdrop of past experiences, it is clear that our responses to the Paris attacks have been selective – disturbingly selective. Since January 7, traditional and social media have powerfully recorded our very real capacity for horror, fury, and determination. But why do some terrible events lead to the energizing of such capacities while others do not? Where were (where are) the mass demonstrations and vigils, where are the marches led by phalanxes of heads of state, in the face of other traumatizing instances of violence and death?

There have been countless recitations of the "Je suis Charlie" mantra, for example – but no "Je suis Raif Badawi" badges being marketed by the *Guardian* on behalf of the Internet commentator facing brutal flogging in Riyadh (or, more distressingly yet, on behalf of the dozens of individuals beheaded in Saudi Arabia each year) (Kermalli 2014).

World leaders flocked to Paris in January – but none have travelled to Poplar Hill First Nation or Webequie First Nation in Ontario to show anguish over the deaths of Reggie Bushie and Jordan Wabasse (only two of the Aboriginal teenagers who have committed suicide at a rate five to ten times greater than the national Canadian average) (Seglins 2012).

And if we can at least identify a Raif Badawi, Reggie Bushie, and Jordan Wabasse – even if we do not let those names prod us to actions like those prompted by the Paris attacks – do we even bother to learn the names of other hundreds and thousands who have been victims of violence and cruelty? If we stop to think about it, would we not readily admit that such hundreds and thousands will almost always remain nameless as they go on dying horrible deaths, with no counterpart to a "Je suis Charlie" declaration, save for friends and families: those killed in political violence in Cairo, for example, or in the drug wars that plague Mexico, or the victims of obscene infant mortality rates in places like Gaza and Somalia (23 deaths per 1000 births in the former, 100 deaths per 1000 in Somalia, vs 3.31 in France and 4.71 in Canada) (Central Intelligence Agency 2015).

To be sure, pointing to the selectivity inherent in the responses to the Paris attacks is not to criticize those responses themselves. The anguish and anger, the desire to stand up or march after January 7 – all are understandable and admirable. But it does not hurt to take a moment to realize – especially for people who have actually had the heart to feel the pain and the vigour to act – that we could be using those emotional and intellectual muscles more often than we do.

II

The selectivity of responses to the Paris attacks is clear. We will need time, though (says the historian, as ever) to know whether there is reason to be concerned about the possibility that some reactions may also be momentary. Will the intensity of anger and determination fade in the months ahead, and if so, with what consequences? At the moment, we can see immediate reactions clearly (and hear them loudly). We can even identify separate strands that may prompt our sympathy or admiration or concern. But we cannot yet know the medium- or longer-term trajectories of those separate strands: will more admirable reactions, for instance, be more temporary than disturbing ones?

Unfortunately, a "long view" backwards suggests that troubling reactions to traumatic events can have greater staying power. This was certainly the fate of responses in the United States to the profoundly disturbing experiences of September 11, 2001. Instantaneous shock and grief in that case rapidly gave way to a complex amalgam of multiplying emotions and actions. There was an understandable thirst for vengeance and the punishment of those responsible for heinous acts – evidenced by the invasion of Afghanistan, George W. Bush's declaration that he wanted Osama bin Laden brought in "dead or alive," and the shootings, fire-bombings, and acts of vandalism that hit mosques in a dozen U.S. states, from California to Connecticut to Florida.

There was steely determination to ramp up security systems in order to prevent further acts of destructive violence – evidenced by the passage of the Patriot Act, the creation of the White House's Office of Homeland Security, and presidential authorization of new counterterrorism methods that included rendition, Guantanamo detention without trial, and waterboarding. And there were calls to develop a "long view" approach that would address the root causes of terrorist recruitment capabilities: witness British Prime Minister Tony Blair's passionate October 2 address at the Labour Party Conference in which his listing of many necessary actions ended with the declaration that what was needed "above all" was "justice and prosperity for the poor and dispossessed."

Fourteen years later, of course, we know which of these impulses was more temporary than others. Military action in Afghanistan was soon followed by war in Iraq – and each theatre continues to be active in bloody forms to the present day, supplemented now by regional actions against the so-called Islamic State and an expanding use of drones (among other things). Security programs and regulations have continued to grow, with Edward Snowden's NSA revelations giving a glimpse (but only a glimpse) of the vast surveillance apparatus that grew during both the Bush and Obama presidencies. But a Blair-like recognition of the desirability of attending to root causes of terrorism has withered on the vine. Rhetoric concerning activism against poverty and political corruption or on behalf of development, health, and women's rights was certainly present in the years immediately following 9/11. Condoleeza Rice has recounted her early desire to have the "historical narrative" of the war in Afghanistan emphasize the pursuit of freedom and the advancement of women, for example, and she also touts the far-sightedness of an early $1.2 billion aid package for Pakistan. But the post-9/11 period saw steady evidence of either weak follow-through on such impulses or sparse substance in the first place. Discussions of Afghanistan in 2015 might have been very different if such early intentions had been seriously prioritized; and 70 per cent or more of that $1.2 billion U.S. aid package for Pakistan was geared to military programs (Rice 2011; Centre for Global Development 2012).

So what will be the longer-term fate of the complex of reactions that have emerged since the Paris attacks of January 7? What does an attempt at a "long view" forwards suggest? As in 2001–2, we have been seeing for weeks some attention to the logic of "long view" initiatives focused on economic, social, and political reforms. The French government, for example, would point to the relevance of an ambitious "Métropole du Grand Paris" plan (which began to take shape under Nicolas Sarkozy's leadership): it could conceivably transform the way community infrastructure, education, and development funds are allocated to the troubled suburbs lying to the north, east, and south of Paris (where youth unemployment is often 40 per cent or more) (Kimmelman 2015).

On this side of the Atlantic, Barack Obama has explicitly channelled Tony Blair's earlier messaging. In a February 18 address, the president eloquently argued for steps that would go beyond military responses to the tragedies in Paris or the horrors perpetrated by ISIS. We "do have to address the grievances that terrorists exploit," he pointedly said – by trying to "lift up people's lives here in America and around the world," by understanding resentments that fester in order to "eliminate the soil out of which they grew" (Obama 2015).

Only the long view forward will reveal which post–January 7 reactions prove to be the hardier strains. There is already reason to wonder about a repetition of post-9/11 patterns, however. In France, the most visible and concrete immediate responses have included the deployment of 10,000 soldiers to "sensitive" sites in Paris (including tourist meccas and Jewish schools), the preparation of new legislation expanding surveillance programs, and the government decision to increase participation in military operations in the Middle East. In the United States, President Obama has been subjected to especially vicious diatribes (even by the standards operational throughout his presidency) for failing to summon up sufficient outrage by even suggesting that there were deep-seated resentments requiring recognition and attention. And in Canada, of course, it is hard to avoid noting the way in which Prime Minister Harper's government is using the Paris attacks to reinforce its push for approval of Bill C-51.

To zero in on post-9/11 developments and their potential relevance to what will gradually unfold in this period following the January 7 Paris attacks may not be the longest "long view" a historian could offer. Such an example should be complemented by at least a nod toward more deeply rooted comparators, as well. In fact, the furore evident in recent weeks has many counterparts across history – especially in the way in which shock and anger can regularly tilt toward behaviour that is more violent and repressive than remedial.

Traumatic events and strong challenges to the comforts that some enjoy in any given status quo have often had severely negative or counterproductive effects on those whose safety, power, wealth, or status is being threatened. A few examples:

- The intensification of belligerence in the southern United States during the mid-nineteenth century as those who saw their well-being dependent on slavery came to feel the economic, political, and cultural ground shifting under them – with the use of fugitive slave laws and Supreme Court rulings giving way to a belief that bloody rebellion was the only honourable course remaining.
- The brutal crushing of unrest among colonial and subject peoples: an imperial penchant through millennia, the nineteenth and twentieth centuries alone saw countless repetitions of the pattern in (among many others) India, Algeria, Kenya, the Philippines, and Hungary.
- The establishment of repressive legal regimes – and the toleration of extra-legal violence – in the face of revolutionary movements. Two examples from U.S. history: Fears of the 1917 Bolshevik Revolution spurred "Red Scare" government arrests and deportations and

added fire (literally) to the already vicious targeting of Afro-American and Jewish scapegoats by the Ku Klux Klan. The Soviet Union's successful testing of an atomic bomb and the Communist Party's victory in the Chinese Civil War helped pave the way for McCarthyism's abusive excesses in the 1950s.

III

Given what historians might see as they take a long view backwards, what are the odds that a long view forward can be undertaken with optimism? For this historian, at least, the odds are terrible.

Why?

There is no simple answer to this question – and a brief chapter will allow only a bare mention of a few over-simplified observations. With that caveat in mind, however, this historian would say he is pessimistic about the effectiveness of responses to the Paris attacks, because troubling past behaviour remains an effective guide to the thoughts and actions of the present – not least among leaders and voters in countries that actually have the power and wealth to create opportunities for more positive results. If there is any divergence from past behaviour, in fact, it is in a direction that makes it even less likely that there will be satisfying and effective responses to tragedies like those of January 7. It is unsettling to think that we may actually go from bad to worse in our ability to improve the soil in which social ills and grievances can grow into violent, horrible acts – to go back to Barack Obama's phrasing – but that makes it no less appropriate a thought as we try to discern a long view looking forward.

One component of past behaviour that remains all too evident in 2015 – and only one can be touched on here – is the profoundly traditional inclinations of the powerful and wealthy. Within individual nations and in the broader global arena, key leaders in both the public and private sectors have repeatedly shown themselves to be limited in their ability to solve deep-seated social problems like racism, economic problems like unemployment, and political problems like money's corrupting influence. Rhetoric about reform and justice may often be in the air, even sincerely articulated in many instances. When the time comes to actually design and implement public goods initiatives or serious regulatory measures, however, meaningful follow-through can stall or stumble. Tax cuts, higher quarterly profits, maximum "free market" freedoms, etc.: any and all may have greater relative appeal to both leaders and the taxpayers who elect them (in democratic societies). The "opportunity cost" of taking more meaningful action on the problems that aggravate both domestic and global peace is deemed to be too high.

In recent times, as well, the driving power of immediate self-interest calculations has been problematically reinforced by an increasing appetite for quick solutions – even when speed is an unrealistic expectation in the face of the challenges being confronted. Like any historical era, the early twenty-first century has seen the emergence of its own distinctive share of complex problems. The terrorism and violence represented by the Paris attacks is one, to be sure, but there are all too many others: How to regain greater economic dynamism after the crisis of 2007–8? How to protect against pandemic threats like SARS and Ebola? How to coordinate meaningful action to deal with climate change? No one worth listening to would seriously argue that such problems can be solved quickly. And yet, there is a marked tendency in many quarters to grow impatient – and to let impatience seriously weaken policy choices when challenges prove as stubborn as our intellectual assessment should have told us they would be.

An appetite for speed is not at all a strictly twenty-first-century phenomenon, of course. Several centuries of "modern" history have seen almost constant efforts to travel farther and faster, for example, with especially dramatic leaps and bounds coming with the advent of steam power for railroads and ships in the nineteenth century and air travel in the twentieth. (It is hard now to think of Jules Verne's concept in *Around the World in 80 Days* – written in 1872 – as anything but quaint.) Communication technology has also advanced to the point where many of us have come to enjoy routinely instantaneous connectability with friends and colleagues anywhere in the world – as the telegraph has been succeeded by the telephone and the internet. The faster (much faster) world in which we now live certainly has many attributes, not least the way it can fuel human creativity by literally opening the globe to observation and imagination. It also exacts a price, however – with reduced patience for long-haul analysis, planning, and implementation among the darker dimensions.

Logic might suggest, for instance, that the gradual solution of social and economic ills (in both home countries and abroad) would actually be more cost effective and satisfying than war or escalating surveillance. Even if military action and policing were reasonable components of a multifaceted game plan, logic might also prompt appreciation for what Barack Obama has called "strategic patience" (Ratnam 2015). The problems for which remedial measures are being sought, after all, are really not Tweetable matters. Instead, post-9/11 experience shows regular evidence of strategic *impatience*. On one hand, this may entail a desire to start backing away from or functionally ignoring what was formerly prioritized, such as the readiness to drastically reduce military efforts in Afghanistan and Iraq, even though original objectives have not been achieved – or to seriously neglect the war damage and post-traumatic stresses of the societies that served as battlefields and the warriors who fought on them. On another hand – when "out of sight, out of mind" does not work – strategic impatience can generate responses fuelled by anger: for example, more military action, even if earlier forays did not work as they were designed to do (escalating operations designed to "degrade and ultimately destroy" ISIL) (Hudson 2014) or something of a doubling down on surveillance or drone campaigns.

The irony, of course – the tragic irony – is that strategic impatience makes it even less likely that challenges will be met. The more we try to hurry, the greater the odds against our moving at all, at least in the direction that logic and idealism would tell us we want to move. Superimpose this conundrum on the inherited tendencies to make poor policy choices – such as those that followed the trauma of 9/11 – and it is not difficult to understand how pessimism can hover over the delineation of a "long view" forwards from the Paris attacks.

REFERENCES

Central Intelligence Agency. 2015. *The World Factbook,* https://www.cia.gov/library/publications/the-world-factbook/.
Center for Global Development. 2012. "Aid to Pakistan by the Numbers," http://www.cgdev.org/page/aid-pakistan-numbers.
Hudson, David. 2014. "President Obama: 'We Will Degrade and Ultimately Destroy ISIL,'" September 10, https://www.whitehouse.gov/blog/2014/09/10/president-obama-we-will-degrade-and-ultimately-destroy-isil.
Kermali, Shenaz. 2014. "Mr Baird, How Are Saudi Arabia's Beheadings Different from Islamic State's?," October 17, http://www.theglobeandmail.com/globe-debate/mr-baird-how-are-saudi-arabias-beheadings-different-from-islamic-states/article21146919/.
Kimmelman, Michael. 2015. "Paris Aims to Embrace Its Estranged Suburbs." *New York Times*, February 12, http://www.nytimes.com/2015/02/13/world/europe/paris-tries-to-embrace-suburbs-isolated-by-poverty-and-race.html?_r=0.

Obama, Barack. 2015. "Remarks by the President in Closing of the Summit on Countering Violent Extremism," February 18, http://www.whitehouse .gov/the-press-office/2015/02/18/remarks-president-closing-summit-countering-violent-extremism.

Ratnam, Gopal. 2015. "White House Unveils Call for 'Strategic Patience,'" FP, February 5, http://foreignpolicy.com/2015/02/05/white-house-to-unveil-call-for-strategic-patience-russia-ukraine-syria-iraq-china-asia/.

Rice, Condoleeza. 2011. *No Higher Honor: A Memoir of My Years in Washington.* New York: Crown Publishers.

Seglins, Dave. 2012. "Ontario Calls Joint Inquest in Aboriginal Student Deaths." CBC News, May 31, http://www.cbc.ca/news/canada/thunder-bay/ontario-calls-joint-inquest-in-aboriginal-student-deaths-1.1151765.

11 International Law and Transnational Terrorism

JUTTA BRUNNÉE

Introduction

On January 7, 2015, the brothers Saïd and Chérif Kouachi stormed the offices of the satirical newspaper *Charlie Hebdo* in Paris, killing eleven people and injuring twelve others. In the course of the ensuing manhunt, Amedy Coulibaly, in a separate but related incident, took Jewish shoppers hostage at a kosher grocery store, ultimately killing five and injuring eleven. The perpetrators as well as the victims of the terrorist attacks were French nationals.

At first glance, the Paris attacks were a domestic incident – a matter for French law, not international law. In this respect, the Paris events seemed to differ from the attacks perpetrated in the United States on September 11, 2001, which were directed from abroad and executed by foreign nationals who entered the United States in order to carry them out. However, as quickly became apparent, the Paris attacks too had an international dimension. Indeed, they serve to illustrate the adaptable nature of transnational terrorism. Rather than planning and directing large-scale operations abroad, as did Osama Bin Laden's Al Qaeda, or fighting rival combat forces for territorial control, as do the various groups now operating in Syria and Iraq, today's terror networks often resort to training foreign nationals or simply to inducing attacks by "home-grown" terrorists through local contacts or Internet-based propaganda and "how-to" information. In the case of the Paris attackers it turned out that one or both of the Kouachi brothers had previously travelled to Yemen for training with Al Qaeda in the Arabian Peninsula, the organization that later took credit for the *Charlie Hebdo* attack. Amedy Coulibay, for his part, released a video in which he proclaimed his affiliation with the Islamic State in the Levant (ISIL).

This chapter offers a reflection on the challenges that transnational terrorism poses for the international legal order, on how states have sought to improve law's capacity to address terrorism, and on the potentially significant impact of these efforts on international law.

Challenges

It is easy to see why transnational terrorism is challenging for international law. In its basic structure, international law remains focused on the rights and obligations of states. While it envisages rights for individuals (human rights law, refugee law, and so on), individuals have no obligations under international law, other than those enshrined in international criminal law. International criminal law, however, currently knows only certain categories of international crime: genocide, war crimes, crimes against humanity, and, less clearly, the crime of aggression. Although individuals can be held accountable for these crimes, each of them presupposes that the perpetrators acted on behalf of states. In other words, transnational terrorism is not currently a crime under international law.

What then of states' ability to apply and enforce their domestic laws to acts of transnational terrorism? International law actually sets out some limits in this respect, resulting from the fact that states' rights and obligations are generally based on, as well as limited by, jurisdiction over territory or persons. In this framework, a state can apply its laws to acts of terrorism that occur within its territory. A state can also extend the reach of its laws to terror acts that are perpetrated by its nationals abroad, and terrorist attacks against its nationals abroad. However, while states can enforce their laws in their own territories, they have traditionally been limited in their ability to take enforcement action abroad, especially in the territories of other states. Hence, when terrorists manage to slip out of the country or are based abroad in the first place, there is often a practical barrier to the application and enforcement of domestic law. A state wishing to see terrorists held legally accountable for their actions would have to rely on another state's willingness to make arrests, and its willingness either to prosecute or to extradite the perpetrators.

There are many good reasons for this framework of limited national jurisdiction. In a world of sovereign states, extraterritorial application of one state's law, let alone its extraterritorial enforcement, risks encroaching on the sovereign spheres of other states. In minimizing such encroachments, the basic jurisdictional framework not only reflects the sovereignty interests of states, but also provides a measure of protection to their citizens and societies against the imposition of foreign values and standards. But in dealing with a phenomenon like transnational terrorism, the jurisdictional limits inherent in the framework also pose obvious problems. Indeed, transnational terrorist organizations exploit these limits by operating through diffuse networks, by sheltering themselves beyond the jurisdictional reach of target states, and by using cyberspace (in its own right a difficult phenomenon for the traditional jurisdictional framework) to communicate, coordinate, direct, or entice.

Requesting the cooperation of other states in the application of domestic law is one avenue for dealing with a terrorist attack or threat that has a transnational dimension. But case-by-case cooperation, although clearly important, is a cumbersome way to pursue highly mobile actors and address fast-moving threats. What is more, terrorist networks typically seek out "host" states that are either unwilling or unable to suppress their activities, or to cooperate with other states in combatting transnational terrorism. The key question, therefore, is whether international law provides any other options to states for responding to transnational terrorism.

Responses

Given the basic jurisdictional framework sketched out above, there are only two avenues (short of extra-legal action) for overcoming the inherent constraints. The first is to argue that there are circumstances in which a state that is subject to a transnational terrorist attack or threat is permitted to take unilateral, extraterritorial response action. This approach leads to the law of self-defence. The second approach is to promote the harmonization and strengthening of national anti-terrorism regimes by imposing international obligations on states to enact and enforce appropriate laws and to cooperate with other states in suppressing transnational terrorism.

Self-Defence

The scale and severity of the 9/11 attacks, and the initial fear that further attacks might be imminent, prompted the United States to advance, and other states to endorse, the notion that states have a right to self-defence against a terrorist attack. While this proposition may seem intuitive at first glance, it was not actually a foregone conclusion under the rules that governed interstate use of force. Those rules, it is important to recall, grew from the world's experience with two world wars, and the untold suffering and death toll they visited upon soldiers as well as civilian populations – by most counts over 60 million people were killed in the Second World War alone.

To help "save succeeding generations from the scourge of war," the UN Charter placed stringent legal constraints on resort to military force. It imposed an absolute prohibition on the threat or use of force against other states (article 2(4)). In the Charter framework, therefore, recourse to interstate force is legal only under two narrowly defined exceptions to this sweeping rule. First, pursuant to an authorization by the UN Security Council under chapter VII of the UN Charter, states may take collective action to address a breach of or threat to international peace and security (including crises involving grave human rights abuses). And second, states may unilaterally (that is, outside the collective security regime) use force to defend themselves against an armed attack (article 51). The overarching goals of this framework were to protect states against military intervention and to suppress interstate use of force as much as possible.

The pursuit of these ambitious goals, difficult enough in a world riddled with political conflict, was further complicated by the rise of various kinds of irregular forces, sometimes operating at the behest of states and sometimes pursuing their own goals. Beginning with its judgment in the *Nicaragua* case, the International Court of Justice, when confronted with situations involving trans-border operations of non-state forces, has repeatedly confirmed that a right to unilateral recourse to force in self-defence was available only when such actions were attributable to a state, such that it could be said to have perpetrated an armed attack (International Court of Justice 1986). Only then, considered the Court, would the target state be legally justified in taking defensive military action against or in the other state.

All indications are that, in the aftermath of 9/11, international law has come to embrace the right of self-defence against non-state attacks. The United States, to be sure, had asserted for some time that it was permitted under international law to defend itself against terrorist attackers. Whereas this proposition was once subject to debate, most commentators read the UN Security Council as having endorsed it in its Resolution 1368, adopted immediately after 9/11. State practice since then seems to have confirmed this reading. There remains ambiguity on a number of crucial points, however.

First, self-defence against terrorist attacks will almost always involve operations within another state. Even if there is now agreement that an armed attack can be undertaken by non-state actors and trigger the target state's right to self-defence, there still remains a question as to the circumstances under which that state can take response action in another state. Since the 9/11 attacks, some states and a good number of commentators have asserted that strikes against terrorists in another state are lawful when that state is either unwilling or unable to handle the situation. This line of reasoning may seem sensible at first glance. But it extends the right to self-defence considerably beyond the deliberately tight requirement that only an armed attack by the state itself, or attributable to it, legally justifies unilateral military response by the victim state. In any case, what circumstances justify strikes against terrorists in other states remains a murky issue (Weller 2015).

Witness the current military operations against ISIL. The fact that ISIL calls itself a "state" does not resolve the matter, since ISIL does not meet the criteria for statehood and, furthermore, is asserting control over areas that are located within existing states, Iraq and Syria. In respect of the operations in its territory, Iraq communicated to the UN Security Council in September 2014 that it had asked the United States to lead international efforts to strike terrorist sites in its territory. The United States, in turn, asserted that the efforts to help defend Iraq against ISIL extended to attacking its sites in Syria, which had proven to be "unwilling or unable" to prevent the use by ISIL of its territory for attacks on Iraq.

Some commentators have suggested that states always have had the provisional right to take necessary and proportionate action against actual or imminent attacks, including forcible action abroad, without the need for direct attribution of the attacks to the state. If the state in which the terrorists are located takes steps to counter an attack or imminent threat, military intervention by the target state is unnecessary and hence unlawful. In turn, if there is no actual or imminent attack, the mere fact that the territorial state is unwilling or unable to assist cannot carry a self-defence argument. According to this view, operations against ISIL in Syria are necessary and therefore lawful as self-defence because of the close connections between ISIL's ongoing attacks in Iraq and its resources in Syria. It is irrelevant, so goes the argument, whether Syria consented to the operations, or has shown itself unwilling or unable to control ISIL (Weller 2015).

Whether one agrees with this assessment or not, it highlights another area of ambiguity in the law of self-defence: the question whether and under what circumstances states can exercise the right to self-defence in advance of an armed attack. Although, immediately after the 9/11 attacks, more expansive "preventive self-defence" arguments were advanced, the dominant view today seems to be that anticipatory action is justified only when an attack is imminent. The existence of even such a narrowly circumscribed right of anticipatory self-defence was long in dispute, with many states and commentators insisting that an actual armed attack was required to trigger the right to self-defence.

There is much at stake in this debate. After all, the greater the scope for anticipatory action, the more the prohibition on the interstate use of force risks being hollowed out by the right to self-defence. The rise of transnational terrorist networks and their modes of operation have helped reignite, and further complicate, the debate. As we have seen, even leaving aside the thorny question of attribution, the right to self-defence justifies strikes against terrorists only when they have launched an attack or are about to do so. But just what the requirement of imminence means in the context of transnational terrorism is a difficult question, and the push for strikes against terrorists, whenever and wherever they may be located, has been strong. The spectrum of justifications runs the gamut from assertions of much wider concepts of imminence, to reliance on the notion of ongoing attacks, to the much-invoked "War on Terror." Others warn that these arguments fail to legally justify what may really amount to extrajudicial killings, in violation not only of the interstate prohibition of force, but also of humanitarian law and human rights law, let alone the due process requirements of criminal law (O'Connell 2010).

Collective Action and Standard-Setting

The second broad approach to tackling transnational terrorism has been to narrow the gaps resulting from international law's basic jurisdictional framework. In principle, this gap-filling, and the elimination of safe havens for terrorists, can be advanced through international regimes that require states to adopt adequate laws and enforcement measures and to cooperate with other states in combatting transnational terrorism.

Such initiatives would normally require the negotiation of treaties that set out the measures parties have to take to meet their obligations under the relevant agreements. And, indeed, over the years states have negotiated nineteen anti-terrorism conventions, including the Convention for the Suppression of Terrorist Bombings (1997), the Convention for the Suppression of the Financing of Terrorism (1999), and the Convention for the Suppression of Acts of Nuclear Terrorism (2005). Each of these conventions requires parties to criminalize the conduct in question under their own domestic law, to assert jurisdiction over the relevant offences even if they occurred abroad, to either extradite or prosecute the alleged offenders, and to cooperate with other states in criminal matters within the ambit of the treaty.

The treaty-based approach has a number of drawbacks, however. The first may be obvious – states are not required to join treaties, and any treaty can bind only those states that do in fact become parties to it. As a result, the treaty approach cannot guarantee that all states that give shelter, wittingly or unwittingly, to terrorist networks will be obligated to step up their counterterrorism efforts and participate in global efforts to suppress transnational terrorism. An additional difficulty is that the need to engage as many states as possible in the treaty regime may require compromises on the scope and stringency of obligations. One emblematic illustration of this difficulty has been the inability to arrive at an overarching definition of *terrorism*, although some common ground seems have begun to emerge in recent years (Roach 2011; Peters 2014). Finally, leaving aside unwillingness to combat terrorism, many states simply do not have the financial, legislative, and technical capacity to do so. Even if they joined a counterterrorism treaty, therefore, they may find themselves unable to meet their commitments.

The United Nations has pursued a range of strategies to address these ratification and capacity issues. The Terrorism Prevention Branch of the United Nations Office on Drugs and Crime, for example, provides technical and legislative assistance to promote ratification and implementation of the terrorism prevention and suppression treaties. Universal ratification remains elusive, but the UN efforts have borne some fruit. For example, while the Nuclear Terrorism Convention has ninety-nine parties, the Terrorist Bombing Convention and the Terror Financing Convention have attracted the ratification of 168 and 186 states, respectively (United Nations 2015).

A second major plank in the effort to harmonize and coordinate national responses to terrorism, and to turn the patchwork of national counterterrorism efforts into a more seamless global web, is the exercise of UN Security Council powers. Under chapter VII of the UN Charter, in the face of threats to international peace and security, the council can impose legally binding requirements on *all* states. Although this unique power arguably was intended to enable the council to adopt decisions that address specific situations, its post-9/11 decisions on terrorism have taken on an increasingly "legislative" flavour. That is, on the grounds that terrorism constitutes a serious threat to international peace and security, the council has adopted a series of resolutions that impose general, open-ended requirements on states. These resolutions address the various modes of transnational terrorism – attacks directed from abroad, recruitment and training of foreign fighters, and incitement of home-grown terrorism around the world – and require states to take sweeping domestic measures to choke off the staging grounds, mobility, communication, and finances of terror networks.

The strength of the Security Council's recourse to binding resolutions is the very fact that all states now have the same obligations to take domestic counterterrorism measures. However, the existence of universally binding international obligations does not mean that a seamless web of domestic regimes is actually in place. Recalcitrance and capacity limitations pose problems, whether the international obligations are treaty-based or imposed by the Security Council. And, quite apart from these practical challenges, the Security Council's counterterrorism resolutions also raise a number of fundamental questions.

One such question is whether the council does in fact have to power to "legislate." This issue was debated with considerable passion following the adoption in 2001 of the council's first legislative counterterrorism resolution, Resolution 1373 (Talmon 2005). The series of similar resolutions adopted since 2001, however, suggests that the member states of the UN have come to accept the council's power in this respect. Nonetheless, there remains a related question as to the legitimacy of universal lawmaking by a body of limited membership. This legitimacy question feeds into the demands for a more representative Security Council, expanded beyond its current membership of fifteen – five permanent members (China, France, Russia, United Kingdom, and United States) and ten other states on rotating terms.

Another major question concerns the manner in which the council's counterterrorism resolutions have affected individuals. Technically, obligations are imposed only on UN member states. But since member states are legally required to enact the measures mandated by the Security Council, individuals find their mobility restricted and finances cut off. These concerns were most significant in relation to a list of persons and entities associated with terrorist organizations that was drawn up under the auspices of Security Council Resolution 1267. Originally focused on the Taliban and expanded by subsequent resolutions to Osama Bin Laden, Al Qaeda, and related organizations, the list system is managed by a UN committee. On the basis of secret evidence submitted by member states, persons and organizations are added to the 1267 list, which in turn requires states to take stringent measures, including travel bans and asset freezes. As originally conceived, the list system did not provide for any access of the affected persons or entities to information about the reasons for their inclusion in the list, or any avenue for the review or reversal of the listing decision. The criticism of the regime was harsh. National and European courts found ways to reject measures that implemented travel bans and asset freezes, such as on the grounds that they violated domestic or European due process and human rights guarantees. The UN listing regime itself has since seen some reforms, principally through the appointment of an ombudsperson tasked with reviewing petitions by listed individuals. For many observers, the process is not strong enough to allay human rights concerns (Roach 2011). But it has resulted in some de-listing decisions.

Conclusion

Although the tragic events surrounding the *Charlie Hebdo* attacks in Paris were ultimately an all-French affair, they also constituted an encounter with one of the many faces of transnational terrorism. Transnational terrorism, in its many permutations, challenges the state-centric apparatus of international law and has prompted an array of responses that, taken together, entail potentially significant changes to the international legal order.

As between states, the fight against diffuse networks and highly mobile actors has entailed a series of developments that chip away at the legal protections against external intervention in the sovereign spheres of states. This pattern ranges from armed interventions abroad in the guise of self-defence against terrorists, to the imposition of universal legal requirements for domestic counterterrorism measures through Security Council resolutions.

As between states and non-state actors, the intensifying global counterterrorism efforts struggle with the inherent limits of international law. Terrorists do not have obligations directly under international law, although the Security Council, in its most recent counterterrorism resolution, made the unprecedented demand "that all terrorist fighters disarm and cease all terrorist acts and participation in armed conflict"

(Resolution 2178 (2014), para. 1). Meanwhile, as individuals, terrorists and terrorism suspects have human rights and due process rights, rights on which some of the Security Council's counterterrorism measures have trenched. When it comes to dealing with the terrorist actors themselves, therefore, domestic legal systems have turned out to be indispensable, both in criminalizing and suppressing terrorist activity and in protecting the rights of those who are targeted by counterterrorism measures.

International law has a role to play in addressing transnational terrorism, in enabling states to defend themselves while also constraining the impulse to strike back incautiously, and in framing a genuinely global effort to suppress terrorism. But we must remember to step back and examine the cumulative effect on the global legal order of the many smaller and larger shifts brought about in the name of fighting terrorism.

REFERENCES

International Court of Justice. 2014. *Case Concerning the Military and Paramilitary Activities in and against Nicaragua (Nicaragua vs United States)*, (1986) ICJ Reports 14.

O'Connell, Mary-Ellen. 2010. "Unlawful Killing with Combat Drones: A Case Study of Pakistan, 2004–2009." Notre Dame Law School Legal Studies Research Paper No. 09-43, https://www.law.upenn.edu/institutes/cerl/conferences/targetedkilling/papers/OConnellDrones.pdf.

Peters, Anne. 2014. "Security Council Resolution 2178 (2014): The 'Foreign Terrorist Fighter' as an International Legal Person." EJIL: *Talk!*, November 20, http://www.ejiltalk.org/security-council-resolution-2178–2014-the-foreign-terrorist-fighter-as-an-international-legal-person-part-i/.

Roach, Kent. 2011. *The 9/11 Effect: Comparative Counter-Terrorism*. Cambridge: Cambridge University Press.

Talmon, Stefan. 2005. "The Security Council as World Legislature." AJIL 99:175.

United Nations. 2015. "Treaty Collection: Text and Status of United Nations Conventions on Terrorism," https://treaties.un.org/Pages/DB.aspx?path=DB/studies/page2_en.xml&menu=MTDSG.

Weller, Mark. 2015. "Striking ISIL: Aspects of the Law on the Use of Force." *American Society of International Law Insights* 19 (5), http://www.asil.org/insights/volume/19/issue/5/striking-isil-aspects-law-use-force.

12 Looking Back and Looking Forward: Authenticity through Purification

JANICE GROSS STEIN

The world's attention is fixated on *Daesh* (the Islamic State) and its capacity to inspire young people in the Arab world and in Muslim communities around the globe to join its cause. Abu Bakr al-Baghdadi, the ruler of the Islamic State, a descendant of the tribe of the Prophet, is the first to proclaim a caliphate since Turkey ended the last one ninety years ago. The creation of a caliphate that controls territory is for its leaders a seminal moment; the laws of *Shari'a* now apply in their entirety, and Muslims from all over the world are enjoined to come and live under Islamic law.

Recoiling in horror from the brutal violence, the beheadings, the destruction of historic works of art, the enslavement of women who have been captured in battle that has accompanied the creation of the Islamic State, leaders and publics are asking, Who is Islamic State? Who do they speak for? Are their followers amongst us? And how do we cope? Unfortunately, the answers are not straightforward.

In the Arab world, a cacophony of voices has always spoken for Islam. Immediately after the Prophet's death, a struggle for succession and legitimacy broke out, and the Islamic world, small as it was at the time, heard more than one voice that claimed authority through authenticity. At that time, authenticity came from the immediacy of the relationship to the Prophet and the capacity of his heirs who knew him to provide faithful – and "true" – interpretations of his teachings.

Even as the descendants of the Prophet claimed to be the sole, the exclusive, and the authentic voice of Islam, multiple voices spoke in noisy chorus. Almost from the outset, the Muslim world has been pluralist in form, if not in content. As the Muslim Empire expanded and grew, multiple sites of scholarship developed, and seats of learning, science, and law emerged in Baghdad, Damascus, and Cairo. Universities and

communities of legal scholarship became especially important in a religion governed by law, and over time, four major Sunni legal traditions
as well as Shi'a jurisprudence developed, all enriched by arguments,
commentaries, and interpretations.

It is this diversity of voices, and a lively tradition of reform and renewal, that paradoxically opened up space for an impulse by some to
return to fundamentals, to the "true" and authentic Islam, and by others to look forward to apocalyptic redemption. Whether they looked
backward or forward, they shared an emphasis on the purification of
Islam.

When the Islamic world began to bump up against a West that was
undergoing a renaissance of science, the development of revolutionary
new military technologies, and a drive for expansion, Islamic scholars
began to ask how Islam should renew itself to engage with the West but
preserve its distinctiveness. Movements of renewal and reform become
increasingly important in the nineteenth century as the Ottoman Empire began to decay and Western powers forced their way into the heart
of the Arab world.

A vigorous reform movement developed that focused on the renewal
of Islam and its adaptation to a "modern" world. This was far from
the first time that Islam engaged with modernity. Not surprisingly, this
conversation about reform also enabled the rise of those who wanted
not reform, but return, return to the roots of Islam, to the authentic
teachings of the Prophet that were unsullied by encounters with foreign religions and alien cultures and customs. A conversation began
about purification, some urging return and others redemption so that
Islam could fulfil its mission.

In the last few decades, the drive to purify has been amplified by the
failure of Arab governments to improve the lives of their citizens, to
promote basic health and education, to deliver services to their poor,
and to rein in the visible corruption that has so badly infected the auto-
cratic regimes that governed in the Arab world. The anger and despair
evoked by this failure has encouraged the search for the authentic and
the turn to redemption. Young people especially have turned not only
against their own governments, who have enriched themselves while
they exploited their citizens, but also against the *takfir*, the infidel West,
that has sustained and supported these governments. Not all these angry voices, however, are alike.

It is important to distinguish two strains. Those who want a return
to the true faith that is uncorrupted by the modern, especially the West,

look back. There are also those who are apocalyptic and seek redemption through purification; they look forward. Common to both, however, is a militant emphasis on purification, often through violent struggle, and a commitment to fundamentals.

This is not the first time that the Arab world has been galvanized by the search for the authentic and the pure. In the eighteenth century, Muhammad ibn 'Abd al-Wahhab, born in Nejd in the Arabian Peninsula, was determined to "purify" Islam from the corrupting influences of innovation and to return believers to the practices of the Prophet; he looked backward to early Islamic history. Al-Wahhab formed an alliance with the house of al-Saud, and today, the kings of Saudi Arabia, the guardians of the holy places of Mecca and Medina, are the heirs to Wahhabism, the determination to purify Islam. For decades, they have financed and exported fundamentalist movements to the Arab world, while keeping a tight grip on dissent at home. They have done so in the name of purity, as the guardians of the holy sites of Islam, and the custodians of Islam in the face of corrupting foreign influences.

The House of Saud was not alone in claiming to speak for a pure, authentic Islam in the face of modernity. In 1881, the Sudanese Muslim cleric Muhammad Ahmad conquered Khartoum and created a state that lasted until 1898. He invoked messianic writings in Islamic texts and declared himself the Mahdi – a millenarian who would lead Muslims to victory before the end of the world. Muhammad Ahmad gave voice to many of the strains of redemption and purification that *Daesh* articulates today. His was the first millenarian Islamic state of the modern period, the predecessor of today's Islamic State.

In Egypt, in 1928, Hassan al-Banna founded the *Ikhwan* or Muslim Brotherhood, to return believers to the faith in the face of Westernizing British colonial influence and the grotesquely corrupt government of the Egyptian king. The Muslim Brotherhood developed a syncretic form of Islam, combining religious tenets with social welfare. The Brothers not only issued a call to purify the faith, they also ran schools and clinics among the poorest urban and rural populations in Egypt. The Brotherhood would grow to be the strongest Muslim organization in Egypt and across the Arab world, with branches in almost every country, even after they were forced underground by President Gamal Ab'dul al-Nasir. Theirs was an Islam defined against corruption that served the poor and returned the faithful to purity without, however, the millenarian and apocalyptic overlay.

It is no surprise that the House of Saud fears and detests the Brothers, because they are competing largely for the same political and social space. The *Ikhwan* fully returns the enmity. This has been and continues to be a "close in" argument about legitimacy and voice, and between them, there is room for only one. When the *Ikhwan* finally won the presidency of Egypt after the overthrow of President Mubarak, the Saudi monarch allied with the ruling family of the United Arab Emirates and used every possible means to undermine the newly elected President Morsi. The fierce ongoing enmity toward the Brotherhood by some of the ruling families in the Gulf is understandable only as a continuing struggle for the mantle of purifier.

Even within the heartland of Wahhabi Saudi Arabia, militants consider the ruling family corrupt, despoiled by its riches and compromised by its close contact with the West. In 1979, long before *al-Qa'eda* and the Islamic State, an apocalyptic movement led by Islamist militants inside the kingdom seized the Grand Mosque in Mecca and called for the overthrow of the House of Saud; the group claimed one of its own leaders as the Mahdi, the redeemer and purifier. The Saudi royal family crushed the uprising with visceral ferocity.

These angry voices are heard most loudly today through *al-Qa'eda* that operates across the Arab and Muslim world and through *Daesh*, the Islamic State that is attracting recruits from across the Muslim world as well as the West. While they share an emphasis on purification, they are not alike: *al-Qa'eda* largely looks back, while *Daesh* largely looks forward. Neither can live with the other, and the struggle between them is fierce. One competes with the other as the "true" voice of Islam, but both are a beacon to angry young men and women who respond to the call for authenticity or redemption through purification, a call that gives meaning and purpose to their lives.

What makes these contemporary Islamist movements so threatening to Western societies? The Mahdi in Sudan, also an apocalyptic purifier who ruled an Islamic state more than a hundred years ago, alarmed the British but few others.

The first difference is in the ordering principles of the international system. Today, the tight interconnections of the contemporary globalized world, the open societies that encourage people to migrate and form communities abroad, and the digital technologies that allow unprecedentedly quick patterns of communication through social media make impossible the indifference shown to the Mahdi in Sudan in colonial times. The contemporary round of millenarian militancy in the Arab world diffuses outward through online recruitment fuelled by sophisticated social media campaigns, videos that glorify purification through violence, and, finally, through militant attacks in Western cities. Whether these attacks are coordinated or spontaneous, the violence comes "home" to the West.

Globalization has also enabled migration and the creation of diaspora communities that stay connected in ways that would have been impossible even a generation ago. *Daesh* draws on networks of militants, women as well as men, who facilitate travel, visas, and safe passage to recruit and move young people who find little meaning in their postindustrial lives. *Al-Qa'eda* and *Daesh* are the first calls to purification from the heart of the Islamic world that are echoed and amplified through the technologies and networks of a globalized world. It is not the call but the globalizing conditions and technologies that are especially new. It is no small irony that they use the technologies that define our contemporary era of globalization to wage war for purification.

A second and related difference is the weakness, possibly the collapse, of a 100-year-old order built by colonizers who drew borders and created states. It is the fracturing of the states of Iraq and Syria that opened up the political space and the physical territory to create a caliphate. It is inconceivable, for example, that the Islamic State could have been created when Saddam Hussein and Hafez al-Assad ruled their republics of fear. That this violent millenarian movement grew out of the collapse of the authoritarian order should neither surprise nor evoke nostalgia for the past. The collapse of the autocrats was inevitable; no authoritarian order endures forever. In this case, the midwife was the invasion of Iraq by the Bush administration, but the unmaking of the Middle East would have happened sooner or later. The unmaking of orders is quick, brutal, violent, and dramatic, but remaking is slow, arduous, painful, and uncertain. It is the work of generations, and if the outcome is to be legitimate, it can be led only from the inside. The rest of the world can only try to contain the spread of the pathogen of purification and limit its capacity to infect and kill.

How has the West reacted? With understandable confusion, laced with horror at the ferocity of the personalized violence. The West has to reach back a long time to remember the 100-year ferocity of its religious wars, but the memory of the Nazi orgy of blood and violence less than 80 years ago should still be fresh. What seems incomprehensible, even genocidal, is different in form and texture but hardly unique.

There are at least three broad strands in the response of the West to *Daesh*. The first, the criminalization of support for the Islamic State by those living in Western societies, is well analysed in this volume. It ranges from the confiscation of passports of young men and women, often at the behest of their agonized Muslim parents; enhanced surveillance of the speech and actions of suspected supporters; increased sharing of information among intelligence agencies; relaxation of evidentiary standards for intervention; and the criminalization of support for terrorism, all of this without significant increase in civilian oversight and partnership with police and intelligence agencies. This is a dangerous dance in democratic societies. History shows again and again that citizens will turn against their governments when unsupervised agencies inevitably exceed their authority and threaten deeply held democratic values.

The second set of responses, partnership with Muslim communities, should be more prominent than it is. Muslim communities living in Western societies are at an exposed intersection of conflicting fears, needs, and feelings. First, they are the victims of public horror at the incomprehensible brutality of *Daesh,* stereotyped by Westerners who often do not recognize that the overwhelming majority of Muslims who live amongst them reject both the violence and the legitimacy of the Islamic State. Muslims living in Western societies are also frightened that their young people will be seduced by the call of a violent, millenarian organization. Finally, when information is released about young Muslims from the West who have left to join the Islamic State, community leaders at home not only worry about the fate of their young people but about the backlash and hardening of public attitudes that follows after each new case comes to light.

Yet Muslims in Western societies are essential partners, leaders in establishing interpretations of Islam that reject the literal reading of texts that promotes violence. Even as they speak out against the violence, however, Muslims are angered by the demand that they do so and by the collective stigmatization that the request from political leaders implies. There are no easy answers to these conundrums, only the deepening of civility, respect, and commitment to inclusive and shared citizenship.

Finally, the West has created a broad military coalition to contain the Islamic state within its present borders and then gradually to push it back and degrade its capabilities. There is, inevitably, deep concern about the destabilizing consequences of yet another Western military action, but it is essential that the Islamic State be contained. And coalition air strikes have largely accomplished that objective; they have stopped the expansion of the millenarian state and pushed it back in a few critical areas.

The hard part, of course, lies ahead, but paradoxically, despite the sophisticated use of social media and networked patterns of recruitment, the struggle against the Islamic State is a fairly old-fashioned war centred on the control of territory. Once the Islamic State loses control of the territory it now rules, it will no longer be a caliphate and it will lose its legitimacy and its appeal. The loss of territory would constitute a strategic defeat, even though elements of the millenarian ideology would live on, reconstituted in a different form. What distinguishes *Daesh* is the creation of the caliphate, and when that fails, so does *Daesh*, its legitimacy and its capacity to recruit deeply compromised. As the Islamic State continues to struggle to control its borders and fails to expand, over time it loses the magnetic appeal of a truly millenarian movement. Since the moment of redemption cannot be forever postponed, persistent containment is a powerful repudiation of the millenarian claims of Islamic State leaders.

The West, however, cannot lead the attack on the ground against the Islamic State. An all-out assault by Western forces would fulfil the moist violent apocalyptic fantasies of *Daesh* leaders. It must be led by those who live next door, by neighbours who reject the brutality, the violence, and the genocidal impulses. But it must be led in a way that reassures those who now live under the rule of the Islamic State that the violence and the brutality will not continue under the liberators. Here, past performance is not encouraging. The West can only support from behind those who seek to overthrow the Islamic State, even while it restrains from behind those who seek vengeance and reprisals.

Over time, this story is mildly optimistic. The fires of purification burn fiercely for a while, but then are generally quenched by the grinding realities that organizations face. The kings of Saudi Arabia, the partners and inheritors of Wahhabi ideology, make the compromises that they must, and the Muslim Brotherhood that won the election in Egypt a few years ago was but a pale imitation of the *Ikhwan* that was born in the slums of Cairo in 1928. Our own history confirms that the puritans cannot remain puritanical forever.

What can the West do in the face of a struggle that will go on for generations? Endure, with resolve, stoicism, patience, and intelligence. The fight among this generation of purifiers continues, but its primary victims are the hundreds of millions of believing Muslims whose voices are drowned out by this quarrel, the millions who have been made refugees from their homes, and the hundreds of thousands who have lost their lives in the ongoing wars in Iraq and Syria. This quarrel, like all others in history, will eventually be transformed, institutionalized, and routinized. In these early days, as the fires of purification burn strongly, we in the West need to be resolute in our commitment to contain, to prevent the spread of the violent, brutal impulse, but not to lead. Our best protection from the flying debris is the use of our intelligence assets in ways that are compatible with our basic values, the deepening of our open and inclusive societies, and a long view of history.

PART THREE

From Headlines to Analysis: The Media

13 After the Paris Attacks: Reflections on the Media

NATASHA FATAH

Every January we tell ourselves this year will be better. This year *we'll* be better. We make resolutions to be a healthier, thinner, smarter, more productive, kinder, or gentler. And there is a hope that, through our individual acts, our *world* will be a better, kinder place. So it was that we started 2015 with that promise of a better year ahead. But how quickly that resolution was broken, when a hail of bullets and the shouts of Islamist rhetoric were fired out into the streets of Paris outside the offices of a group of provocative cartoonists.

On January 7 – just a week into our new collective promise – two brothers struck terror into the people of Paris, France, Europe, the West, the world, anyone on the side of civility.

As a response, on January 11, forty international leaders linked arms and led a march through the streets of Paris, behind them followed a crowd of millions right across France. Smaller demonstrations were held around the world. Those who could not make it to the streets went to the digital town square, where they declared "Je suis Charlie," a statement of solidarity with freedom of expression and an attempt to unify when the world seems so divided.

The shootings of the cartoonists at the *Charlie Hebdo* magazine was a moment that forced many of us to stop, stare in horror, and try to make sense of what was happening around us. It was not the first attack carried out by Islamist extremists, and sadly it was not the last.

When a tragic, horrifying, and complicated story like this presents itself, we in the media have to tell the story as responsibly as we can and to the best of our ability.

For those who don't work at newspapers, broadcasters, and media offices, it might seem that there are clear rules about how to move forward when reporting a story like this, or any story, for that matter. But the truth is there aren't. There are best practices, corporate guidelines, legal considerations, and common sense. Ultimately it comes down to a group of individuals in the newsroom making those calls, and the answers to those calls can vary widely, depending on the values of the individuals involved.

Below I offer my assessment, based on my experience as a journalist and as a consumer of news, of what the media in Canada got right, what we got wrong, and what we need to do better surrounding the coverage of the *Charlie Hebdo* attacks and beyond.

What We Got Right

This section is short and easy. The Canadian media gave the story a tremendous amount of coverage; it was the lead story for several days, across all media platforms. This was absolutely the right way to handle this story. The attack on *Charlie Hebdo* cartoonists was an attack on freedom of expression and freedom of the press, but that's not all that it was. It was an attack on the rules of civilized society.

In the Western world, where the Kouachi brothers grew up, there are agreed upon rules of engagement. If a magazine publishes an image that you find offensive, you are welcome to write an op-ed, and if you can't find a publisher, then the Internet provides the ability to self-publish. You can take legal action, as one group did in 2007. The Grand Mosque of Paris filed a lawsuit against the editor of *Charlie Hebdo* on the basis that the depictions of Islam's Prophet Muhammad were tantamount to hate speech. The tribunal did not find in the mosque's favour, but the point had been made that the cartoons were offensive to some.

Those offended also have the option to lobby politicians, run for political office, change the laws, or create another publication that counters the offending content. But nowhere in our collective rules of engagement do we accept physical violence and murder as a suitable response. It isn't just about "Western" values, it is about civility, decency, and rationality. Most of us were offended on all those fronts, which made the attacks highly harmful to our society and made them worthy of an exceptionally high degree of news coverage.

I think reporters, writers, and broadcasters presented the information fairly, quickly, responsibly, and for the most part got the facts right.

What We Got Wrong

Following the attacks on *Charlie Hebdo*, only a handful of Canadian news outlets published illustrations of Muhammad from the French satirical magazine: the *National Post*, Sun News Network, CBC's French network services Radio-Canada, and multiple French-language newspapers based in Quebec. They got it right, and I applaud them for it.

But for the most part, English-Canadian broadcasters and newspapers chose not to publish the *Charlie Hebdo* cartoons of the Prophet Muhammad, or the cover of the *Charlie Hebdo* issue following the attacks that featured the Prophet holding a sign in French that read "All Is Forgiven." This decision was wrong on two fronts: It was the wrong decision for journalists, whose responsibility it is to tell the story and let the facts speak for themselves. It was also wrong because the notion that there is a religious edict against showing images of the Prophet is invalid, which I will explain in further detail below.

In choosing not to publish the illustrations, some suggested that you don't need to see the images to understand the story. However, that argument can be used for any story. And when it comes to visual media like TV and print, where the picture can boost the understanding of the story for the public, there is an obligation to show the picture, particularly in this case, where the images were an essential element of the story.

This was addressed by Andrew Coyne of the *National Post*, who participated in a panel discussion on CBC Radio's show *The Current* on the issue of publishing the cartoons. Coyne said, "This is the news story. The story here is that this magazine was slaughtered for publishing cartoons that some people found objectionable. It's a little precious to write about it but then not show people what the fuss is about." He went on to say that this issue is near and dear to many journalists, that this is a broader issue of freedom of press and expression. Coyne said we can't have religious fanatics dictating what we can and cannot publish. We can't apply rules selectively. We cannot bend our freedoms for one religious group.[1]

---

1 "Media Split on Publishing *Charlie Hebdo* Prophet Muhammad Cartoons," *The Current*, January 9, 2015, http://www.cbc.ca/radio/thecurrent/.

Some media managers have said they were not publishing the cartoons the day before the *Charlie Hebdo* attacks, so why change the policy after the attacks? The answer to that question is that the day before the attacks, the cartoons themselves were not newsworthy. The parameters of the story changed after people were gunned down in the street and in their workplaces. When the story changes, the policies on the coverage might have to change, and they often do.

Denise Bombardier of the *Journal de Montreal* was also on *The Current*'s panel. She described the decision by most broadcasters to not publish the cartoons as "gutless." She went on to point out that not all Muslims feel that depictions of Islam's Prophet are offensive, and that the media should not be kowtowing to a fundamentalism and radical interpretation of Islam.[2]

That brings me to the most common argument presented for not publishing the cartoons: illustrations of Prophet Muhammad are strictly forbidden in Islam and will offend Muslims. The former is false.

This highlights that Muslims themselves were, and continue to be, absent from much of the discussion about these editorial decisions.

CBC News Network's show *Power and Politics* hosted a discussion with two Muslims about the publishing of the *Charlie Hebdo* cartoons. Shahid Mahmood is a political cartoonist, who had to flee his native Pakistan because of the lack of freedom of expression in that country, and the danger it had posed to his life. He corrected a common misconception: "In early Islam, the Prophet was depicted. It was only in the eighth century that you have a stream of fundamentalists, not unlike the Wahhabi culture that we have in much of the Middle East, that started to control the religion and what was portrayed to the public … This is detrimental to faith and detrimental to society. You have to be able to speak your mind."[3]

Christine Gruber is one of the foremost authorities in North America on the issue of artistic representations of the Prophet Muhammad. Gruber is a professor of Islamic arts at the University of Michigan and is writing a book called "The Praiseworthy One: The Prophet Muhammad in Islamic Texts and Images."

---

2 Ibid.
3 "*Charlie Hebdo* Controversial Cartoon," *Power and Politics*, January 14, 2015, http:// www.cbc.ca/news/politics.

During an interview on Public Radio International Gruber offered the following arguments:[4]

1. Nowhere in the Quran, Islam's holy book, does it forbid the depiction of the Prophet.
2. Muhammad has been depicted in illustrated manuscripts dating back to the thirteenth century, created by both Sunnis and Shias. And she points out that at the time these illustrations were created, there were no negative reactions amongst Muslims.
3. Islamic texts give detailed notes about the Prophet's appearance, referred to as "Characteristics Texts." They describe Muhammad's height, eye shape, complexion, beard length, and so on. So an understanding of his appearance is important for Muslims.

Gruber makes the distinction that, in Islam, it is strictly forbidden to worship idols. So perhaps over the years, and as the most conservative voices of Islam have become the loudest, depictions of Muhammad have been forbidden to avoid idolatry. But depictions are not forbidden in the Quran or in the *hadith*s, which are religious writings and teachings from the Prophet that Muslims use as supplementary resources.

In fact there are images of the Prophet Muhammad on display at the New York Metropolitan Museum.[5] The Bibliothèque Nationale in France recently had a display of Islamic art in which the Prophet was represented.[6] There is a large volume of Muhammad illustrations at the Edinburgh University Library in Scotland. Depictions of the Prophet by Muslim artists have been found in regions currently known as Iran, Turkey, Uzbekistan, Afghanistan, and India.

Then some would argue that those paintings of Muhammad are respectful, whereas the vulgar satirical cartoons are hurtful. Well, either the depiction is forbidden or it is not. And it is not. As it relates to hurt feelings, Rosie DiManno, a columnist with the *Toronto Star*, put it this way: "Sometimes journalism involves taking risks. And that doesn't

---

4 "You Can't Draw Muhammad – Unless You're One of the Many Muslim Artists Who Did," PRI, January 15, 2015.
5 "The Birth of Islam," Metropolitan Museum of Art, New York, http://www.metmuseum.org/toah/hd/isla/hd_isla.htm.
6 "Muhammad: dans la tradition islamique," Bibliothèque Nationale, Paris, http://expositions.bnf.fr/parole/zoom/110/01.htm.

just mean reporting from war zones. It means taking a stand ... We are a secular profession. We do not make a habit of cowering before any other faith. We do not allow potential ramifications to pre-censor. We do not defer to the *hurt*."[7]

And just to cover the entire ground, let us say, for the purposes of argument, that the Quran did clearly prohibit the depictions of Prophet Muhammad, thereby making it a duty of Muslims to not present him in an illustrative way. Even then, the cartoons should have been printed. A newspaper or broadcaster has no religion: these are secular, public institutions, and why should the rules for religious believers be forced on them or adopted by them? In extreme cases, if a Muslim reporter or editor did not feel comfortable with the story, which should be respected, then he or she should not be assigned it, as though it were a matter of conflict of interest. If Muslims are ordered to not show Muhammad, then what does that matter to the Christians, Jews, Hindus, Sikhs, Buddhists, atheists, and agnostics in the newsroom?

If I were in the position to make the decision, I would have published the cartoons and the *Charlie Hebdo* covers. Not to offend, but to inform – which is my primary responsibility as a journalist.

What We Need to Do Better

One of the main goals of journalism is to hold people to account. When covering Islamist extremism stories, we need to be braver, be bolder, and push harder. Journalists must continue to work on improving the coverage of these stories and not allow the fear of being labelled anti-Muslim dictate our analysis of news events, particularly around the motivations of the attackers, and what is demonstrably a rise in Islamist extremism in the West.

Canadians have a well-deserved reputation for being open-minded and tolerant, particularly to visible, ethnic, and religious minorities. In that same vein, the media in Canada, located largely in Toronto, mostly white, liberal, insulated, and homogeneous, share common values. And in the business of storytelling we often present someone – with or without intention – as the good guy or the bad guy. Because there

---

7 Rosie DiManno, "Star Should Have Published Charlie Hebdo Front Cover," *Toronto Star*, January 13, 2015. http://www.thestar.com/news/gta/2015/01/13/star_should_have_published_charlie_hebdo_front_cover_dimanno.html.

is a history of minorities being the victims of actions of the dominant communities, journalists have fallen into the familiar and lazy pattern of presenting Muslims as victims. This is a form of well-meaning, unintentional racism, to presume that all Muslims are victims at all times. Muslims are as varied, as complicated, as kind-hearted, and as mean-spirited or vicious as any other community. They must be seen as individuals, not as a group.

Following the *Charlie Hebdo* attacks, Canadian media turned to the "Muslim community" for their reaction – again, as though there is one community or a singular reaction. Average daily news reporters are under a tight deadline, and if they need a "Muslim voice," it's easy to go to the local mosque and ask the imam what he thinks. But then what "Muslims are thinking" is misrepresented. Like most people born into Christianity or Judaism, most Muslims do not attend religious service. They are, for the most part, living their lives like mainstream Canadians, but their voices and opinions are shut out. If the media overwhelmingly turn to mosques and Islamic organizations that represent a narrow, often conservative perspective of what it means to be a Muslim, and they speak on behalf of the thousands of Muslims in Canada, then we're painting a highly skewed picture.

Once that imam, or representative, or spokesperson starts talking on behalf of Muslims, there has to be accountability. If every interview with a politician is in some way an accountability interview, then the same should be true for those who claim to represent a religious group, especially when that religious group has political aspirations, like the implementation of sharia law, for example.

On more than one occasion, following the *Charlie Hebdo* attacks, on national broadcasts, representatives from Islamic organizations said that, while they deplored the violence and bloodshed of the attack, the actions were explicable because of U.S. or Western involvement in Muslim countries. And often the journalist conducting the interview did not challenge this assertion. If a white supremacist or a conservative politician had made similar remarks, the reporter would be obliged, in fact emboldened to challenge. But my sense is that a fear of appearing racist or Islamophobic has prevented Canadian journalists from asking Muslim representatives tougher questions.

It is not good enough to have a "Muslim voice" say, "This has nothing to do Islam" and "Islam is a religion of peace." There is evidence that there is a strain of Islam that is radical and violent, and it is building momentum.

After the *Charlie Hebdo* attacks, the BBC conducted a poll of British Muslims about their perspectives on the attacks, and on life in the West in general. While 95 per cent of British Muslims polled felt a loyalty to Britain, there were disturbing numbers that need further analysis:[8]

- 24 per cent feel violence can be justified against those who depict Prophet Muhammad.
- 11 per cent feel sympathy for the people who want to fight against Western interests.
- 8 per cent know Muslims who are sympathetic to ISIS or Al Qaeda.
- 45 per cent feel there is some justification for clerics to preach violence against the West.

There was a much more comprehensive, five-year, "Six Country Immigration Integration Comparative Survey" done by a German research institute, WZB Berlin Social Science Center, which surveyed Muslim communities in Austria, Belgium, France, Germany, the Netherlands, and Sweden. Some of the findings suggest a disconnection between "Muslim" values and "Western" values:[9]

- 65 per cent of Muslims interviewed say Islamic/sharia law is more important to them than the laws of the country they live in.
- 54 per cent believe that the West is out to destroy Islam.
- 60 per cent reject homosexuals as friends, 45 per cent say Jews cannot be trusted.
- 20 per cent of non-Muslim Europeans expressed Islamophobia, whereas 54 per cent of Muslims expressed Occidentophobia or anti-Western sentiment.

No similar national survey has been conducted in Canada since 2006. Nevertheless, these Western surveys give reporters scientific, research-based evidence that there is a schism between Western values and those

---

8 "BBC Radio 4 Today Muslim Poll," ComRes, February 25, 2015, http://comres.co.uk/polls/bbc-radio-4-today-muslim-poll/.
9 "Six Country Immigrant Integration Comparative Survey (SCIICS)," WZB Berlin Social Science Center, December 11, 2013, http://www.wzb.eu/en/research/migration-and-diversity/migration-and-integration/projects/six-country-immigrant-integration-comparat.

of some Muslims who live in those countries, including here in Canada. And increasingly that is leading to sympathy towards anti-Western terrorist organizations, which could be resulting in the steady stream of young Muslims joining the global, violent, armed jihad.

Of course we need to understand what is driving hundreds of young people, born and raised in the Western world, to leave their lives of promise and freedom to fight and die alongside a "death cult," as so described by former foreign affairs minister John Baird, U.S. President Barack Obama, U.K. Prime Minister David Cameron, and Australian Prime Minister Tony Abbott. But we need to acknowledge that it is happening and not minimize the issue in the first place.

As journalists it our responsibility to be neutral, to not show bias or take sides. However, there are occasions, particularly when talking about an extremist ideology, that we do not need to offer balanced coverage, to present the other side of the argument for the purposes of seeming fair. For example, when the Taliban shoot a fourteen-year-old girl in the head because she wants to get an education, there is no need for balance. When Boko Haram kidnap more than 200 girls from a Nigerian village, forcing the Christians to convert to Islam, and then selling them into sexual slavery, there is no other side to this story. When ISIS militants slit the throat of a Japanese war reporter, there is no other side to this story. These acts are disgusting and go against our very understanding of decency. The same I would say can be applied to the murders at the *Charlie Hebdo* offices.

Rosie DiManno said it brilliantly: "I'm tired of being told this is not Islam. I *know* this is not Islam. But it is a strain of and a stain on Islam."[10]

That extremist stain is smeared each and every day across the headlines of our national newspapers and on our TV screens during broadcast reports. Three middle-class British girls go to Syria to become jihad-brides. A group of chocolate shop customers are held hostage in Sydney. A young man is shot in the head at a synagogue in Copenhagen. A Bangladeshi-American atheist is hacked to death in Dhaka. A Canadian military officer is gunned down in our capital. If we can tell each story individually, then we also have a responsibility to offer the analysis of the shared ideology that ties these stories together and ask for accountability. Think of it as a New Year's resolution.

---

10 DiManno, "Star Should Have Published."

14 Journalism and Political Decision-Making in an Age of Crises

BRIAN STEWART

Introduction

The Paris shootings and latest security alarms in Europe and North America were profoundly important events, yet such brutal happenings are scarcely isolated shocks anymore. Rather, they are part of what journalists see as the "terrible torrent" of crises in a hyper-alert age.

It's difficult to analyse the Paris shootings and our response to them without taking into account the unprecedented influence mainstream and social media news coverage has on governments, which are determined to "seize the narrative" by promising rapid, effective action. The race is to both calm an anxious public and grab political gain by appearing bold.

It never stops, does it? Our 24/7 all-news environment has become a vortex in which the increasing mass of information and an unprecedented velocity of communications produce a force that threatens to overwhelm media and government alike. We are starting to feel we are in a permanent state of siege.

We have struggled just within the past twelve months to grasp everything from the rise of ISIS and the near-collapse of Iraq to the emergence of a possible new Cold War in Europe, as Russia has seized the Crimea and supported insurgency in the Ukraine. There's been Boko Haram in Africa and an Ebola crisis as well. Add to that a mysteriously missing airliner yet to be found and another shot down, as well as a new Canadian military mission abroad and new terrorist acts at home, along with Paris and its aftermath.

Since 9/11 we have really lived within an Age of Crises, so our public discourse is severely distorted by a tempo of upheavals that tend to exacerbate an obsession with short-term dangers while drawing attention away from critical long-term issues. It's often said it was ever thus in the world, but it really wasn't – this is overdrive as never seen before.

I can remember long ago, in November 1956, being fascinated by what seemed media frenzy as the Suez Invasion and Hungarian uprising exploded at the same time, and of course in 1962 by the extraordinary drama of the Cuban Missiles Crisis. But when I view archival news footage from those times, media stakeouts and once-a-night newscasts seem almost languid compared to the media bombardment today.

The Surge in Information

The whole manner in which crises are covered changed irrevocably in the 1980s when both the Internet and satellite TV feeds married near-instantaneous information to real-time or live reporting. A more transparent and well-informed world was at hand, or so it was hoped, but for politicians and journalists it arrived as both a blessing and curse. It meant governments could grab attention more often, while TV journalists could feed same-day stories from a distant famine or an artillery duel in Beirut into that night's newscasts. The new immediacy had immense attractions.

The curse, as politicians found out, was that the sheer number of problems needing urgent answers offered up not only the possibility of political gain, but also far more opportunities to stumble in public. Major resources were shifted into public information operations to stick-handle, or more often just block, the media inquiries now pouring in. Crisis-mode management became far more a preoccupation of those near the centre of power.

For reporters, the downside soon arrived in an escalating demand for stories from now-insatiable news departments at the very time media began to chop back the number of journalists employed and even whole foreign and domestic bureaux. Foreign reporters who once had days to research reports found themselves often asked to file shorter, same-day reports, sometimes for all morning, noontime, and evening newscasts, which often were expected to include almost instant analysis.

More alertness and rapid-fire analysis has unfortunately not meant an end to misjudgments. There is still a media tendency to exaggerate good news (admittedly rare) or the more common bad happenings. Both journalism and government remain myopic to a surprising degree

– we did not foresee the collapse of communism around 1990; failed to really forecast the rise of China in such spectacular form; certainly did not predict the Great Global Recession of 2008; were astonished by "the Arab Spring"; and were mystified by stumbling upon the spectre of Cold War Two, as well as still another Iraq War.

In fairness, however, nothing prepared policymakers or journalists for the shock effects of our time. Even if the unbelievable savagery of the war as waged by ISIS and Boko Haram and seen often on YouTube had been foretold, who would have believed such gory predictions?

We believe ever more information should enlighten out darkness, but American political scientist Philip Tetloch has studied the misfires of pundits and notes that the immediacy of more information does not seem to increased accuracy of predictions, but rather the reverse (2005).

This is the turbulent environment in which we try to absorb current events such as the Boston Marathon bombing and Paris shootings, and in which governments naturally seek to act as if firmly in charge of events, even as our decision-makers are increasingly overwhelmed by cascades of seemingly incomprehensible problems.

At one level it is a problem of sheer numbers. The list of independent countries in the world has tripled to 196 since I graduated as a journalist a half-century ago, all with problems, causes to defend, and demands to make at international forums. At last count 50 of these nations are failing or failed states, hollowed out by years of conflict, corruption, and rule by oligarchs, and most in an almost permanent state of ruinous internal conflicts.

The demands on the attention of leaders and advisors is unprecedented. It's not just countries, of course, that need attending to, but also economies as well, global health emergencies, along with an ever-expanding number of non-state actors in national and global affairs – tens of thousands of NGO and volunteer groups, diaspora and commercial lobbies, all seeking, demanding attention for their cause and increasingly skilled in using Internet and social media campaigns to influence opinion. To this we should add the remarkable growth of outside consultants of all kinds that governments are now reliant on to help handle the sheer volume of issues they face.

Talk to former policymakers in almost any democratic government and one senses nostalgia for a slower pace of decision-making in a time when leadership still had moments for calm reflection, even for blue-sky sessions when long-term strategy could be devised. Madeline Albright, President Bill Clinton's secretary of state, stresses that it's not just the volume of international problems, it's also the fact they all urgently "need fixing." Forty years ago, few in office likely cared overly about an distant upheaval in East Timor or Somalia, or Yemen, but today any small nation can suddenly threaten world stability and so launch yet another diplomatic emergency.

So turbulent is our world that leaders need a strong, supporting body of knowledge already in place before they take office. It's a common complaint of policy advisors, albeit deeply off-the-record, that many of today's younger crop of leaders arrive in power with little if any concept of strategy and are deficient in the historical knowledge that strategy requires (and to some extent similar complaints are made of many journalists today).

More Information, More Pressure to Act

The greater transparency that media provide has benefited the world in many ways, and there is much to be said for bringing foreign and security problems, once the preserve of highly trained, elite public servants, at least partially into the "public market place of ideas," as the media like to call it. But it has also significantly increased pressure on government to often react, even to directly intervene, in distant trouble spots they know too little about.

As Robert Bothwell, Canadian historian and distinguished Munk School professor, wrote of the 1990s era of post–Cold War interventions, "The Canadian public, spurred on by the media and by special-interest non-governmental organizations was prone to demand action as one crisis after another was perceived and adopted by journalists – sometimes for good reason, sometimes not" (2006, 519).

Canada was hardly alone in this development. As the Cold War defrosted, numerous political and global affairs commentators have complained of a lack of coherent strategy, or even clear policy or doctrine evident in top government circles. The complaint is often heard that today governments seem most guided by a series of news strategies to appease a media hungry for drama and the public's demand for quick results whenever the latest headline crisis erupts.

According to Canadian Donald Savoie, the much-quoted analyst of governance, some recent prime ministers often seem to govern through "bolts of electricity" – hurried actions meant to keep both party followers and Parliament in line at a time of such fast-moving and complex events. "For the centre of government, coordination now means operating an early warning system for the prime minister, anticipating and managing political crisis, and pursuing prime ministerial priorities. The emphasis is less on policy coherence and more on keeping the lid on, so that the prime minister and the centre can get this done" (2000, 336).

Government actions are shaped at a time when too much information increases the difficulty in setting clear strategy. The undeniable benefits of the computer's information floodtides coincide with a loss of perspective, even a weakening of our capacity to separate merely important issues from the most critical ones.

"Because information is so accessible and communications instantaneous, there is a diminution of focus on its significance, and even on the definition of what is significant," Henry Kissinger writes in *World Order*. "This dynamic may encourage policy makers to wait for an issue to arise rather than anticipate it, and to regard moments of decision as a series of isolated events rather than part of a historical continuum. When this happens, manipulation of information replaces reflection as the principal policy tool" (2014, 351).

The old diplomacy had many faults, including failure to support deserving political forces, he concedes. Governments today, however, too often plunge into commitments they scarcely understand. It is not difficult to think of some recent Canadian operations when reading from Kissinger, "The new diplomacy risks indiscriminate intervention disconnected from strategy. It declares moral absolutes to a global audience before it has become possible to access the long-term intentions of the central actors, their prospects for success, or the ability to carry out a long-term policy" (2014, 357).

This tendency is happening at a time when the various news organizations supposed to cover government, even the best of them, are straining to provide balanced reporting in such a period of deep financial constraints and reduced staffs. The media have less ability even to analyse and give context to the material government feeds them.

Both print and television journalism can still provide brilliant moments, often under enormous stress, as they did during the immediate hours and days following the Ottawa and Paris shootings. When the need for deeper information and understanding is required, however, we are often left dissatisfied.

The arrival of access to information had admittedly increased the power of some journalists to penetrate more deeply into government workings. Yet, with few exceptions, skeletal news organizations have ditched detailed examination of how government functions in favour of highlighting party clashes in the restricted "gotcha circus" of televised Question Periods or media scrums.

This reality has collided with those increasingly powerful power circles mentioned by Savoie, here primarily the Prime Minister's Office, that are at all times determined to ensure government wagons are in a circle, protected from any slip of the lip or release of information that might rebound to the opposition's favour. Even very senior officials are restricted from speaking freely to media, while departments either clam up entirely or merely hand out position-paper talking points.

Yet while attempts to manage media have increased significantly in Canada under Prime Minister Stephen Harper, even strong critics of such control admit it's not just a Harper problem or even a Conservative problem, but rather a tendency in governments generally. There is little optimism that another party in power might act very differently, for there's a dynamic at play that increasingly pits inner power circles against media. As Mark Bourrie, author and media expert notes, "The reporters in Obama's White House are treated with the same contempt that Harper holds for the Parliamentary Press Gallery and subject to the same kind of controls" (2015, 7).

In his just released *Kill the Messengers: Stephen Harper's Assault on Your Right to Know*, Bourrie sees new restraints on media as a threat to democracy, not just here but in most Western countries: "The use of corporate communications strategy to hide public information, the development of retail politics, the invention of intrusive technology and the defanging of media and other governmental watchdogs have become normal … a new kind of controlling, arrogant, and often vindictive government has emerged since the 1980's and is getting more emboldened and entrenched" (2015, 7).

What is deeply worrisome is that governments today, beset by a sense of continuous siege, and media driven by hunger for the dramatic, will find it ever harder to avoid falling back on superficial answers or bumper-sticker slogans to explain the deeply complex dangers facing us.

In this extraordinary period of rapid change, political writer Joshua Ramo titled his study of such risks *The Age of the Unthinkable*. He argues that ideas and institutions once relied on are failing, "and the best ideas of our leaders seem to make our problems worse, not better. A global war on terror produces, in the end, more dangerous terrorists" (2009, 9–10).

After Paris I was reminded of something historian and author David Fromkin predicted fully forty years ago in his *Foreign Affairs* article, "The Strategy of Terrorism." He warned that an age of terrorism would flourish in the rapidly expanding world of global, instantaneous communications that was even then on the near horizon. As terrorists garnered more news coverage, they would continually increase shock tactics in attempts to goad governments into overreacting. "All too little understood, the uniqueness of the strategy lies in this: – that it achieves its goal not through its acts but through the response to its act" (1975). More psychologically shocking, more deadly attacks will dangerously rattle our societies. He added, "Increasingly we will be under pressure to abridge our laws and liberties, in order to suppress the terrorist. It is a pressure that should be resisted."

Conclusion

One can sympathize with leaders today with all that they confront. Still, as we now face a new cycle of shocks over the Paris shootings, Iraq, and our domestic security, one would surely wish for more considered and transparent examinations of issues. One cannot be hopeful, given current time restrictions on debate in Parliament and the deep freeze that has settled over government and media.

New technology seems in many cases to be actually hardening political attitudes and cultural divides, rather than softening them by bringing factions closer, a tendency towards bitterness and distrust found not only nationally, but internationally as well.

We face major challenges at a time when the public seems deeply disenchanted with governments and media alike.

A yearning for improved dialogue may have positive effects, over time. Certainly academia has a renewed responsibility to provide deeper, more balanced, and calmer study of issues, and social media as well can sometimes provide important new insights. On the plus side, the Canadian public appears to have so far embraced the need for social resilience in the face of so many new anxieties. We'll need plenty of this quality in future.

However, it's hard to escape the conclusion that the latest batch of crises only highlights for us: we have profound weaknesses in our public discourse and no consensus yet how to fix them.

REFERENCES

Bothwell, Robert. 2006. *The Penguin History of Canada*. Toronto: Penguin Canada.

Bourrie, Mark. 2015. *Kill the Messengers: Stephen Harper's Assault on Your Right to Know*. Toronto: HarperCollins Canada.

Fromkin, David. 1975. "The Strategy of Terrorism." *Foreign Affairs Quarterly*, July, http://www.foreignaffairs.com/articles/24584/david-fromkin/the-strategy-of-terrorism.

Kissinger, Henry. 2014. *World Order*. New York: Penguin.

Ramo, Joshua Cooper. 2009. *The Age of the Unthinkable: Why the New World Order Constantly Surprises Us and What Can We Do about It*. New York: Little, Brown.

Savoie, Donald J. 2000. *Governing from the Centre*. Toronto: University of Toronto Press.

Tetloch, Philip. 2005. *Expert Political Judgement: How Good Is It? How Can We Know?* Princeton, NJ: Princeton University Press.

PART FOUR

Canada: Security and Society

15 Legislating in Fearful and Politicized Times: The Limits of Bill C-51's Disruption Powers in Making Us Safer

KENT ROACH AND CRAIG FORCESE[1]

Introduction

The high, though apparently declining levels of public support for Bill C-51, the Canadian government's proposed Anti-Terrorism Act, 2015, in the face of sustained criticism can best be explained by growing concerns about the increased risk of terrorism. These fears are understandable. Alas they can be exploited for political gain. The result may well be legislation that threatens rights without advancing security.

Since its release on January 30, 2015, we have written and released over 200 pages of legal analysis of several parts of the omnibus bill (Forcese and Roach 2015). We have tried to discuss both threats to rights and threats to security, including unintended or second-order consequences of the legislation to security operations and terrorism prosecutions. In this chapter, we will focus on the latter.

We will argue that the new powers that Bill C-51 provides to CSIS and the police are best understood as powers of disruption. As such, they provide only partial and temporary solutions to real security problems presented by those radicalized to violent extremism.

The first part of this chapter will examine the context in which C-51 was introduced and debated. It will also situate C-51's new disruption powers in a broader continuum of counterterrorism strategies from prevention to prosecution. The second part will critically examine the new

---

1 We thank Leah Sherriff for excellent research assistance and Professor Roach acknowledges the generous support provided by his 2013 Fellowship granted by the Pierre Elliott Trudeau Foundation.

disruption powers that will be given to CSIS, the role that judges will play in granting and supervising such powers, and the unintended and harmful effects that the powers may have on terrorism prosecutions. The final part will critically examine C-51's enhanced preventive arrest and peace bond powers with a focus on their limited role and efficacy.

The Context: Fearful and Politicized Times

The UN Security Council in Resolution 2178 has recognized terrorist foreign fighters as a threat to international peace. Estimates of Canadians who have joined foreign terrorist fights range from 30 to 130. These are significant numbers, albeit much fewer than those who have left Europe to join the forces of ISIL's brutal regime that is trying to impose a caliphate in parts of Syria and Iraq. The two "lone wolf" terrorist attacks in Quebec and Ottawa in October 2014 shook Canadians. The ability of an armed gunman to enter Parliament both scared and embarrassed Canadians.

The threat then seemed to get even worse. The Paris and Copenhagen attacks of January 2015 were symbolic and unsettling. In Canada, there were constant domestic echoes of these threats. The police charged two people with conspiracy to commit murder by shooting people in a Halifax mall. The minister of justice stated that this was not an act of terrorism because of the absence of a "cultural" element – a peculiar turn of phrase, given the absence of such a concept in the law. For some, it was a coded suggestion that invoked a double standard for Islamic terrorism (see Fadel, this volume), but the arrests also increased fears.

Al Shabaab, the al Qaeda–linked Somalia terrorist group, issued threats to shopping malls, including the West Edmonton Mall. This led to thirty-five teams withdrawing from a cheerleading competition that was fortunately still held with 2700 competitors and without incident. This threat was cited by the government as an indication of the need to enact Bill C-51 in a hurry. In March, a permanent resident was held in immigration detention, pending deportation to Pakistan, with allegations that he told an undercover officer of plans to bomb the American consulate in Toronto. In other developments, a mysterious tunnel near a Pan Am Games venue turned out to be a man cave, and a white powder sent to Quebec ministers turned out to be innocuous, but these incidents still stoked fears.

Bill C-51 was also introduced in highly politicized times. Prime Minister Harper introduced the bill in an election-style rally in a highly sought after "905" riding in suburban Toronto. He used the rhetoric of war by suggesting that "violent jihadism is not a human right. It is an act of war, and our government's new legislation fully understands the difference" (CBC News, 2015). Although the official Opposition eventually opposed the bill, other parties did not, in part to avoid a wedge issue in the upcoming October 2015 election.

Though some recent polls suggest a sharp decline in support, Bill C-51 seems politically popular, especially in Quebec, where some supporters have rekindled a divisive debate about the Quebec Charter of Values and debates about secularism. The Paris attacks may have had a greater effect in Quebec than the rest of Canada.

The fearful and politicized context in which C-51 was introduced and debated is not conducive to clear thinking or recognition of its long-term and unintended implications. Indeed, the government's "common sense" approach rejected key recommendations from the 2006 Arar Commission report, the 2010 Air India report, and a 2011 report by a Special Senate Committee. C-51, like much of the government's criminal justice agenda, was not evidence-based, and proudly so.

Situating Disruption Powers in a Broader Continuum of Counterterrorism Strategies from Prevention to Prosecution

Disruption needs to be situated in a continuum of counterterrorism measures that, as outlined in Canada's 2012 counterterrorism strategy, range from prevention to detection, denial, and response. At the softer preventive end of the spectrum are multidisciplinary interventions of the type contemplated in the United Kingdom's *Crime and Security Act*, 2015 c 6. As in the United Kingdom, these measures are often implemented not by police or intelligence agencies, but by schools, health services, local authorities, prisons, and even universities. They may best be implemented by and with close cooperation from community groups.

The fact that some of the Paris and the Copenhagen attackers had spent time in prison underlines the need for prison de-radicalization programs. The problem of prison radicalization may be particularly acute in Europe, but it is not limited to Europe.

Ali Mohamed Dirie went to jail for his role in the Toronto 18 terrorism plot. He remained radicalized and perhaps became more radicalized while serving two years in a special handling unit with others convicted of terrorism in Canada. He was released, and though restricted under a peace bond from possessing a passport, he subsequently joined ISIL forces and died in Syria. C-51 makes it easier for judges to impose the type of conditions that Dirie breached, but it does nothing to address radicalization within prison even though deradicalization programs may provide more lasting and effective remedies than peace bonds. This is another example of C-51's failure to take a comprehensive or balanced approach to counterterrorism.

Bill C-51's powers of disruption include increased periods of preventive arrest and lowered standards for both preventive arrests and peace bonds. Such powers do nothing to address the factors that may motivate terrorism or to facilitate actual terrorism prosecutions. Bill C-51's focus on disruption is unfortunate, because there is need for both preventive counter-radicalization and terrorism prosecutions, including prosecution of four new criminal offences that Parliament enacted in 2013 that apply to those who attempt to leave Canada to engage in terrorism abroad. Bill C-51, combined with Bill C-44, which allows CSIS human sources to veto their participation or identification in terrorism prosecutions (Roach 2014a), may have the unintended effect of making it more difficult to apply these valuable new offences.

CSIS can disrupt and perhaps even detain, but even under C-51, it cannot arrest or charge. The police can use preventive arrests, and judges can impose peace bonds that may prevent travel and certain associations. If they are violated, under C-51 a terrorist suspect can be jailed for a maximum of four years. However, such a person will not be jailed for terrorism but for the less serious offence of breaching a peace bond.

Bill C-51's new powers of disruption are designed to be used in cases where there is not enough evidence to justify laying criminal charges under the fourteen existing terrorism offences and related offences. Disruption will be used when criminal charges are not possible. From a security perspective, criminal charges are generally better than disruption. An accused will often be denied bail awaiting trial and will often receive a long sentence if convicted. From a rights perspective, charges ensure that the accused will receive a fair and public trial.

Increasing False Positives by Using Disruption

Bill C-51's increased disruption powers are designed to avoid one variety of security failure: cases where CSIS or the police were able to identify suspected terrorists but were unable to charge them or take other actions to prevent them from engaging in terrorist violence. Below we will address the limited efficacy of C-51's disruption powers in preventing terrorism, but at this juncture we note that the new powers raise the problem of false positives: the disruption or detention of those who may not be terrorists. In the United Kingdom, only 34 per cent of over 1500 individuals subject to preventive arrests since 9/11 have been charged with an offence (United Kingdom 2012).

Following the late Ronald Dworkin, we should recognize that in determining balances between security and liberty, sacrifices of the latter in the post-9/11 terrorism context will be distributed unequally, and the burden will fall on Muslim persons, often on the basis of so-called extremist beliefs and associations (Dworkin 2002). The increased false-positive rates of disruption raise important issues of community relations and the adequacies of review and oversight of the security agencies whose disruption activities may often not be scrutinized by courts in the context of a criminal trial.

The New CSIS Powers of Disruption

CSIS engaged in "soft" forms of disruption before C-51 by contacting family members or community leaders close to a terrorist suspect. SIRC expressed the view that such actions were within the CSIS Act. It recommended that ministerial guidelines manage the risk of such measures, but it is not known whether any were issued, because many ministerial directives remain confidential (SIRC 2010). In 2011, a Special Senate Committee recommended that the CSIS Act be amended to clarify CSIS's powers of "lawful disruption" (Senate 2011).

For reasons that the government has yet to explain or justify, C-51 dramatically ramps up CSIS's powers to engage in disruption. Although the government has used the example of CSIS interviews to dissuade persons from leaving to join ISIL as an example of the new CSIS powers under C-51, the powers are actually much greater. They include powers to violate both the law and the Charter under a judicial warrant granted by the Federal Court.

When C-51 is enacted, CSIS will be expressly authorized to "take measures, within or outside Canada, to reduce" very broadly defined "threats to the security of Canada." These threats are not limited to terrorism but include espionage, clandestine or deceptive foreign-influenced activities, or the undermining of the constitutionally established system of government in Canada by covert unlawful acts or by violence. Where authorized by Federal Court warrant, these "measures" may "contravene a right or freedom guaranteed by the Canadian Charter of Rights and Freedoms" or may be "contrary to other Canadian law." The only categorical restriction is that such measures must not intentionally or by criminal negligence cause death or bodily harm, violate sexual integrity, or wilfully obstruct justice. A judge must also determine that illegal disruption is reasonable and proportionate, having regard to the threat and the reasonable availability of less drastic measures.

The CSIS changes are dramatic, even radical. In 1984, in the wake of illegalities, including the burning of a barn and theft of Parti Québécois membership lists by the Security Service of the RCMP, Parliament created CSIS and gave it the powers only to collect intelligence. Parliament accepted CSIS's broad mandate because it lacked what we have called "kinetic" or physical powers – the powers to do things to people in the physical world (except as necessary to, for example, install a wiretap or listening device).

That will change with Bill C-51. The bill superimposes kinetic powers on the broad mandate CSIS has had for the last thirty years to be a pure intelligence agency. Perhaps the new powers could be justified to respond to new terrorist threats, but they will be available for CSIS to take physical measures to reduce all threats to Canadian security, including those relating to subversion that may touch on protest and advocacy that does not comply fully with the law.

CSIS will also be able to enlist or deputize domestic and foreign partners when engaging in such disruption. Again, this may be an appropriate response to whole-of-government and transnational responses to terrorism. But we are extremely troubled by the fact that C-51 leaves in place the 1984 review structure, where the independent reviewers in SIRC have no jurisdiction to review CSIS's security partners, including those who are deputized into assisting in the execution of new disruption warrants.

Giving Judges New Powers to Authorize Charter Violations in One-Sided and Secret Warrant Hearings

Jason Kenney has argued that C-51 does not really grant CSIS new powers: it grants them to judges. Such arguments are disingenuous. First, C-51 requires only a warrant if CSIS must break a law or violate the Charter to reduce threats to security. It will expand CSIS's warrantless powers.

Second, the idea of judicial oversight will understandably invoke images of public adversarial hearings subject to appeal, ultimately to the Supreme Court of Canada. This is not the case under C-51. Judicial oversight of CSIS's new powers will be conducted in a secret hearing with only a judge and a government lawyer. The target of the disruption will not be present and will never be informed. No civil rights group can weigh in. There will be no appeals.

At best, the Federal Court judge might appoint a security-cleared special advocate to challenge the government's case, but even this is not specifically provided for in C-51. Even if this occurs, there is hardly an equality of arms between the special advocate and the government's lawyer. Indeed special advocates' constitutionally required access to information will be significantly reduced under the immigration law amendments in C-51, so that they may no longer be able to detect that some human sources used by CSIS have not been reliable. C-51 also does not contemplate that special advocates will be able to challenge the secret intelligence used to place someone on a no-fly list. When secret intelligence is used as evidence, the problem of false positive looms large.

We have concerns about what will happen in one-sided CSIS disruption warrant hearings. There are an alarming number of judicial decisions finding that CSIS has failed to meet its duty of candour in closed door proceedings. It is very difficult to know whether these reports represent the sum total of CSIS shortcomings – a failure to be candid is something that is, by definition, very difficult to detect.

The government will argue that all warrants proceedings are one-sided and the new CSIS warrants are no different. But the quick and facile analogy to search-and-seizure and surveillance warrants breaks down upon reflection. Judges who grant such warrants are trying their best to prevent Charter violations – it is the warrant that makes the search constitutional.

C-51 is different and radically so. It contemplates that the Federal Court will be able to grant warrants that authorize CSIS to contravene a Charter right. To imagine that a court can pre-authorize a violation of any Charter right in response to an open-textured invitation to do so is to misunderstand the way our constitution works, on a fundamental level. This is especially so when the contravention of the Charter will be justified by the judge in a secret one-sided hearing without any right of appeal.

For instance, a judge could in theory be asked to authorize a violation of the right against cruel and unusual treatment under the Charter. In the present security context, with its focus on foreign terrorist fighters, we expect that the first Charter right to be violated by a new CSIS warrant will be the section 6 Charter right of Canadian citizens to leave or return to Canada.

Imposing restraints on returning foreign fighters is a controversial issue. The U.K. Parliament recently had a robust debate about whether temporary exclusion orders can be justified to prevent citizen foreign terrorist fighters from returning to the United Kingdom. No such debate is happening in Canada – but C-51 will allow this result to be achieved covertly, through a one-sided judicial process.

All rights, including section 6 Charter rights, can be subject to reasonable limits under section 1 of the Charter. Nevertheless, the restraint on the right is usually spelled out in advance in legislation that can be debated by the public and interpreted by the courts. But C-51 contains only an open-ended and generic reference to authorizing violations of any Charter right, so long as the violation is reasonable and proportionate to the threat and the reasonable availability of less drastic measures.

C-51's new CSIS disruption warrants differ dramatically from investigative hearings that were one of the most controversial parts of the post 9/11 terrorism law. Investigative hearings are consistent with the Charter, because they are presumptively held in open court, with the target represented by counsel. Those safeguards do not exist in C-51. Even then, a strong minority of the Court concluded that investigative hearings did violence to the role of judges by turning them into police investigators (*Re Section 83.28*, 2004). This concern about the fusion of judicial with executive powers is even more true in the context of new disruption warrants. Moreover, a Federal Court will be asked to do Parliament's work by fleshing out how and why Charter rights must be limited to reduce security threats. The judges are being asked to do the dirty work of both the executive and Parliament.

Our expectation is that the Federal Court will do its best to ensure that the government justifies the need for illegal measures, and our hope is that it will resist the notion that the executive can violate the Charter in this novel manner. Nevertheless, C-51 places the Federal Court in a very awkward position, one that may reflect the government's lack of understanding of the judicial role. The judiciary is traditionally expected to uphold the rule of law and the Charter. It will now be asked to provide ex ante justification and cover for their violation. We suspect all this will be anathema to the Court. It will rightly worry about its reputation, especially if a Court-authorized "Charter breach warrant" is associated with an operation that goes wrong and generates public scandal.

In any case, the Federal Court will have to devise ad hoc procedures to ensure that CSIS and other individuals who assist it do not go beyond the terms of the warrant in what may be a dynamic and dangerous context, sometimes in foreign lands.

We expect that the Federal Court will also do its best to issue redacted versions of its judgments in these novel warrant cases. Nevertheless it will have to respect the need for secrecy to protect both ongoing and perhaps international investigations. Under Bill C-44, it will also have to ensure that no identifying information about CSIS human sources is revealed. The warrant decisions will be made by specially designated Federal Court judges, generally acting without the benefit of appellate guidance.

The Need for Judicial Oversight to Be Complemented by Adequate Review

The Federal Court will not automatically know what is done under its authorization. Past experience suggests that what it authorizes and what is actually done may not always line up. Justice Mosley found that surveillance that he had authorized CSIS to conduct had been subcontracted to foreign intelligence partners. He learned of this subcontracting only from reading review body reports (*Re X* 2013).

The Federal Court would be well advised to reach out to review bodies for monitoring and feedback. Alas they will find the existing ones to be overburdened and stuck in twentieth-century silos. SIRC will be mandated under C-51 to annually examine one aspect of the new powers, but it has only seventeen people and a budget under $3 million. C-51 also contemplates that judges may authorize and CSIS may unilaterally deputize any person, including foreign persons, to assist in the execution of their warrants. It will be very difficult for the Federal Court or SIRC to supervise their actions if these deputies violate rights or do not do their jobs well.

CSIS will appropriately work with CSE, our signals intelligence agency, but SIRC and the CSE reviewer, contrary to the Arar Commission's 2006 recommendations, still cannot share secret information or conduct joint investigations. There will be no independent review of the actions of other officials such as foreign, border services or the military who will likely assist CSIS in disruption at home or abroad. The case of Maher Arar case and other Canadians tortured in Syria remind us that all bets are off once CSIS enlists foreign agencies to assist it.

In a populist manner, the government has painted enhanced review as duplicative red tape and as the enemy of those who do very difficult jobs in our security forces. But security agencies recognize that informed review bodies can assist them, to defend them from unfair criticism, to ensure adequate resources, and to improve performance. The accountability gaps that existed before C-51 may become significantly wider after its enactment.

Unintended Effects of New CSIS Powers That May Harm Security

The government is banking on Canadians dismissing the concerns of rights groups and "so-called experts," in part because Canadians are understandably scared about terrorism. The government may be right in this political calculation, but C-51 may have unintended effects that will harm security efforts, especially terrorism prosecutions, which remain the best means to incapacitate and denounce terrorists. Here are some of our concerns:

- *Criminal trials*: CSIS's operation and new powers are often "pre-criminal." As such, they may overlap, affect, and perhaps taint a subsequent RCMP investigation and evidentiary record. A criminal trial may be mired in questions arising from the Federal Court authorization of violations of the law and the Charter and doubts about whether the CSIS operation contributed to the alleged crime or constituted an abuse of process that requires a terrorism prosecution to be terminated.
- *Interaction with informer privilege*: Bill C-44, now in the Senate, will give CSIS "human sources" broad privilege from being compelled to be a Crown witness or having identifying information disclosed in court proceedings. Crown prosecutors may find this frustrates their witness list. Good defence lawyers will fight the new privilege, especially when the first thing they suspect is that a CSIS kinetic operation lies at the heart of a subsequent criminal case. They will argue, as they have done with success in criminal cases, that informers have lost the protective shield of privilege by becoming active agents or even agent provocateurs with respect to the criminal trial. They will demand disclosure of CSIS material to make such claims.

Disclosure disputes and abuse of process claims may make terrorism trials – already long and complex – even more difficult.

- *Interaction with the RCMP*: The RCMP already have legal powers under section 25.1 of the Criminal Code to engage in disruptions. Peace officers in these situations likely remain preoccupied with the effect their conduct might have in any future criminal proceedings. For cultural and institutional reasons, the Air India Commission concluded in 2010 that CSIS was still not sufficiently aware of its evidentiary obligations and the effects of their actions on criminal investigations and prosecutions. How will CSIS and RCMP arrange their affairs so that CSIS's kinetic activities do not undermine RCMP criminal investigations, either ongoing or prospective?

- *Lack of police independence*: CSIS, unlike the RCMP, does not have constitutional protections of police independence designed to ensure that governments do not order the police to investigate and charge their enemies or to investigate or charge their friends. CSIS's new powers apply to attempts to reduce all threats to the security of Canada, including threats associated with its counter-subversion mandate and threats that may be conducted in conjunction with even lawful protest and advocacy. Especially when read in tandem with the even broader definition of security threats in C-51's proposed information-sharing act, this raises concerns that government may use their legitimate powers of providing political direction to CSIS effectively to encourage the service to focus on "enemies," such as Aboriginal, environmental, "anti-petroleum" protesters, or certain diaspora groups.

- *Institutional skills and culture*: CSIS is a security intelligence organization. If it gears up kinetic activities, it will presumably require skills and aptitudes that presently are not part of its arsenal. C-51 allows them to use "any person" to carry out activities that reduce security threats – not just their own employees. Intelligence assets gone rogue is one thing, but rogue behaviour by individuals charged with physical interventions with targets might be even more concerning. CSIS is a law-observant service, adhering to legal expectations is an important part of its culture, and it remains to be seen what effects C-51 will have on this culture.

- *Social licence*: The world is rife with misunderstandings and conspiracy theories about spy services, including CSIS. With the new measures, many conspiracy theories move from the "implausible because they require compounded illegal steps" to "within CSIS's powers in principle." There will be a consequence in social licence for a clandestine service empowered to act in violation of the law and the Charter, especially in communities that feel targeted.

- *Limited efficacy of disruption powers*: A likely scenario is that CSIS will obtain a warrant to do illegal acts to prevent would-be or former foreign terrorist fighters from exercising their rights as Canadian citizens either to leave or return to Canada. The new warrant will, subject to one renewal, allow CSIS to violate the law and the Charter for 120 days. But what if, after this time, the person is still determined to leave or return to Canada? Criminal prosecutions under the 2013 foreign terrorist fighter provisions may be the answer, but CSIS actions may frustrate rather than facilitate such prosecutions.

Summary

CSIS already engages in "soft" forms of disruption by making people, their families, and friends aware that they are being investigated. C-51 deliberately goes far beyond the Special Senate Committee's 2011 recommendation that "legal disruption" powers be codified. It does so by authorizing disruptions that may even violate the law and the Charter, and stop only at the outer limit of bodily harm, obstructions of justice, and violation of sexual integrity. These new powers may have far-reaching and unintended consequences, for rights but also for security, including subsequent terrorism prosecutions that may be necessary to deal with foreign terrorist fighters not amenable to CSIS's persuasion.

New Police Powers

Bill C-51's new police powers are even more of a temporary fix than CSIS's disruption powers. Although the police, unlike CSIS, must collect evidence for criminal charges, C-51 does little to encourage or facilitate terrorism prosecutions, as recommended by the Air India Commission. Instead, it will make it easier for the police to engage in temporary disruption in the form of preventive arrests and peace bonds.

Preventive Arrests

Under C-51, it will be easier to make preventive arrests, and the maximum period of detention will be increased from three to seven days.

Preventive arrests can also be used as investigative detention, because judges will be required after three and then five days' detention to determine whether the investigation is being conducted diligently and expeditiously in order to justify an extension.

The standards for preventive arrest will be lowered from the current reasonable grounds that a terrorist activity "will" be carried out, to a requirement that it "may" be carried out. In addition, the current requirement that the imposition of controls on the person is "necessary" to prevent a terrorist activity will be lowered to the standard that such controls are "likely" to prevent such a terrorist activity.

Preventive and investigative detention should always be used with restraint. The original preventive arrest provisions enacted after 9/11 allowed a maximum of three days' preventive arrest. In any event, they were not used before the powers expired in 2007 or after they were re-enacted in 2013. The Canadian approach was comparatively restrained (Forcese 2010). With C-51's increased maximum period of seven days, Canada is now drifting towards the upper end of the spectrum in comparative duration of detention without charge (Liberty 2010).

The government has not responded to Gary Trotter's criticisms of original post-9/11 preventive arrests for refusing to regulate where a person will be detained under the now extended period (Trotter 2001). We have recommended to the committee studying the bill that Australian legislation provides a useful template, either in restricting interrogation during the period of preventive detention or in ensuring that it is conducted in a humane and transparent manner (Forcese and Roach 2015). The U.K. experience suggests that increased use of preventive arrests – which have never been used in Canada – will increase false positives in the form of detention of those who are never charged and may never have an opportunity to clear their name.

Recognizances and Peace Bonds

The end result of a preventive arrest is not designed to be a charge but a judicial imposition of a recognizance commonly known as a peace bond. This is an order that allows a person to live in the community, but under judicially imposed conditions. Such conditions can be imposed by a judge, either following a preventive arrest or as a result of an independent judicial proceeding under the Criminal Code. Bill C-51 quite sensibly instructs judges to consider new conditions such as preventing a person from having a passport.

C-51 will allow peace bonds when there are reasonable fears that a person "may" – as opposed to "will" – commit a terrorism offence. In other words, the state will now have to establish only a reasonable basis to conclude that there is a possibility that a terrorism offence will be committed as opposed to a probability.

It is difficult to criticize these provisions because almost six months later, the public still has not been given details about why prosecutors refused to consent to a request that Martin Couture-Rouleau, the terrorist attacker in St Jean-sur-Richeleau, be subject to a peace bond. If there was clear evidence that the requirements of reasonable fears that a terrorism "will" be committed was the stumbling block, this would constitute evidence in support of the proposed lowering of the standard. Unfortunately, the government has not made public information about this security failure. Again, however, the lower standard in C-51 increases the risk of false positives.

The Limited Efficacy of Peace Bonds for Terrorists

We join Professor (now Justice) Trotter in questioning the efficacy of what he called "peace bonds for terrorists" (Trotter 2001). In other words, even if a peace bond could have been imposed on Couture-Rouleau, it is not clear that it would have prevented him from using his car to kill Warrant Officer Patrice Vincent.

Ali Mohamed Dirie was subject to a peace bond that prohibited his possession of a passport, a condition encouraged under C-51. Nevertheless, Dirie was still able to leave Canada and join ISIL in Syria, where he was killed. Dirie is not the only example of someone who walked away from a peace bond. Mohammed El Shaer has apparently left Canada for Syria in what would be his second breach of a recognizance not to leave the country (Bell 2015).

The very limited efficacy of peace bonds for determined terrorists suggests the continued need for criminal prosecutions. A criminal charge will generally result in long-term pre-trial detention, because the accused must establish that bail is consistent with public safety and public confidence, as well as attendance at trial (Roach 2014b).

Questions abound about why Couture-Rouleau was not prosecuted for terrorism offences. Why was there enough evidence to seize his passport and prevent him from flying to Turkey in July 2014, but not enough evidence to prosecute him under the new law for attempting to leave Canada to participate in foreign terrorist offences enacted in 2013?

Canada was ahead of the foreign terrorist fighter curve in enacting these offences, but it lags behind other democracies in converting secret intelligence into public evidence. One hypothesis is that the continued problems of converting intelligence into evidence may have been a factor in the failure to prosecute Couture-Rouleau for attempting to leave Canada to join foreign terrorist fights. In truth we do not know. These are precisely the sort of questions that a parliamentary committee that was given access to secret information (which no committee now has) should ask.

Preventive arrests and peace bonds are emergency powers of temporary disruption. The most lasting and most effective intervention for those prepared to engage in terrorism is a criminal prosecution. Canada has a troubled history of terrorism prosecutions, caused in large part because of conflicts between CSIS's mandate to produce secret intelligence and the mandate of the police and prosecutor to produce public evidence, dramatically seen in the ill-fated investigations and prosecutions of the 1985 Air India bombings.

Although there have been some improvements, the Air India Commission warned in 2010 that many problems remained. The government has chosen to ignore many of the commission's major recommendations. The result may well be to make it more difficult to conduct terrorism prosecutions precisely at a time when they are most needed. Successful terrorism prosecutions can denounce and de-glorify terrorism and incapacitate would-be terrorists in a way that temporary disruption measures cannot.

Control Orders by the Back Door

The eased standards in C-51, combined with increased radicalization, may well lead to increased use of preventive arrests and peace bonds. But will this be a success in fighting terrorism? In some cases, temporary disruption may be necessary and might even avert serious violence. Preventive arrests may buy police officers a few days' more time to find evidence. But the endgame is a peace bond that will control a suspected terrorist in the community. If the person is not a terrorist, the controls may turn out to be harsh and disproportionate. The United Kingdom's experience with control orders, as well as Canada's experience with community controls on security certificate detainees, indicates that the controls may be controversial and challenged as violating human rights. Conversely, if the person subject to a peace bond turns out to be a terrorist, community controls may be too weak.

In the end, C-51 offers only one type of strategy – temporary disruption – to an emerging and serious security threat that requires a holistic and evidence-based strategy, ranging from community engagement and prevention, including prison de-radicalization, through to the unique ability of criminal prosecutions to provide sustainable incapacitation and denunciation of terrorism.

Conclusion

Bill C-51 is not about putting terrorists in jail: it is about sharing information and giving both CSIS and the police new powers to engage in temporary disruptions. To be sure, we are deeply troubled about the adverse effects of C-51 on freedom of expression, liberty, privacy, equality, and other rights, but we also genuinely believe that, in light of the publicly available evidence, including the Air India Commission's report, C-51 will not make us safer. C-51 should not be oversold, because it does nothing at the front end to prevent people from becoming radicalized, and it does nothing at the back end to facilitate terrorism prosecutions.

Disruption measures can make us safer for only relatively short periods. They may also have the unintended consequences of making terrorism prosecutions more difficult. This deprives us of longer-term incapacitation of those who intend to commit violence and the unique ability of criminal prosecutions to denounce, de-legitimize, and de-glorify violence for political or religious ends. The government's reputation as tough on crime has blinded many to seeing the real security deficiencies in its rushed legislative response to the October 2014 and Paris attacks.

The result is a bill that threatens rights and freedoms without offering obvious or robust security gains. This no doubt reflects the rushed and politicized nature of the legislative process. A fearful public may be reassured for a time, but this will likely not be the last of panicked amendments to our security laws that are unsupported by evidence. The result may be a slow-motion self-immolation on the rights side and counterproductive incoherence on the security side.

REFERENCES

Bell, Stewart. 2015. "Windsor Extremist Who Had No Passport and Was a 'High Risk Traveller' Joins Jihadists in Syria." *National Post*, March 10.

CBC News. 2015. "Stephen Harper Makes His Case for New Powers to Combat Terrorism." CBC News, January 30, http://www.cbc.ca/news/politics/stephen-harper-makes-his-case-for-new-powers-to-combat-terror-1.2937602.

Dworkin, Ronald. 2002. "The Threat to Patriotism." *New York Review of Books*, February 28.

Forcese, Craig. 2010. "Catch and Release: A Role for Preventive Detention without Charge in Canadian Anti-Terrorism Law." IRPP Study, no. 7.

Forcese, Craig, and Kent Roach. 2015. "Backgrounders 1–5 on Bill C-51 and Submissions to Commons Committee on National Security," http://www.antiterrorlaw.ca.

Liberty. 2010. "Terrorism Pre-Charge Detention: Comparative Law Study." National Council for National Liberties, United Kingdom, https://www.liberty-human-rights.org.uk/sites/default/files/comparative-law-study-2010-pre-charge-detention.pdf.

Re Section 83.28 of the Criminal Code [2004] 2 SCR 248.

Re X 2013 FC 1274 affd 2014 FCA 249 leave to appeal SCC granted.

Roach, Kent. 2014a. "Be Careful What You Wish For?: Terrorism Prosecutions in Post-9/11 Canada." *Queen's Law Journal* 40:99.

– 2014b. "The Problems with the New CSIS Human Source Privilege in Bill C-44." *Criminal Law Quarterly* 61:451.

Security Intelligence Review Committee (SIRC). 2010. *Annual Report 2009–2010*. Ottawa: SIRC.

Senate. 2011. *Interim Report of the Special Committee on Anti-Terrorism Law*, Hugh Segal, chair.

Trotter, Gary. 2001. "The Anti-Terrorism Bill and Preventive Restraints on Liberty." In *The Security of Freedom: Essays on Canada's Anti-Terrorism Bill*, ed. Ronald Joel Daniels, Patrick Macklem, and Kent Roach. Toronto: University of Toronto Press.

United Kingdom. 2012. *Pre-Charge Detention in Terrorism Cases*. House of Commons Library.

16 What Lessons Have We Learned about Speech in the Aftermath of the Paris Attacks?

DAVID SCHNEIDERMAN

I fear that we may have learned the wrong lessons in the aftermath of the attacks in Paris and Ottawa. We seem to be operating under the fantasy that if we clamp down on expressive activities having only a tangential relationship, or none at all, to actual terrorist activity, we will somehow make ourselves safer. There is no necessary relationship between criminally proscribed silence and the cessation of terrorist threats.

It is undoubtedly true that communication via social media is made easier and faster than ever and that it facilitates the spread of beneficial, benign, and harmful speech. There also is no question that the sophisticated use of social media by ISIS and other jihadist groups is offensive and potentially harmful, underscoring that "we are not safe even in our own land," according to Canada-based and now deceased terrorist Michael Zehaf-Bibeau. The challenge for Western liberal democracies is to devise a response that is effective and proportionate to the threat that this sort of communication poses, without, at the same time, prohibiting speech that liberal democracies should be loath to restrain.

The first widespread response to the Paris attacks among the citizens of Western democratic states was to proclaim "Je suis Charlie." The slogan likely had different meanings for different people – from "we are all secularists" to the condemnation of murder in the name of religion. The slogan, I think, was commonly understood to support freedom of expression, even forms of expression of which one might not approve and might even loathe.

The second response was to clamp down on speech construed as being supportive of terrorism at home or abroad. Within one week, up to one hundred people were under investigation in France for making or posting comments that glorify, or amount to an *apologie* of, terrorism. Those arrested included drunken and disturbed individuals who shouted out their support for jihad in public streets, to a fourteen-year-old girl who threatened to "bring out the Kalashnikovs" in response to a request to produce a ticket for public transit. The anti-Semitic comedian Dieudonne M'bala M'bala posted "Je me sens Charlie Calibouly" on his Facebook page and was given a suspended two-month jail sentence for being a terrorist apologist.

The government of Canada has embraced a similar sort of response. To be sure, with the experience of home-grown, if lone-wolf, terrorist attacks like Zehaf-Bibeau's, coupled with the phenomenon of young Canadians travelling abroad to join ISIS, there is a felt need to do more than we have been doing to respond to these threats. Bill C-51's prohibition on the "promotion of terrorism in general" is an example of the sort of wrong lesson drawn from these threats. Similar concerns can be expressed about proposed new powers to seize "terrorist propaganda," which is defined with reference to the same language of promoting terrorism in general. The new proposed power for CSIS to disrupt "threats to the security of Canada" as defined in the CSIS Act also gives rise to serious concerns about freedom of expression. Judicial warrants will be required only if, in the view of CSIS, a measure violates Charter rights and freedoms. Given the available space, my focus here will be on the proposed offence of promoting terrorism in general.

The omnibus anti-terrorism law, Bill C-51, proposes that the Criminal Code be amended to make it an offence to communicate statements that "knowingly" advocate or promote the commission of "terrorism offences in general," knowing that those offences "will be committed or being reckless as to whether those offences may be committed." Those convicted of the offence are liable to a penalty of imprisonment for up to five years (section 83.221).

Though narrower than the French offence of apologizing for terrorism, the proposed offence raises disturbing free speech concerns: it is vague and overbroad, contemplates no good faith defences, and is drafted to catch as wide a swath of speech – legitimate or illegitimate – as possible. It evinces no concern with the fact that freedom of expression is a constitutionally protected right.

In a free and democratic society, we should be loath to ban speech that merely is offensive and poses no real or substantial risk of harm to anyone. Yet the proposed offence is drafted so that there need not be any connection between the words spoken or written and the commission of terrorism offences. There need not be, in other words, any causal connection between words and deeds. It is sufficient that someone merely "promotes" something called "terrorism in general" and is reckless about its consequences. We are, in short, punishing speech that we fear.

An array of speech acts having a closer and more intimate connection to the commission of terrorist activities are already caught by the criminal law. Criminal conspiracies, attempts or threats to commit, being an accessory after the fact or counselling the commission of terrorist activities are caught as a consequence of Canada's first anti-terrorism law in 2001 (Roach 2001). Mr Namouh, a hard-core Al Qaeda supporter, was convicted of "participating" in a terrorist group and "facilitating terrorist activity" by, among other things, calling for support of the group, distributing its materials, and "singing the praises" of jihadi leadership. In Mr Namouh's case, we have the prohibition of speech acts more closely connected to the commission of terrorist activities. If the criminal law already catches speech that facilitates the commission of terrorist acts, what else is intended to be caught by the new "promotion of terrorism in general" offence other than merely offensive speech?

What does it mean, then, to promote "terrorism in general'? This is not a term of art nor is it defined anywhere in the proposed bill or in the Criminal Code. The term "terrorism offence" is defined with some precision in the Criminal Code: it encompasses offences already included within the code. There is no definition, by contrast, of terrorism offences "in general." Why such vague language? We are given some insight into the matter by virtue of two explanations that were offered by the Department of Justice and the minister of public safety, respectively. First, the federal Justice Department explains that the prohibition is intended to fill a gap in the present law, namely, those circumstances where "someone who instructs others to 'carry out attacks on Canada.'" As "no specific terrorism offence is singled out," no one can be charged, claims the Department of Justice, hence, the need to construct a new, more general, offence (Canada 2015). This indicates that the rationale behind the law is to move beyond the list of prohibited terrorist activities already listed in the Criminal Code to include something called "terrorism in general." The new offence clearly is intended to lower the bar for offensive speech acts. The backgrounder otherwise provides no further guidance.

A similar sort of rationale was offered by the minister for public safety, Steven Blainey. When someone calls for the "killing of all infidels," he explained, "we would not be able to charge them." As they would be "threatening in broad terms all Canadians," there would otherwise be no criminal law with which to ensnare them. In his testimony before the House of Commons Committee on Public Safety and National Security, Minister Blainey clarified that such calls amounted to "hate propaganda ... and the time has come for the government to take our responsibility."

One wonders why propagandizing along these lines, with the aim of participating in or facilitating terrorism offences, would not already be caught by the Criminal Code. Why wouldn't such a call to arms – "kill all the infidels" – also be caught by the Criminal Code's prohibition of the promotion of hatred? "Infidels" are an identifiable group distinguished by "religion," which is one of the grounds mentioned in the hate promotion provisions. At least the existing prohibition on the promotion of hatred has the benefit of being better drafted – it is cabined in by a number of good faith defences, such as speaking out on matters of public interest. It also requires the threshold consent of the attorney general for a prosecution to proceed.

In addition to the vagueness of the offence of promoting terrorism in general, there is the problem of overbreadth and chilling effect. The offence, as mentioned, is not tied specifically to any of the fourteen terrorist activities that are already labelled criminal. Rather, "terrorism in general" is an opaque standard nowhere defined. It has the potential of catching those who express support for insurgent activities around the globe. Those activities for which support is expressed need not even be violent ones. Activities that cause "substantial property damage" or "serious disruption of an essential service" fall within the wide definition of "terrorist activity" in the Criminal Code (Schneiderman and Cossman 2001). Expressions of support for the overthrow of the Somoza government in Nicaragua by the Sandinistas would have run afoul of the proposed offence, as would support for the Free Syrian army during the Syrian uprising in Homs. One wonders how well Bruce Cockburn's song, "If I Had a Rocket Launcher," rising to number eighty-eight on the 1984 Billboard charts, would fare in the current environment.[1] One can reasonably envisage expressions of support for

---

1 In his recent autobiography, Cockburn describes a crowd of 600 Chileans erupting in response to the song's lyric "Some son-of-a-bitch would die," in Bruce Cockburn, *Rumours of Glory: A Memoir* (Toronto: HarperOne, 2014), 262.

liberation movements in various locales running afoul of the prohibition. The more likely response is that folks will choose to remain silent – the phenomenon of the chilling effect. A democratic society should be expected to do otherwise: to allow people the courage to tell their own truths.

There also is the reasonable likelihood that the law will not even have its desired effect of silencing the promotion and advocacy of jihadi terrorism over the Internet. ISIS beheading and recruitment videos do not originate from within Canada. They are stored and available on servers offshore. The proposed law does not contemplate an effective means of policing these offshore servers unless these sites are under the control of persons resident within Canada (Zundel 2002). Nor does the proposed law contemplate preventing access to these sites in Canada. In other words, if the motivation for the proposed law is to silence jihadi speech, it will not be capable of securing its objective without the cooperation of jurisdictions that host offshore servers.

Documents released by American whistle-blower Edward Snowden reveal that Canada's communication security establishment has the capacity to engage in cyber sabotage in order to disrupt and disable Internet activities at home and abroad (CSEC 2015). These are capabilities in addition to those proposed under Bill C-51: those that enable judges to order the deletion of terrorist propaganda (including material that promotes "terrorism in general") from computer systems within the court's jurisdiction or that authorize CSIS to take measures, with or without judicial warrant, to reduce security threats "within or outside Canada." Setting aside the considerable oversight and review problems that follow upon the Snowden disclosures, if there is no apparent correlation between securing the law's objectives and the proposed offence, it hardly justifies enactment of a law having such chilling effects. Moreover, on those occasions when the law might presumably have some effect, for messages and images originating within Canada, law enforcement agencies will be denying to themselves one of the few means of identifying and tracking the sentiments of lone-wolf extremists (Benson 2014, 327–8).

Indeed, the empirical evidence to date reveals that the Internet plays a modest role in the rise of jihadism. The evidence indicates, instead, that it is "peer group leaders" who are likely to secure recruits from among family, friends, and extended social networks (Dalgaard-Nielson 2010, 807). Take, for instance, Hamaad Munshi, Britain's eighteen-year-old terrorist. He had an active online presence but was radicalized in person at the Dewsbury central mosque. It was a combination of personal recruitment together with communications over the Internet with like-minded jihadists that fuelled Munshi's extremism (ICSR 2009, 14).

Not only will the law be unlikely to secure its desired outcomes, it may undermine efforts at counter-radicalization. Forcese and Roach (2015) argue that the new "terrorism in general offence" likely will deter participation in de-radicalization strategies currently promoted by security intelligence agencies. The concern is that, for these strategies to be successful, they need to be pursued where young Muslim men are likely to congregate, namely, in mosques. Imams are expected to bring youth together to speak frankly about issues of concern to them. There is less likely to be genuinely frank, or any, talk if there is a concern that participants could run afoul of such an excessively broad law.

The new offence appears to be drafted without regard for the fact that freedom of expression is a constitutionally protected activity. In short, there are no qualifications attached to the new promotion of "terror in general" offence. This disregard of constitutionally protected freedoms is all the more striking when the offence is contrasted with the Australian law, a jurisdiction without constitutionally protected rights that appears to have inspired the Government of Canada's Bill C-51. In Australia, the advocacy of terrorism is tied specifically to advocating the commission of terrorism offences that are defined in the Australian Criminal Code. There is no legally untethered crime of "terrorism in general." Significantly, defences for the promotion of terrorism offence are included for "acts done in good faith," including pointing out mistaken beliefs, good faith errors, or seeking to remove conditions that give rise to "feelings of ill-will or hostility between different groups." Courts are directed to take into account a variety of factors when considering these defences, including whether the acts are done with a "genuine" artistic, academic, or scientific purpose, or for the purpose of "disseminating news or current affairs."

The absence of any defences – or any seeming consideration that the new offence may chill legitimate speech that a democratic society should be loath to inhibit – gives rise to more overbreadth problems. We are led to wonder, for instance, whether the Conservative fundraising effort on Facebook, which reproduced a screen shot from an Al-Shabaab video calling for violent attacks on shopping malls in various locales around the Western world, including the West Edmonton Mall, might not run afoul of the proposed law. The Conservative Party of Canada is knowingly disseminating a message that advocates the promotion of a very specific act of terrorism and are reckless about whether an act of terrorism may come about by promoting this message. Of course, we can expect no charges will be laid against the CPC. If they were, a court might draw an adverse inference that no statutory defences, such as dissemination of information concerning matters of public interest, are available. On the other hand, a court could just as well read in new defences deliberately omitted in order to salvage the law and so work around its overbreadth problems.

In that case, if the act is passed in its current form, there is no question that it will be up to the courts to clean up the mess. It is hard to predict precisely what the Supreme Court would do with this new offence. It has indicated that "threats of violence" associated with existing terrorism offences are not constitutionally protected speech (Khawaja 2012, ¶70). It would be surprising, however, if the Court were to exempt speech from section 2(b) protection that is so far removed from threats of actual violence. As well, given the Court's past response to vague and overbroad laws, it can be expected to read down the broad language and perhaps read out certain categories of speech. Whatever the case, it is a serious neglect of parliamentary duty not to anticipate these constitutional concerns and not to address them in the course of drafting and then enacting this law.

All of this raises suspicions about the motivation for the new offence and related ones in Bill C-51. It seems reasonably clear that the primary motivation for the law is not to silence jihadi speech – as mentioned, it will not reach offshore websites and is as likely to have the perverse result of stifling efforts to counter radicalization in Canada. Rather, as the Conservative Party of Canada fundraising effort reveals, this is part of a concerted effort to create winning conditions for the re-election of the Conservative government in 2015. By appealing to the basest fears and instincts of the Canadian electorate, the Conservatives are betting that voters will cast their ballots in favour of the party that takes the heaviest hand to the terrorist threat. Any political party that proposes doing less is labelled as being more concerned with protecting terrorists than Canadians.

There is a further suspicion. In the context of other recently enacted Conservative laws – for instance, Bill C-25, enacted in response to the Supreme Court's Bedford decision (2014), which prohibits the purchase of sexual services – one can see a pattern emerging, pointing to a subsidiary motivation. The Conservative government seems to be laying the groundwork for recurring invocations of the notwithstanding clause. If re-elected – that is, if the above-mentioned plan works – one can predict that the fourth Conservative government, whether a minority or majority one, will be the first to shield federal law from the Charter's application. That laws are enacted notwithstanding the Charter for five-year renewable terms, also conveniently lays the groundwork for a Conservative re-election campaign next time around.

REFERENCES

Bedford, Canada (Attorney General) v. 2013. 3 Supreme Court Reports 1101.
Benson, David. 2014. "Why the Internet Is Not Increasing Terrorism." *Security Studies* 23:293–328.
Canada, Government of. 2015. "Backgrounder: Criminalizing the Advocacy or Promotion of Terrorism Offences in General," http://news.gc.ca/web/article-en.do?nid=926049&_ga=1.92265369.2078202319.1410971187.
Dalgaard-Nielsen, Anja. 2010. "Violent Radicalization in Europe: What We Know and What We Do Not Know." *Studies in Conflict and Terrorism* 33:797–814.
Forcese, Craig, and Kent Roach. 2015. "It's Good to Talk." *National Post*, February 10, A11.
International Centre for the Study of Radicalisation and Political Violence (ICSR). 2009. *Countering Online Radicalisation: A Strategy for Action*. London: ICSR.
Khawaja, R. v. 2012. 3 Supreme Court Reports 555.
Roach, Kent. 2001. "The New Terrorism Offences and the Criminal Law." In *The Security of Freedom: Essays on Canada's Anti-Terrorism Bill*, ed. Ronald J. Daniels, Patrick Macklem, and Kent Roach, 151–72. Toronto: University of Toronto Press.
Schneiderman, David, and Brenda Cossman. 2001. "Political Association and the Anti-Terrorism Bill." In *The Security of Freedom: Essays on Canada's Anti-Terrorism Bill*, ed. Ronald J. Daniels, Patrick Macklem, and Kent Roach, 173–94. Toronto: University of Toronto Press.
Zundel, Citron, and Toronto Mayor's Committee v. 2002. CanLII 23557 (CHRT), canlii.ca/t/1g95g.

17 C-51 and the Canadian Security and Intelligence Community: Finding the Balance for Security and Rights Protections

WESLEY WARK

Canada faces a universal challenge shared by all democracies confronting national security threats. That challenge is to provide sufficient protections for both the security of the state and its inhabitants, and for civil liberties and privacy. The challenge is further enlarged through international law obligations and global collective action against borderless threats. The notion that we must balance security and rights is not a new one, and it has resounded through public debate on national security for a very long time. In recent times, Canadian society grappled with these issues in 2001, in the aftermath of the 9/11 attacks and during the passage of Canada's first anti-terrorism legislation. The security-rights conundrum has continued to command some attention ever since, especially in the context of arrests and trials with regard to terrorist plots and to the privacy impacts of Edward Snowden's leaks about global electronic surveillance conducted by the United States and its partners. Now the security-rights balance is the focus for renewed and intense scrutiny once again, in the context of a succession of recent terrorist attacks in Canada in October 2014, in Sydney, Australia, in December 2014, and in Paris in January 2015.

In the aftermath of the Canadian terror attacks of October 2014, the government began to assemble new anti-terrorism legislation, which was tabled in the House of Commons on January 30 2015 as Bill C-51. The Canadian prime minister, Stephen Harper, has argued, "To fully protect Canadians from terrorism in response to evolving threats, we must take further action ... as the terrorists refine and adapt their methods, our police and national security agencies need additional tools and greater coordination."[1]

In considering the construction of a current balance between security and civil liberties protections, we need to keep in mind two things. One is that the Canadian security and intelligence community has been radically transformed since the 9/11 attacks. The other is that Canadian national security legislation has been put on a strong foundation through previous parliamentary debate, through subsequent legislative enactments after 2001, and through the adversarial process of Charter of Rights challenges and trial proceedings in terrorism cases.

It is also important to understand that while we have the tools to be appreciative, even on occasion hyper-vigilant, about our civil liberties and privacy protections, the same cannot be said for the other side of the equation – figuring out the nature of security threats and what might comprise reasonable and proportional responses to them. There are real-world limits to our understanding of a fast-changing terrorism threat environment, and how we might appropriately respond through the capacities of our intelligence and security agencies. We also lack a framework for democratic expectations of national security agencies.

Understanding the role of Canadian security and intelligence agencies in responding to threats is made challenging by two phenomena – the entrenched problem of high levels of official secrecy, and the unacknowledged scale of the transformation of the intelligence sector in the years after 2001. The Canadian security and intelligence system is now much more fully resourced, more capable, more globally engaged, and more important to decision-making than was the case prior to the 9/11 attacks. With greater power have come greater challenges to its management, greater challenges in potential abuses of power, and greater public expectations of transparency.

Our ability to assess what the prime minister described as the need for additional tools and greater coordination for a "mature" security and intelligence system would have benefited from three things. One would have been an update to the government's counterterrorism strategy, which was last released in August 2014, prior to the recent wave of global terror attacks. A second would have been the availabil-

---

1 "PM Announces Anti-Terrorism Measures to Protect Canadians," text of speech delivered in Richmond Hill, Ontario, January 30, 2015, http://pm.gc.ca/eng/news/2015/01/30/pm-announces-anti-terrorism-measures-protect-canadians-O.

ity of any inquiry report into the terror attacks in Ottawa and Quebec in October 2014, so as to be able to better assess any shortcomings in operational, intelligence, or lawful powers that affected these first successful terrorist attacks on Canadian soil since 9/11. The third thing would have been the publication of more detailed explanations for the development and rationale for the various elements of Bill C-51. We are left instead with generalities.

The generalities problem is not restricted to the rationale for the bill itself. It also extends to an understanding of the new threat environment. There can be no question that the nature of terrorism threats is evolving rapidly, and that we are now in a post–Al Qaeda age. The debate on C-51 tends to pay lip service to this reality.[2] We face serious threats to international security from jihadist terrorist groups, such as ISIL and Boko Haram, engaged in sustained insurgency campaigns abroad to seize territory and acquire the resources and capabilities of a state. We face threats from jihadist terrorists inspired and mobilized by cyber communications to engage in attacks at home. There can be no more chilling expression of this threat than the video exhortation delivered by the ISIL media lieutenant, Abu Muhammad al-Adnani, in September 2014, which urged jihadist supporters of the so-called Islamic State: "Do not let this battle pass you by wherever you may be. You must strike the soldiers, patrons, and troops ... Strike their police, security, and intelligence members, as well as their treacherous agents. Destroy their beds. Embitter their lives for them and busy them with themselves. If you can kill a disbelieving American or European, especially the spiteful and filthy French, or an Australian, or a Canadian, or any other disbeliever from the disbelievers waging war, including the citizens of the counties entered into a coalition against the Islamic State, then rely upon Allah and kill him in any manner or way, however it may be."[3]

The overseas threat posed by jihadist groups attempting to seize and build states and the domestic threat posed by individual terrorists are not completely distinguishable; they threaten to fuse. We face threats

---

2 For example, the "Open Letter to Members of Parliament on Bill C-51," organized by the Nathanson Centre at York University, simply states that the signatories are "not dismissive of the real threats to Canadians' security that government and Parliament have a duty to protect."

3 Helen Davidson, "ISIS Instructs Followers to Kill Australians and Other 'Disbelievers,'" *Guardian*, September 23, 2014, with excerpt from the al-Adnani video message.

posed by the literal and figurative bridge between overseas jihadist insurgencies and home-grown attacks, in the form of the foreign fighter problem.

The three broad strands of the current terrorist threat suggest the nature of the necessary responses. One is to find ways to prevent jihadist terror groups from seizing territory and becoming state-like. A second is to find ways to diminish the capacity for cyber recruitment and incitement of domestic jihadist terrorism. A third is to dismantle the bridge that connects domestic and overseas jihadist campaigns by stopping the flow of foreign fighters.

The Canadian legislative response to the terrorist threat clearly attempts to speak to the second and third imperatives. It contains measures to deal with cyber recruitment and incitement, and measures to deal with the foreign fighter phenomenon, layered on top of existing legislative powers. Bill C-51 does not address the international challenge of jihadist insurgency campaigns abroad directly. It is domestically focused, and operationally focused on tactical as opposed to strategic capabilities.

To measure Bill C-51's supposed security enhancements against our understanding of the current terrorist threat is a starting point for assessing how a security-rights balance might be achieved. From this perspective, we can position the new powers proposed in Canadian legislation into two categories:

1. Enhanced powers to deal with jihadist terrorist cyber recruitment and incitement
2. Enhanced powers to deal with the foreign fighter problem

Enhanced powers to deal with cyber recruitment and incitement include Criminal Code amendments to allow for seizure of terrorist propaganda and dismantlement of web-based sites, a new criminal sanction against promoting and advocating terrorism, an extended reach for peace bonds and preventive arrest, and possibly proposed new powers for the Canadian Security Intelligence Service (CSIS) to engage in "disruption."

Enhanced powers to deal with the foreign fighter problem would include all of the above measures, as well as changes to Canada's "no-fly" list, officially known as the Passenger Protect Program.

In the background, not designed specifically to deal with either the cyber recruitment or foreign fighter problems, but presumably meant to facilitate both elements of counterterrorism, are the provisions in the bill for a new information-sharing regime.

Among these measures, a reasonable case can be made that security enhancement would follow from improvements to the no-fly list, including a new definition of the construction of the list itself to encompass those who might engage in threats to transportation security and those who might attempt to use air travel to engage in terrorism abroad. The no-fly list would thus supplement existing powers to arrest and charge persons who attempt to travel abroad to commit terrorism, and executive powers to refuse or cancel passports. Equally a case could be made for security enhancements that might follow from the extension of the provisions for peace bonds and preventive arrest. Seizure of terrorist propaganda and the dismantling under court order of jihadist websites based in Canada are likely of limited efficacy and should be focused on the greater dangers posed by website propaganda.

An enhanced information-sharing regime is also a reasonable method for security change but is imperilled in the current legislation by a bad construct that overburdens the system and under-protects privacy and rights. This part of the legislation could be saved by a tightening of the baseline definition of threats, greater transparency reporting, mandated engagement by the privacy commissioner, and a strengthening of provisions for use of caveats and respect for the principle known as "originator control" of information.

Measures that do not clearly enhance security capabilities include new sanctions against promoting and advocating terrorism, and CSIS disruption powers. With regard to the former, the operational burdens of sweeping up speech offences, compared to the likely security benefit, strike me as too high. With regard to CSIS disruption powers, disruption or threat diminishment powers are a necessity and are already practised by Canadian security and intelligence agencies, but the domestic lead should be left to the RCMP. It is important that CSIS stick to its mandate – challenging enough – as an agency charged with collecting and assessing information about threats to the security of Canada, and advising government. What CSIS requires domestically, as the Security Intelligence Review Committee argued in its 2009–10 annual report, is proper ministerial accountability and strong internal policies and controls around threat diminishment.[4]

---

4 Security Intelligence Review Committee, *Annual Report 2009–2010*, "SIRC Review: CSIS's Use of Disruption to Counter National Security Threat."

With regard to overseas operations, there may be a stronger case for a lead CSIS role, and clarification of its legal mandate, not least as its operational footprint is expanding abroad and as other Canadian agencies such as the RCMP would have only a small overseas reach. But even in overseas threat diminishment operations, perhaps targeted at Canadians engaged in the foreign fighter pipeline, or involved in facilitation, or engaged in jihadist propaganda, the CSIS mandate needs to be more narrowly defined, and such operations should not be allowed to distort CSIS's intelligence-focused mandate.

Measures that pass muster as potentially enhancing security still require scrutiny of their impact on rights protections, including privacy rights. In my view, none of the measures that promise security enhancements in Bill C-51 need involve negative impacts on rights and privacy protections. They have the power to do so only if improperly framed. Here there is clearly a role for a parliamentary process that seeks to improve national security legislation through amendments, with the goal of ensuring that the best form of legislation emerges, one that might secure a social consensus. But in the context of an election year with political passions running high, such a high-minded parliamentary role may be out of reach.

If an un-amended Bill C-51 ultimately passes, the results will not be disastrous for Canadian democracy. The reasons are to be found in the overall maturity of our intelligence and security system, in the maturity of our national security legislation, on which this bill will be layered, and in the fortunes of electoral politics. National security issues, most importantly the security-rights balance, have now been raised to a position of political prominence, and so long as terrorism threats remain persistent, may stay there for Election 2015 and beyond.

Bill C-51, touted as omnibus anti-terrorism legislation and as a major response to a changing threat environment, is also, strangely, narrowly focused and tactical. Despite elements that might enhance security, and despite all its more negative features, it may be less than meets the eye. It is not genuinely adaptive, as betrayed by its many missing elements, and it lacks any underlying strategic vision of how a democracy should use its security and intelligence system to meet threats, from terrorism or other sources.

The missing elements in the Canadian legislative response to the new terrorism threat are many and include the lack of measures to strengthen the accountability regime for security and intelligence to match greatly expanded powers; the obdurate refusal to increase federal transparency on national security matters in the face of heightened public expectations; the secret "elephant" in the room that is the Communications Security Establishment, with its impressive technological powers to intercept communications, its established counterterrorism mission, and its creaky enabling legislation, dating back to 2001 and untouched by Bill C-51; the lack of attention to improving Canadian threat-assessment capabilities; and the divorcing of new powers from new resources. The security-rights balance is engaged by all of these elements, especially in strengthened accountability and increased transparency. Of all of these missing elements in Bill C-51, only accountability questions have really engaged our attention, on the legitimate assumption that strengthened accountability might help rescue the security-rights balance. As the collective open letter on Bill C-51 by four former prime ministers put it, "A strong and robust accountability regime mitigates the risk of abuse, stops abuse when it is detected, and provides a mechanism for remedying abuses that have taken place."[5] As for the other missing elements, they have remained invisible in the public debate. But accountability cannot function without reasonable transparency; the significant role played by CSE has to be acknowledged and better legislated; collection of tactical information and intelligence is of little or no value without strong capabilities for strategic threat assessment; and intelligence, despite historic Canadian tendencies in this direction going back to the dawn of the Cold War, cannot be done on the cheap if it is to be done well.

As we deal with a more complex threat environment blending state-actor and non-state-actor threats, and threats that have no nexus with either but encompass such things as climate change impacts and pandemics, we will increasingly require a strategic "social contract" on the democratic conduct of security and intelligence power. Such a social contract should be an expression of the security-rights balance that transcends individual pieces of legislation. It may be too much to expect signs of such a social contract in a politically contested bill such as C-51. But what might such a contract look like? In essence it would borrow from the long-established doctrine of "just war" to furbish a doctrine of ethical "just intelligence." Relating an ethical doctrine of just intelligence to legislation is easy. As Sir David Omand has said,

---

5 Jean Chrétien, Joe Clark, Paul Martin, John Turner, and other signatories, "A Close Eye on Security Makes Canadians Safer," to the *Globe and Mail*, February 19, 2015.

"Primary legislation should set down limits on what the intelligence machine can be used for, to remove fears that the power of modern intelligence methods will become ubiquitous and thus seriously erode individual liberty."[6] The key components of a "just intelligence" doctrine include just cause (determining the right priorities for the deployment of security and intelligence powers); right authority (having the proper command and control systems in place and ensuring lawfulness); proportionality of methods (using security and intelligence powers in ways appropriate to the seriousness of the threat and the harm to human security); and reasonable prospect of success (including a calculation of the benefits and costs of deploying security and intelligence powers). A more controversial transfer from just war doctrine might be the requirement of "last resort" use. While this makes eminent sense for a classic doctrine of war prevention and limitation, it may make less or little sense for an age of complex threats where intelligence can be both a knowledge and preventive tool.

The more we are exposed to reactive national security legislation, the more we are exposed to a fast-changing world of threats, the more important it will become to have an anchoring doctrine for the use of intelligence powers in a democracy.

---

6 David Omand, *Securing the State* (London: C. Hurst, 2010), 286.

18 Freedom and Security: The Gordian Knot for Democracies

HUGH SEGAL

Perspective

While it may well appear that the end of the Cold War and the concurrent bipolar world has bred a series of new asymmetric, non-state-actor threats to global security, embracing this appearance too fully may well deny some pre-1990 hard facts, as would, by the way, any association of the asymmetric non-state-actor menace exclusively with extreme Islamic violent jihads.

One need only list entities like Spain, Corsica, Northern and Southern Ireland, Indonesia, Malaysia, the pre-1948 British Palestinian protectorate, various South and Central America insurgencies, or India before 1948 to assemble a generous list of places where civilian security was seriously threatened by armed non-state actors intent on using violence to advance political or denominational goals. This meets the present determination of what constitutes "terrorism" under the terms of the Anti-Terrorism law legislated under the Chrétien government after the 9/11 attacks. The notion that the terrorist threat or phenomenon is new is without foundation.

When, over forty-five years ago, the Trudeau government initiated the War Measures Act, sending troops into the streets of Quebec cities and Ottawa, suspending the de facto Bill of Rights, and arresting, without charge, hundreds of Quebecers in the middle of the night, we saw a massive overreaction and dilution of freedom. This far oversteps the nature of even a worst-case interpretation of what present, proposed anti-terrorist legislation might cause to transpire.

It is in that context, and with appreciation of the ultra vires provisions of the post-9/11 Chrétien laws, which were amended by a Senate committee on which I sat from 2005 to 2012, that the debate over present measures in Parliament, the Senate, and, in a very short time, the courts, should be engaged. To ignore the recent post-war history is to weaken any intellectually coherent context for the present debate.

Critical Balancing

The tendency of post–Second World War Canadian governments to re-frame the search for the right balance between security and freedom is consistent without regard to which of the two major political parties are in government. The general tendency of the security agencies, the bureaucracy, or the Privy Council Office and Prime Minister's Office to limit any parliamentary role in the pursuit for the right "balance du jour" is also quite consistent. This tendency, both to search for new balances and constrain who is actually part of the search, comes, in my view, from some devastatingly strong historic tendencies at both the agency and bureaucratic level.

The "Need to Know Exclusionary Cultures"

This is endemic to many intelligence, surveillance, military, or police operating units and reflects the "knowledge is power" bias of most hierarchies, equating the internal fidelity of a closed circle with the ultimate efficacy of the agency or an operation engaged or underway.

Points of access to the "need to know" circle were usually defined by who reported to whom, or who had vital technical data essential to the operation. Also, who does or does not provide the money and authorization and who takes the rap for failure are both serious parts of this exclusionary, if on occasion necessary, operational bias.

Who Can Be Trusted

Within any military, intelligence, police, or criminal intelligence force, however high and compelling the prevailing ethical standards, distrust of elected politicians and aides and advisors close to them is endemic. Concluding that "the less 'they' know about operations, risks, strategies, tactics, threats, or detailed deployments, the better it would be" is the normative stance. This is not a deep-seated contempt in any subversive or disloyal sense. It is usually a sadly self-reverential view that some political actor will leak, or will be unable to manage or cope with the truth, or that some of the political clan will want to meddle without the skill or expertise to do so constructively. This last part about expertise becomes a self-fulfilling defining exclusion that continues to imperil any constructive accountability for our national security services.

The Executive vs Legislative Branch

In the United States the clear division between the Executive Branch and the legislative-congressional (and funding branch) makes some legislative oversight essential to the funding of security, military, or clandestine activities. In the United Kingdom or Canada, the blending of ministers in Parliament makes that requirement, at least for funding purposes, not that clear. A majority parliamentary government from which ministers responsible for security matters would come, essentially controls the funding rates required through their majority in Parliament and on committees. Hence, funding and oversight are not necessarily joined up.

As well, as all funding is approved (albeit in a pro forma way when there is a majority government) by Parliament, its two Houses and committees and ministers are subject to questioning in the House, and some modest, narrow, and resource-limited extra-parliamentary oversight does exist, a plausible (if shallow) case that oversight is present can be, and has been, made.

The problem here is that with this stance, Canada is at odds with the balanced oversight apparatus of its major NATO allies, including the Westminster Parliament. This also suggests that the regular in-camera statutory and legislative oversight faced by MI6, CIA, DSA, the NSA, MI5, and others in the anglophone world does not exist for Canadian national security operations. It means that elected Canadian legislators, unless ministers, are essentially out of the loop, lacking and having no way to acquire the expertise and facility necessary to conduct competent, diligent, and discrete legislative oversight on behalf of Canadian taxpayers.

Practices in Other Countries[1]

To put intelligence practices in Canada, my focus in the following sec-

---

1 Gabriel Reznick, "Looking Ahead: Creating a Legislative Oversight Committee on National Security," research paper for the Special Committee on Anti-Terrorism, 2011.

tion, into context, it is helpful to review practices in other Western countries.

In the *United Kingdom*, the Intelligence and Security Committee (ISC) was, at its inception a quarter century ago, made of nine members drawn from both the House of Commons and the House of Lords. This committee is not like a regular parliamentary select committee because it reports directly to the prime minister and then he or she reports to Parliament, as opposed to reporting directly to Parliament. The ISC meets once a week and is tasked to "examine the expenditure, administration and policy of the main three intelligence agencies." Under the Official Secrets Act 1989, ISC is given access to classified materials.

Germany's intelligence agencies have a long history dating back to the 1950s when the first intelligence agency was created in West Germany. The Bundesnachrichtendienst (1956), the Militärischer Abschirmdienst (1956), and the Bundesamt für Verfassungsschutz (1950) make up the German intelligence community. All of these intelligence agencies are overseen by three intelligence oversight committees. The Confidential Committee currently comprises ten members of the Budget Committee, who are legally bound to secrecy. The main purpose of this committee is to establish the budget for the intelligence agencies.

Italy has two main intelligence agencies: Agenzia Informazioni e Sicurezza Interna (AISI) and Agenzia Informazioni e Sicurezza Esterna (AISE), which have been under the direct control of the prime minister since 2007. AISI gathers intelligence within the border, and AISE gathers intelligence outside the border. In order to oversee these agencies, the Parliamentary Committee for the Security of the Republic (COPASIR) was created.

French parliament passed a law in 2007 establishing a parliamentary oversight committee for security/intelligence, the Délégation parlementaire au renseignement (DPR), which oversees the General Directorate for External Security, as well as a few other intelligence agencies. The purpose of the DRP is to allow members of the national assembly and senators to follow the general activity of intelligence agencies. The committee is made up of eight members of the senate and national assembly.

In the *United States*, intelligence agencies, especially the CIA, play a very significant role in government. In order to oversee these powerful intelligence agencies, the U.S. government created the House Permanent Select Committee on Intelligence as well as the Senate Select Committee on Intelligence. There are three subcommittees of the HPSCOI:

the Subcommittee on Oversight, the Subcommittee on Technical and Tactical Intelligence, and the Subcommittee on Terrorism.

Australia's six main intelligence agencies are the Australian Security Intelligence Organization, the Australian Secret Intelligence Service, the Defence Intelligence Organization, the Defence Signals Directorate, the Defence Imagery and Geospatial Organization, and the Office of National Assessments. In order to oversee these organizations, the Parliamentary Joint Committee on Intelligence and Security (PJCIS) was created in 2002. According to section 29 of the Intelligence Services Act, 2001, there are two main activities that the PJCIS is tasked with: conducting a Review of the Administration and Expenditure of the Australian Intelligence Community and preparing an Annual Report of Committee Activities for the Parliament. PJCIS may review any matter that relates to the Australian intelligence community if they are requested to do so by the Parliament or the Executive.

The Expertise/Discretion Construct: Contrasting the U.K. and Canadian Models

The U.K. Intelligence and Security Committee, the model upon which the Special Senate Committee on Anti-Terrorism framed its parliamentary oversight recommendations, is a joint committee of the Commons and the Lords. Its members were not only elected MPs with prior expertise as home secretary, defence secretary, foreign secretary, and similar posts in prior governments, but also appointed peers who had been Cabinet Office permanent secretaries, chief of the defence staff, etc. It has operated for over twenty years without a leak. It is made up only of parliamentarians, has a separate set of offices away from Westminster, and a separate staff. Over two decades, the prior expertise of many of its members, as well as the acquired expertise from meeting with senior security agency heads and staff have increased the committee's activity and impact. There is no similar capacity in Canada at the legislative level.

The Security and Intelligence Review Committee (SIRC) is appointed (with consultation) by the government. Its membership, while usually worthy, brings no particular security oversight expertise. It is part-time, has a small staff, and is retroactively complaint driven. The U.K. committee is a weekly meeting of experienced legislators with expertise looking prospectively and retroactively at security agency plans, budgets, strategies, and operations. The notion that, even for purposes of accountability, parliamentarians with expertise sufficient to provide competent oversight is, of course, quite self-fulfilling in an analysis and prophecy. Part of the awkward and, on occasion, dysfunctional relationship between security services (RCMP, CSIS, CSEC, military intelligence, etc.) and Parliament is advanced by this expertise cul-de-sac. For a complex, modern parliamentary democracy to be caught in this sort of roundabout is, to be kind, highly problematic.

For all of the above reasons, the Special Senate Committee on Anti-Terrorism made the following recommendation in its 2011 report entitled *Security, Freedom, and the Complex Terrorist Threat: Positive Steps Ahead.*

(16) That, consistent with the practices in the United Kingdom, Australia, France, the Netherlands, and the United States, the federal government constitute, through legislation, a committee composed of members from both chambers of Parliament, to execute Parliamentary oversight over the expenditures, administration and policy of federal departments and agencies in relation to national security, in order to ensure that they are effectively serving national security interests, are respecting the Canadian Charter of Rights and Freedoms, and are fiscally responsible and properly organized and managed.

The proposed committee of Parliamentarians shall have the same right to access information as the Security Intelligence Review Committee. Members of the Committee shall be appointed by the Governor in Council, and will hold office during periods of prorogation. Meetings of the Committee shall be held in camera whenever the Chair, a majority of members present or the Minister considers it necessary for the Committee to do so. Members of the Committee shall be required to swear an oath of secrecy similar to that found in the schedule to the Canadian Security Intelligence Service Act or to the Oath of a Privy Councillor, or both, and be permanently and statutorily bound to secrecy for purposes of application of the Security of Information Act. The Committee shall report to the Prime Minister, who would make that report public within 60 days of receipt. When matters in the report need to be removed for national security reasons, the report, when made public, must indicate that this has transpired.[2]

---

2 Chap. 3, 5.

The Courts and the Charter

When, in 2011, the Special Senate Committee on Anti-Terrorism (in the same report referenced above) recommended that CSIS be given the capacity by statute to "lawfully disrupt" terrorists and terrorist activity (including conspiracy to commit terrorist acts), it did so on the basis of the recommendation of the Major Inquiry into the Air India Terrorist bombing. Mr Justice Major found unacceptable delays in the transmissions of sensitive surveillance information between CSIS and the police and less than rapid execution of appropriate police action once the information was received. Hundreds died as a result.

The use of the adjective "lawful" was both very explicit and purposeful. It was anticipated that the Charter of Rights and Freedoms would apply with all the interdictions and implications appropriately associated therewith. There are many ways to "lawfully disrupt" a potential conspiracy – as by chatting with parents or teachers – in a fashion that contributed to the famous "Toronto Eighteen" being only eighteen.

After 9/11, when the Chrétien government brought in its anti-terrorism laws, senior officials received representations regarding the potential and value of using the "notwithstanding clause" in our present constitution for the new anti-terror law. The notion advanced was "this would signal to the country that this law is extraordinary and not permanent, it would automatically expire etc." The official response was that there was an expiry/sunset clause built into the act and it was "Charter proof."

As the Special Senate Committee on Anti-Terrorism spent much of its subsequent time rewriting the anti-terror laws with significant amendments, accommodating a series of court decisions based on the Charter that had struck down key provisions and imposed more protections for privacy and rights, it was clear that the post-9/11 law was far from "Charter proof." The same may be said for the present law before Parliament. Whatever its final form, legal challenges will inevitably follow, and some will in all likelihood be successful.

Conclusion

The critical bias about "need to know" and "who can be trusted" runs deep and hard within the upper and middle echelons of Canada's security services. It is encouraged and fertilized by the usual predisposition in the PCO and PMO du jour. A new government, regardless of pre-election commitments, would most likely fall prey to the same preju-dices. And until and unless we have a legislative oversight role, man-dated by law and made up of parliamentarians who will, over time, acquire expertise and demonstrate due discretion, the existing biases will carry the day.

While Charter of Rights judicial victories, and the general respect for the law by the able men and women in our security services, will moderate undue excess, there will be no structural impact either in pro-phylactic influence or protection from impunity as part of our national security parliamentary framework without statutory parliamentary oversight.

19 Anti-Terrorism's Privacy Sleight-of-Hand: Bill C-51 and the Erosion of Privacy

LISA M. AUSTIN

Introduction[1]

One of the components of Bill C-51, the federal government's proposed anti-terrorism legislation, is the Security of Canada Information Sharing Act (SCISA). SCISA would facilitate information sharing between government institutions. In its backgrounder on SCISA, the Canadian government claims two things: that this legislation responds to the Air India Inquiry, and the fact that the Privacy Act continues to apply to government information sharing ensures the appropriate balance between privacy and national security. Neither claim withstands critical scrutiny. SCISA facilitates broad information sharing that goes far beyond the kind of coordinated investigations the Air India Inquiry called for and does so while ignoring important recommendations of both the Air India Inquiry and the Arar Commission. There is no privacy protection on offer for this broad sharing. The Privacy Act has always offered weak privacy protection in the context of national security and law enforcement, and SCISA further and rather dramatically undermines that protection. It does so in disregard of the constitutional framework for privacy protection.

Although the lack of effective oversight is, for many, one of the chief defects of C-51 as a whole, the lack of substantive privacy protection is a more serious defect with respect to SCISA. Without such substantive

1 I would like to thank Edward Iacobucci, Christopher Prince, Denise Reaume, Arthur Ripstein, Kent Roach, David Schneiderman, and Martha Shaffer for their very helpful comments on an earlier draft. All errors remain mine.

protection, better oversight risks achieving little but the official confirmation of the erosion of privacy. SCISA cannot be saved through tinkering, either with its provisions or by addressing oversight more generally. The government has not offered a public justification for SCISA that withstands public scrutiny, and its statements regarding privacy mislead. SCISA should be scrapped, and the government should instead *actually* implement the recommendations of the Air India Inquiry as well as those of the Arar Commission.

Collecting Haystacks

SCISA authorizes any government institution to share information with one of seventeen recipient institutions where that information is "relevant" to the recipient's responsibilities "in respect of activities that undermine the security of Canada" (section 5). Three aspects of this are crucial: first, this is not about information sharing *between* institutions with national security responsibilities; second, the understanding of national security here is extremely broad; and third, allowing sharing when information is "relevant" sets a very low standard and enables bulk data collection. Put together, SCISA authorizes a "collect it all" philosophy with respect to all personal information held by the government, enabling government to build "haystacks" of personal information, to then analyse and share access to these haystacks with foreign partners (Nakashima and Warrick 2013).

The information-sharing recommendations in the Air India Inquiry Report were quite specific when compared with what is contemplated by SCISA. They did not involve all seventeen of the recipient national security institutions listed in SCISA, and they did not involve sharing by all government institutions with these recipient institutions. Justice Major recommended greater and even mandatory information sharing between CSIS and the RCMP in particular. In fact, an important recommendation was to *require* CSIS to share investigatory information with the RCMP in order to avoid turf wars between the two agencies. There is no such requirement in SCISA, or anywhere else in C-51. Justice Major also discussed information sharing between Transport Canada and the RCMP in relation to transport security clearances. In other words, all the information sharing recommendations from the Air India Inquiry concern specific and targeted sharing *between* a small subset of SCISA's recipient institutions, not the broad sharing contemplated by SCISA.

The breadth of the national security definition in SCISA is striking and goes well beyond the focus on the prosecution of terrorism offences of the Air India Inquiry. Under SCISA, an "activity that undermines the security of Canada" encompasses activities that undermine "the sovereignty, security or territorial integrity of Canada or the lives or the security of the people of Canada" (section 2). This is also much broader than the definition of "threats to the security of Canada" that constrains the scope of CSIS's authority to collect intelligence under the CSIS Act. SCISA's broad understanding of national security is underscored by the fact that there are seventeen recipient institutions – all thought to have some responsibility in relation to national security. There is an exception for "lawful protest" activities, although the qualifier of "lawful," in combination with the broad understanding of national security, has led many to query whether a broad range of protest activity may actually be caught rather than excluded.

The threshold for all of this information sharing is "relevance" to the recipient institution's "jurisdiction or responsibilities" in relation to national security. It is important to note that this provides a much broader scope than permission to share information that an institution suspects or believes pertains to activities that undermine national security. SCISA attenuates any direct link between the information and national security by asking merely whether the information is connected to the recipient institution's responsibilities. Moreover, it links this information to those responsibilities on the very low threshold of "relevance." To put the "relevance" threshold in perspective, it is important to note that the controversial U.S. phone metadata program, which aims to collect the phone metadata of all domestic calls in the United States, was authorized under section 215 of the Patriot Act, which allows the government to collect information "relevant" to "an authorized investigation." This is not discrete and targeted information collection but bulk collection in order to create databases that can be queried in various ways. This is what the federal privacy commissioner pointed to recently as the Big Data potential of SCISA (OPC 2015). It goes well beyond the concern that a person or group will be wrongly subjected to increased surveillance. Big Data thrives on bulk collection, and bulk collection is non-targeted, suspicion-less collection. For example, if you want to analyse who is at risk of joining ISIL, it is relevant to examine data on all people who have *not* joined ISIL.

This information sharing is further augmented by section 6 of SCISA, which indicates that SCISA is not meant to prevent the recipient institution from "further disclosing it to *any* person, for *any* purpose" (emphasis added). This would include foreign partners. While section 6 adds the qualification that sharing be "in accordance with the law," the Privacy Act permits government institutions to share information with foreign governments and their institutions under an "agreement or arrangement" with that government and does not even require that such arrangements to be in writing (section 8(2)(f)).

If we put all this together, a potentially vast amount of information held by all government institutions is quite easily available to the seventeen national security recipient institutions, and these are quite free to share this with foreign partners. None of this sharing requires that a government institution actually suspect any particular terrorist activity, even broadly construed. In other words, SCISA is about building and linking haystacks, both domestically and internationally.

Privacy Exceptions

If the Snowden revelations have shown anything, it is that the shift away from targeted surveillance towards bulk data collection remains highly controversial from the perspective of privacy and human rights. If SCISA enables bulk collection from all government institutions, then the government must show that this is necessary, likely to be effective, has a review mechanism to assess its effectiveness, and ensures that privacy or other civil liberties and human rights concerns are proportionately balanced. Unfortunately, SCISA does none of these things.

According to the government's backgrounder, because the Privacy Act continues to apply, privacy and national security will be appropriately balanced. What the government fails to acknowledge is that the Privacy Act contains both privacy protections and exceptions to those privacy protections. In the context of national security, or even more routine law enforcement, the exceptions dominate. What SCISA does is extend the scope of these exceptions. In other words, the government is not extending privacy *protection* so much as expanding *exceptions* to privacy protection. There is no "balance" here between privacy and national security – there is simply the erosion of privacy that is given the illusion of protection because most people think that if the Privacy Act applies then privacy is being protected.

How does this work?

The Privacy Act has two main purposes. First, it protects privacy through a set of rules regarding the state's collection, use, and disclosure of personal information. For example, the act requires that the collection of personal information "relates directly" to a program or activity of the government institution (section 4), that where possible the information be collected directly from individuals (section 5(1)), that individuals be told the purpose of the collection (section 5(2)), that the information be accurate (section 6(2)), that the use of the information is for the purpose for which it was obtained (section 7(a)), and that the information not be disclosed without consent unless authorized by the act (section 8(1)).

The second purpose of the Privacy Act is to provide individuals with a right of access to their personal information held by the state. The act provides individuals with a right of access to personal information held by a government institution (section 12(1)), along with the entitlement to request corrections to inaccurate information (section 12(2)(a)). This right of access is central to the scheme of the act. Both the individual complainant and the privacy commissioner can apply to the Federal Court for judicial review of a government decision to refuse access, whereas there is no such review for violations of the collection, use, and disclosure rules (sections 41 and 42).

In the national security context, few of these protective provisions apply. Indeed, the Office of the Privacy Commissioner of Canada has stated that "the antiquated nature of the *Privacy* Act renders it of little significance to the public debate on security and privacy in Canada" (OPC 2008, 7). For example, information does not need to be collected directly from an individual, with notice of the purposes of collection, where this would result in inaccurate information (section 5(3)(a)) or "defeat the purpose or prejudice the use for which information is collected" (section 5(3)(b)). Most national security activities would fit within this exception. Exceptions to the right of access include information obtained in confidence from another government (section 19), information where disclosure would be injurious to international affairs and defence (section 21), law enforcement (section 22), and information where disclosure could threaten the safety of others (section 25). Again, most national security activities would fit within these exceptions.

Use or disclosure of personal information without the consent of the individual and for a purpose other than the purpose for its original collection, is governed by the exceptions listed in section 8 of the Privacy Act. These include disclosure for a "consistent use" (section 8(2)(a)), for law enforcement purposes (section 8(2)(e)), and where the public interest in disclosure outweighs privacy interests (section 8(2)(m)).

These were all mentioned by Justice O'Connor in the Arar Commission as appropriate exceptions whose specific terms did not impose undue impediments to information sharing but ensured that privacy received at least some minimal protection. For example, the law enforcement exception requires a written request from an investigative body that "specifies the purpose and describes the information to be disclosed." If the issue is about targeted information sharing in the context of co-ordinating shared and overlapping duties, then the "consistent use" exception already suffices.

Instead of relying on these existing exceptions, SCISA effectively nullifies any use and disclosure protections offered by the Privacy Act. Section 8(2)(b) of the Privacy Act permits disclosure "for any purpose in accordance with any Act of Parliament or any regulation made thereunder that authorizes its disclosure." Section 7(b) allows for any of the section 8(2) exceptions to also apply to the use of personal information without consent. In other words, SCISA is a grant of authority that effectively allows for the use and disclosure of broadly defined national security information without any further protections. Because it does so through engaging section 8(2)(b), the government can also misleadingly claim in its backgrounder that SCISA "does not override existing legal restrictions on information sharing."

One aspect of the protective portion of the Privacy Act that remains applicable is the obligation of accuracy (section 6(2)). However, this scope of protection is limited. The obligation is engaged in the context of the *use* of information "for an administrative purpose." The act defines "administrative purpose" as "the use of that information in a decision making process that directly affects that individual" (section 3). This would not catch cases of information disclosure to other countries – the very context that the Arar Commission was concerned about. Sharing information with a foreign partner is a disclosure rather than a use, and when the disclosure is in the context of an ongoing investigation or for other intelligence purposes, it is not necessarily a "decision making process." Even in the contexts where this accuracy obligation might have some purchase, such as the granting or denying of security clearances, it is far from clear that the Office of the Privacy Commissioner is the most appropriate body to review for compliance – under the CSIS Act, it is SIRC that hears complaints regarding the denial of security clearances.

The Arar Commission pointed to the importance of caveats when sharing information with foreign states in order to prohibit the dissemination of information to third parties without originator consent. While caveats are mentioned in the guiding principles outlined in section 4 of SCISA, their use is not obligatory, and it is unclear what legal effect the guiding principles are supposed to have or how they relate to what Roach and Forcese have aptly named the "anti-caveat" language of section 6 of SCISA, which permits further sharing with any person for any purpose (Roach and Forcese 2015). As already mentioned, SCISA also does not adequately address the issue of accuracy. Instead, SCISA hides behind the Air India Inquiry, while failing to implement its actual recommendations.

Not only does SCISA eradicate the use and disclosure protections of the Privacy Act, it also disregards the constitutional framework for privacy protection. It cannot be that there is no "reasonable expectation of privacy" in the information at issue because it is somehow routine administrative data. The Supreme Court of Canada recently held that warrantless access to basic subscriber information held by telecommunications providers violated the Charter (*R v Spencer*, 2014 SCC 43). I suspect that most Canadians would think the information they provide to various government departments is more private than that. Nor can the government claim that because the government already holds this information that there is no remaining constitutionally protected interest in it. Numerous cases have affirmed the Supreme Court's statement from *R v Mills* ([1999] 3 SCR 668, ¶108), that "Privacy is not an all or nothing right. It does not follow from the fact that the Crown has possession of the records that any reasonable expectation of privacy disappears. Privacy interests in modern society include the reasonable expectation that private information will remain confidential to the persons to whom and restricted to the purposes for which it was divulged." Information collected by the state can have a residual reasonable expectation of privacy that attracts Charter protection against unreasonable uses, including uses for different purposes and without appropriate safeguards. The Supreme Court has even recently accepted that some cross-border data sharing attracts Charter scrutiny (*R v Wakeling*, 2014 SCC 72). SCISA looks as if it was drafted in deliberate disregard of all of this.

Conclusions

The Privacy Act as it stands does not offer strong privacy protection in the context of national security, and SCISA further, and rather dramatically, undermines that protection. SCISA does so while also ignoring the lessons learned from the Arar Commission regarding the need for safeguards when sharing information with foreign partners. It also does so without any attention to the Canadian constitutional framework for privacy protection. And it does all of this in the name of implementing the lessons of the Air India Inquiry when that inquiry called for none of this. This is smoke and mirrors, an exercise in "privacy sleight-of-hand" that distracts from what SCISA really accomplishes: the facilitation of bulk surveillance.

This sleight of hand is all the more puzzling when one considers that this is the same government that scrapped the long-form census in Canada out of privacy concerns. And yet the Statistics Act includes fines and jail terms for the misuse of information, whereas SCISA provides civil *immunity* for "good faith" disclosures under the act (section 9).

When addressing information sharing in the national security context, Canadians should expect their government to do two things: to follow the recommendations of the various commissions that have looked into information sharing or publicly indicate why they are not; and to respect constitutional rights. In proposing SCISA, the government does neither. There might be appropriate amendments for other parts of C-51, but SCISA should be scrapped in its entirety, as the government has not been able to articulate a coherent public reason for its introduction nor to articulate a framework for the protection of privacy.

REFERENCES

Nakashima, Ellen, and Joby Warrick. 2013. "For NSA Chief, Terrorist Threat Drives Passion to 'Collect It All.'" *Washington Post,* July 14, http://www
.washingtonpost.com/world/national-security/for-nsa-chief-terrorist-threat-drives-passion-to-collect-it-all/2013/07/14/3d26ef80-ea49–11e2-a301-ea5a8116d211_story.html.

Office of the Privacy Commissioner of Canada (OPC). 2008. "Addendum to Government Accountability for Personal Information: Reforming the Privacy Act." https://www.priv.gc.ca/information/pub/pa_ref_add_080417_e
.pdf.

– 2015. "Bill C-51, the Anti-Terrorism Act, 2015." Submission to the Standing Committee on Public Safety and National Security of the House of Commons. https://www.priv.gc.ca/parl/2015/parl_sub_150305_e.asp.

Roach, Kent, and Craig Forcese. 2015. "Bill C-51 Backgrounder #3: Sharing Information and Lost Lessons from the Maher Arar Experience." http://papers.ssrn.com/sol3/papers.cfm?abstract_id=2565886.

20 Who Knows What Evils Lurk in the Shadows?[1]

RONALD DEIBERT

Introduction

Charlie Hebdo. Ottawa. Peshawar. Westgate. Mumbai. Acts of terror such as these have become an unfortunate by-product of the hypermedia world in which we now live. Governments worldwide have responded to these incidents with a sense of urgency: new anti-terrorism laws and expanded law enforcement and intelligence capabilities.

Canada's version is now before us as Bill C-51, an omnibus crime and anti-terrorism bill that introduces two new security laws and amends fifteen existing laws, including the Criminal Code and the CSIS Act. C-51 sets out to counter not just "terrorism" but the vast undefined expanse C-51 describes as "threats to the security of Canada." The Harper government has pushed variations of these laws unsuccessfully for years. But it was the Ottawa attacks, followed quickly by those in Paris, that created a window of political opportunity prior to federal elections to throw together the package. These measures are the most sweeping change of Canadian national security laws since the 2001 terror attacks on the United States (9/11). As the law is being debated, it is important that Canadians understand the full implications.

Many stakeholders and experts have weighed in on various aspects of C-51 as the proposed legislation has touched off a vigorous public debate. I am going to focus on the role of Canada's Communications Security Establishment (CSE), our country's main signals intelligence

---

1 I am grateful to Ed Iacobucci, Christopher Parsons, Chris Prince, and John Scott Railton for comments on earlier drafts.

(SIGINT) agency and the subject of significant media coverage since June 2013, and the disclosures of former National Security Agency (NSA) contractor Edward Snowden.

As one of Canada's principal security and intelligence agencies, CSE would factor into C-51 in a substantial way. One of the most contentious parts of C-51, the Information Sharing Act, would relax rules on information sharing among at least seventeen government agencies, CSE included. As the lead agency charged with gathering intelligence from the global information infrastructure (the Internet and all Internet-connected systems), protecting Canadian networks from threats abroad, and providing "technical assistance" to Canada's other security agencies, CSE will be front and centre in the Big Data analysis opened up by C-51 and would take on an even more prominent role than it has today in our security, foreign intelligence, and law enforcement. In order to make an informed opinion, it is imperative that Canadians understand how this highly classified agency operates, what the statutory limits are to its authority, and how it will change, should C-51 pass into law.

What Is CSE?

Little is known about CSE because of secrecy. Just about everything regarding the CSE and its operations are among the most highly classified in the Canadian government. Although CSE traces its origins to the Second World War, it was not officially acknowledged as existing until 1974, when a CBC investigative news program disclosed details about the agency that led to questions in the House of Commons. Even so, public officials rarely publicly mentioned its name or acknowledged its existence before 9/11. It was only once Snowden's disclosures opened up a steady stream of media reporting about the CSE that many Canadians even heard about the agency. Even now, CSE remains a mystery to most citizens and many policymakers.

What should Canadians know? First, CSE is a very large agency with an enormous budget, which continues to grow. CSE holds the largest operational budget of all of Canada's intelligence and security agencies. Its annual budget has grown from roughly $100 million annually prior to 2001 to about $600 million today. Its new headquarters in Ottawa is enormous – roughly 89,000 square metres – and cost more than one billion dollars, leading some government insiders to refer to it as the "Taj Mahal." One reasons the new headquarters facility is so large is that it must house supercomputers and data storage equipment, and ensure a reliable stream of power and water to keep them all running and cool.

Second, CSE possesses extraordinary capabilities that have been transformed since 9/11. Part of the changes are increased financial and other resources outlined above. But the more important part of the transformation is a function of the Big Data universe in which we now live, and a corresponding philosophical change after 9/11 to collect as much of that Big Data universe as possible. Former NSA director Keith Alexander infamously summed up this approach as "collecting the entire haystack." Practically speaking, "collecting the entire haystack" translates into gathering as many data as possible from as many sources as possible of our daily digital exhaust.

Like all Western SIGINT agencies, CSE collects unimaginably vast quantities of data, as much as them legally allowed to collect (which, as I will explain below, is a *very* large window). It also has truly global reach: this is not a passive SIGINT agency scanning the horizon for stray radio signals, as we might nostalgically recall from the Cold War. CSE is engaged *across the globe,* tapping into undersea cables, insecure routers, Internet service providers, telecommunications companies, computers, and even mobile devices in dozens of countries and regions. One slide-deck from the Snowden disclosures, for example, shows that CSE operates a global data-mining operation code-named EONBLUE that collects data at "backbone Internet speeds" from "200 sensor points around the globe."

Third, part of CSE's extraordinary capabilities and global reach comes from the fact that it is part of the "Five Eyes" (FVEY) alliance and is thus closely integrated with the operations and data collection of not only the NSA, but the United Kingdom's Government Communications Headquarters (GCHQ) and the SIGINT agencies of New Zealand and Australia. The FVEY partnership goes back to the Second World War and has been increasingly integrated after 9/11. The FVEY agencies convene regularly to share tradecraft and best practices, to benefit from each other's data collection, and to improve their access to and integration of the massive databases each agency develops and maintains. In many respects, it is more accurate to conceive of CSE as part of a single FVEY machine than it is a stand-alone national agency. When CSE's analysts gather intelligence or target specific individuals or groups, they routinely access NSA and GCHQ databases as part of that exercise.

Oversight, Public Accountability, and Review

By widespread acknowledgment, Canada's signals intelligence program has the least rigorous oversight, review, and public accountability system of all FVEYs. First, there is no "independent oversight" in the proper definition of the term. CSE has no outside, independent body double-checking its operations or looking over its shoulders. Nor does it have meaningful public accountability, meaning that it does not officially report to Parliament. No security-cleared MPs can compel CSE to testify before them, and, unlike in the United States or United Kingdom, Canada has no standing committees designated to scrutinize CSE's activities or budgetary allocations. Instead, there is only a system of annual "review" undertaken by the Office of the CSE Commissioner to ensure that CSE is operating *lawfully*. That review is delivered in classified form to the minister of defence, with a redacted version delivered to Parliament. The CSE Commissioner's Office is staffed by a retired judge who is assisted by eleven employees (at the time of writing). While it may be tempting to focus on the "single retired judge" part as the questionable aspect of the setup, more important than the person, his age, or his present employment status is the structure, power, independence (or lack thereof), and culture of the review mechanism itself.

A little digging reveals some dubious characteristics. Although the commissioner emphasizes his office can review anything concerning CSE, he has admitted it does not review *everything* that CSE does to ensure compliance – only a *selection* of activities. Of that selection, commissioners have noted that records essential to determining compliance are missing or not properly recorded by the CSE. But rather than asserting that such poor record-keeping indicates non-compliance with the law, the commissioner instead shelves the issue for "further discussions" between the CSE and the himself. Even on the rare occasions when concerns about potential non-compliance have been tepidly broached, the government is given wide latitude to correct the issue – in some cases, many years. But by far the biggest problem is that the CSE commissioner does not act as a court of law or make legal determinations; instead, he only confirms that the CSE follows its own secret interpretations of secret laws. While, in theory, a retired judge can disagree with CSE's interpretation of the law, in practice he rarely does because the deck is stacked against him. As one CSE commissioner noted, "With respect to my reviews of CSE activities carried out under ministerial authorization, I note that I concluded on their lawfulness in light of the Department of Justice interpretation of the applicable legislative provisions" (Office of the Communications Security Establishment Commissioner 2006). In other words, the CSE commissioner is basing assessments of legality on the government's own interpretation of the law (see also Robinson 2015). Should it come as any surprise, then, that in all of the years the commissioner has undertaken reviews, there has been not a single finding of non-compliance with the law? This arrangement is highly convenient for CSE, of course, but terribly misleading for Canadians and the rest of the world, who are routinely assured by repeated public pronouncements from the Government of Canada that CSE is and always has been *in compliance with the law.*

And what about those secret interpretations of secret laws themselves? It is on this basis of friendly "review" that prime ministers, CSE spokespeople, and commissioners can say on the one hand that CSE is prohibited by law from spying on the communications of Canadian citizens, while on the other it routinely collects limitless amounts of metadata of those very Canadians (metadata being a record of IP addresses, phone numbers, email addresses, websites visited, timestamps and geolocation information, social media identifiers, cookies, and more). Why? Because, according to the government's own legal definition, metadata are not "private communications," and what the government is doing when it collects all of that Canadian metadata is not "targeted" or "directed at" Canadians. Never mind that according to common sense and most English dictionaries, that is precisely what they are doing. The government uses its own vocabulary according to its own legal interpretations, and the CSE commissioner affirms year in and year out they are, well, *compliant.* One feels compelled to ask, under such a setup, what else could CSE be but compliant?

Many who have commented about C-51 have noted concerns about boosting the powers and information sharing among seventeen security agencies when only three of those agencies has any type of oversight or review, and the three that do (CSE, CSIS, and RCMP) are "stovepiped" (meaning they do not share or coordinate with each other). While I share those concerns, it is also important to understand that for oversight, review, and accountability of arguably the most well-resourced and powerful of those security agencies (the CSE), we have in the CSE commissioner what is clearly a deferential, inherently limited, and thus fatally flawed "review" body. Given that C-51 will mean an expansion of CSE's activities, these flaws are deeply disturbing and a sure recipe for abuse.

The Information-Sharing Black Hole

As mentioned above, one of the more controversial aspects of C-51 is the Information Sharing Act, which would permit sharing of information among seventeen security agencies, including CSE. Under its Mandate C, CSE already provides technical assistance to domestic federal agencies when they are acting under their lawful mandate, such as possessing a warrant to collect a targeted person's or group's communications traffic. C-51 would amplify this assistance mandate in light of the broad "threats to national security" that could justify intelligence gathering by law enforcement and other security services. The other sixteen agencies will find CSE to be an irresistible source to which to turn, given its formidable collection powers and links to the FVEY resources. Should other agencies make more requests of CSE, the Establishment will likely request – and receive – more federal dollars to enhance its already enormous spying capabilities.

Even notwithstanding C-51, there are aspects of how information is acquired and shared by CSE *now* that are a mystery, and what little we do know already raises some disturbing questions.

First, even under existing law and practice, there have been concerns raised about how often, when, and how CSE provides this type of technical assistance. In one landmark case, Canadian Justice Mosley reprimanded CSIS and CSE when he discovered that a warrant he gave CSIS to seek technical assistance from CSE led to CSE tasking its FVEY allies with the job (Freeze 2013). The only problem was that neither CSIS nor CSE told Justice Mosley they would be doing that. Records obtained by the *Globe and Mail* under freedom of information requests revealed that CSE has received hundreds of such requests for technical assistance from CSIS, the RCMP, and other agencies over the years. CSE tried (unsuccessfully) to block the release, which ended up being highly redacted, leaving Canadians with only a vague sense of what type of "technical assistance" is provided and how often.

Second, CSE operates in close coordination with the other FVEY agencies, to the point of CSE analysts routinely accessing databases operated by the GCHQ and NSA, and vice versa. Whatever limitations there are on CSE's collection of Canadian communications (and recall how questionable these controls are), they do not apply to CSE's allies. As a result, should Canada share data with allies, the information about Canadian citizens could be used by our allies to target Canadians. In plain terms, such sharing could put Canadian citizens or permanent residents at bodily risk as they travel abroad and pass into our allies' sovereign territories (see the Mahar Arar case). Moreover, CSE also receives data from allied SIGINT agencies and these data might be provided to domestic authorities acting in their legal mandates; what the NSA collects about Canadians, in other words, could be provided to the RCMP, CSIS, or other agencies CSE supports. It could even mean that RCMP, CSIS, and other security agencies, through CSE's assistance, directly access databases operated by the NSA, GCHQ, and other allied SIGINT agencies. Even the CSE commissioner (not normally inclined to worries) has raised concerns about such arrangements, warning that beyond "certain general statements and assurances" between CSEC and the FVEYs, the Commissioner's Office was "unable to assess the extent" to which the four partners "follow the agreements with CSEC and protect private communications and information about Canadians in what CSEC shares with the partners" (Bronskill 2013). The review agency for CSIS – SIRC – recently raised the same sort of concerns. Clearly, information sharing among the FVEYs is extensive, but the full extent of that sharing is shrouded in secrecy, even from the review bodies themselves, and thus takes place largely without public accountability.

Third, while CSE (and other security agencies) have long operated their own eavesdropping and wiretapping equipment, today most of what they acquire comes from the private sector: the telecommunications, mobile, Internet, social media, advertising, and search engine companies that own and operate cyberspace and are the frontline sensors of our digital exhaust. Probably the most infamous of such arrangements is the PRISM program, outlined in one of the first Snowden disclosures and showing how the NSA and FBI had acquired direct access to data clouds of major U.S. Internet companies, like Google, Yahoo!, Facebook, and others. A glance through many of the CSE-related slides reveals that similar arrangements are in place for Canadian operations, though no details about specific companies are given outside of the oblique reference to a "special source" (intelligence parlance for a compliant telecommunications company). How often and under what legal authority these Canadian "special source" companies share data with security agencies is a mystery. What little evidence has emerged has been shocking. A recent confidential report undertaken by the law firm Gowlings and involving the participation of several Canadian telcos, acquired through a freedom of information act request by Ottawa Law Professor Michael Geist, estimated that Canadian security agencies request user data from telcos in the order of millions of times a year ... *all without a warrant.* Reports like these strongly suggest that a culture of informal sharing between at least some Canadian telcos and government agencies is common. Given how much data we routinely share hourly with the private sector as we go about our daily lives, these revelations should be alarming.

Before further enhancing inter-agency information sharing, we need to first clarify what information is allowed to be shared, and how, with whom, and from where, in the first place. With respect to existing CSE's practices in this respect, we are in a big black hole.

Digitally Enabled Disruption

Part of C-51 includes new proposed new powers to "disrupt" threats to national security, including preventing individuals from travelling abroad, interfering with money transfers and financing, disrupting websites, manipulating and removing content on computers, and countering propaganda and social media messaging. As the lead agency with the most advanced capabilities of disruption in cyberspace, CSE would be a principal player in these disruptions. Here it is essential to grasp CSE's already formidable offensive capabilities to appreciate just what type of operations could be unleashed if such powers were exercised by CSE at the behest of domestic agencies.

SIGINT agencies like CSE typically have responsibilities that cover a broad spectrum of activities in cyberspace, from defence at one end to computer network exploitation, attack, and sabotage at the other. The offensive parts of the toolkit are easily among the most highly classified, since they routinely involve operations that can violate other countries' local laws or involve the manipulation of the normal operations of computers and devices. As the U.S.-Israeli Stuxnet on Iran's nuclear enrichment facilities demonstrated, computer network attacks like these can even bring about real physical damage to critical infrastructure.

If Canadians believe that our SIGINT agency only passively scans the digital horizon looking to vacuum up data, they are sorely mistaken. The Snowden disclosures have shown that CSE possesses an impressive arsenal of offensive weapons, and a willingness to use them. For example, an August 2014 report on the Snowden disclosures provided a detailed list of FVEY offensive capabilities that included previously classified slides from a CSE presentation on a program called "Landmark." Landmark is the codename for CSE's massive covert global botnet of thousands of compromised computers, which it calls "Operational Relay Boxes" or ORBs. Why does it need ORBs? To disguise whatever computer network exploitation and attacks CSE and its allies may be engaged in. Whose computers are compromised? Hard to say from the slides, but it appears these are the computers of whatever unwitting individuals outside of the FVEYs alliance CSE's clever hackers can manage to infiltrate and take over – in "as many non 5-Eyes countries as possible." Another Snowden disclosure shows that while the Canadian government publicly chastises China-based cyber espionage as a major threat to security, intellectual property, and a violation of international norms, CSE covertly "piggybacks" on those very same cyber espionage networks behind the backs of the Chinese operators, making their own copies of the same data exfiltrated by China. Several Snowden disclosures show that CSE has fashioned a suite of tools to infiltrate and take over mobile phones, under the codename WARRIOR PRIDE, a federated project among the FVEYs. Some of these tools were invaluable in GCHQ's hack of Belgium's main telecommunications network (a NATO ally) and are integrated into NSA data collection. As part of its collaboration with the NSA and GCHQ, CSE has helped subvert encryption standards worldwide to make the job of signals intelligence collection easier (while weakening everyone else's security), and likely hoards known computer vulnerabilities as exploits (instead of disclosing them in the public interest). Another slide deck suggests Canada is familiar with and may use a powerful technique called "QUANTUM," known to be used by NSA and GCHQ in which agents insert malicious packets into data streams at national scales, which then allow them to take effective control of any device that happens to connect to unencrypted content on the Internet.

These are just a few examples of the offensive toolkit that CSE now controls and will be available to the RCMP, CSIS, and several other Canadian security agencies as part of their legal mandate to "disrupt." Considering C-51's broad definition of "threats to national security," it seems logical to conclude that these tools will be used more frequently, against more targets, and with many unintended side effects. Such a pronounced emphasis on "offensive" measures such as this will inevitably result in an escalating arms race in cyberspace, as Russia, China, and other adversaries work to catch up, and a litany of grey market companies profit on lucrative defence contracts for computer network attack and exploitation products and services. It would mean more covert efforts to weaken the security of information systems in the interest of national security. Given Canada's long-term interest in an "open and secure cyberspace" for commerce, communications, and human rights, Canadians must deliberate about whether our goals would be better served by the promotion of norms of mutual restraint in cyberspace instead. At the very least, we should fully appreciate just what "disruption" will mean in practice.

Conclusion

Notwithstanding C-51, Canadians are long overdue for a serious discussion about the proper legal limits of powerful security agencies like CSE in the era of Big Data. Within a few short years we have fundamentally transformed our communications environment, turning our digital lives inside out and leaving a trail of highly revealing personal information around us wherever we go. Meanwhile, CSE and other signals intelligence agencies have reoriented their mission and capabilities to "collect it all" without public debate, and without any corresponding adjustment in the Cold War–era limitations that ostensibly safeguard citizens from potential abuse.

C-51 takes us in a direction that is dramatically different from the one we need to take: more covert collection and disruption against a broader range of targets at the behest of a larger number of security agencies; looser information sharing practices among a broader range of domestic and foreign intelligence agencies; less, rather than more, rigorous checks and balances, oversight, and public accountability. To be sure, societies face serious threats and need properly trained and equipped state security services to deal with them. But without proper checks and balances, we lose sight of what those services are ostensibly designed to secure in the first place. Twenty-first-century SIGINT agencies like CSE are massive electronic omnivores. They are extraordinarily powerful arms of the state. C-51 will boost CSE's capabilities, resources, and reach. Canadians need to ask themselves, is 1950s-era oversight still the right fit for a twenty-first-century signals intelligence agency?

REFERENCES

Bronskill, Jim. 2014. "CSE Commissioner Calls for Safeguards on 'Five Eyes' Info Sharing." Canadian Press, July 14, http://www.huffingtonpost .ca/2014/07/15/csec-commissioner-five-eyes_n_5585530.html.

Freeze, Colin. 2013. "CSIS Not Being Forthcoming with the Court, Judge Says." *Globe and Mail*, November 25, http://www.theglobeandmail.com/news/national/csis-not-being-forthcoming-with-court-federal-judge-says/article15599674/.

Office of the Communications Security Establishment Commissioner. 2006. "2005–2006 Annual Report," http://www.ocsec-bccst.gc.ca/ann-rpt/2005–2006/activit_e.php#5.

Robinson, Bill. 2015. "Does CSE Comply with the Law?" Lux Ex Umbra, http://luxexumbra.blogspot.ca/2015/03/does-cse-comply-with-law.html.

21 The Complex Ecology of Policing, Trust, and Community Partnerships in Counterterrorism

RON LEVI AND JANICE GROSS STEIN

Over the course of three days in early January 2015, Paris experienced the deadliest attacks in France since the Second World War, at *Charlie Hebdo*, in the southern suburb of Montrouge, and at a kosher supermarket in the twentieth arrondissement. Faced with these parallel and connected attacks, the police ordered stores closed in the classic Jewish neighbourhood of the Marais, and put nearby schools in lockdown, until they stormed both locations later that day and killed all the assailants inside.

Days later, the Obama administration announced that an international counterterrorism summit would be held in Washington the next month. There were widespread calls for new research methods, de-radicalization programs, and data-gathering techniques to prevent future terrorist attacks. At the summit, a consensus emerged that law enforcement, or everyday municipal policing, needs to partner with relevant community groups to prevent terrorism. Relying on examples of programs in U.S. cities such as Boston, Los Angeles, and Minneapolis, White House officials at the conference emphasized the benefit of community outreach to Muslim-American groups. The claim was not uncontested: in response to privacy concerns voiced by the American Civil Liberties Union, a Los Angeles Police Department Official insisted, "This has nothing to do with intelligence, it has nothing to do with surveillance, this is about developing healthier, resilient communities" (Acosta and Liptak 2015).

We argue that the importance of community information for policing should not be reduced to a notional trade-off between efficacy and privacy. Nor are formal, legally driven review mechanisms for information sharing and review likely to be the most effective way of engaging in counter-terror policing, particularly given the pressures on police, government officials, and community leaders to prevent future attacks. Instead, what is needed is a framework for information sharing that enhances a culture of legitimacy around policing by greater integration – rather than increased separation – of community and policing groups. We are already seeing evidence of this approach within France. We argue that the question of *how* to build community feedback and trust in policing across community groups should shape the analysis of how to build legitimate information-sharing approaches for counterterrorism policing.

We begin with two data points from the French context. The first is that Tunisian neighbours of the Kouachi brothers who attacked *Charlie Hebdo* had long been concerned by the cache of weapons they found in the Kouachi home in the weeks prior to these attacks – but they did not report these weapons or their concerns to the Paris police because of what one reporter called the "chasm" between the French police and the Muslim community of the Paris *banlieus* (Mackinnon 2015). Given the massive resources required to closely monitor individuals known to police as potential threats, this lack of trust between community residents and local police – a strained relationship in which charges of community treason and threats of reprisal carry particular weight – is particularly problematic for successful counterterrorism.

The second data point comes from the relationship of policing to potential victim groups. In the wake of an outpouring of concern from the French Jewish community over its safety, a provocative call by Israeli Prime Minister Benjamin Netanyahu to the Jews of France to come home to safety in Israel, and French Prime Minister Manuel Valls's impassioned plea that "if 100,000 Jews leave, France will no longer be France," and the "French Republic will be judged a failure" (Goldberg 2015), a new policing position was created. On January 12, the French Minister of the Interior Bernard Cazeneuve appointed a police prefect, who is charged with the protection of religious sites across the country (Cazeneuve 2015). The prefect's mandate is over and above the increased security vigilance and dedication of resources through the Vigipirate security system.

Often referred to in the media as prefect for the Jews of France, Patrice Latron's role appears to instead turn in great measure on building police-community trust across community groups. His mandate is to maintain regular contact, at the highest levels, with representatives of different religious groups in order to enhance the protection of community members and of religious and cultural sites. Jewish sites as well as mosques are specifically delineated in the appointment letter. Early reports suggest that this building of police-community ties may be having some positive effects on building confidence in the police.

Although these two data points may appear unique to the Parisian context, there is much to learn from them. Each draws on robust social psychological and criminological evidence to emphasize the importance of police legitimacy for achieving cooperation in investigations – a legitimacy that turns on people's assessments that law enforcement is conducted in procedurally just and respectful ways, and that law enforcement policies are enacted through consultation and coordination with their communities. Research led by Tom Tyler at Yale Law School demonstrates that when police behave in procedurally fair ways, trust persists, even when residents do not believe in the efficacy of police actions, and even when they do not believe that the problem is one that warrants serious attention. In other words, community members do not identify a trade-off between police efficacy (requiring information and cooperation) and privacy (in which police outreach is regarded as suspicious and as surveillance). Rather than a zero-sum game between efficacy and privacy, when police officers engage with community members in ways that are perceived to be fair, participatory, and even-handed, residents are more likely to regard the police as legitimate and are more likely to engage with police investigations (Tyler 2012).

When we unpack the empirical components of procedural justice, the legitimacy of criminal justice institutions turns to a significant extent on the quality of face-to-face interactions with community members. Tyler and his colleagues have identified the importance of neutrality, respect, trust, and the opportunity to have voice for institutional legitimacy. Research in New York City demonstrates that perceived fairness also explains why people cooperate with the police, including the willingness to report suspicious activity and help police to locate suspects (Tyler and Fagan 2008).

The most recent research from their team explicitly examines the impact of these same processes on counterterrorism investigations. Drawing on studies that include Muslim communities in London and New York, Tyler and his colleagues find that belief in fair and equal treatment predicts the willingness to cooperate in counterterrorism investigation, while the political views of respondents have limited impact. While there are differences between the two sites, people's willingness to cooperate with the police turns largely on their perceptions of how law enforcement policies are implemented, with weaker importance attached to community consultation and community voice in the policy-making process itself. In addition, there is also a relationship between the general belief that one ought to defer to legal authorities and the willingness to cooperate – though here too, this belief in legitimacy is predicted largely by one's interactions with law enforcement, and even then it is more relevant among Muslims in New York than in London. In contrast, perceptions of foreign policy, even when appearing to exert influence on police legitimacy, are not related directly to this willingness to cooperate with the police (Tyler, Schulhofer, and Huq 2010; Huq, Tyler, and Schulhofer 2011a, 2011b).

We anticipate that the public assessment of the quality of data collection and information sharing protocols would have some effect on the general belief that one ought to obey the law and the public's attributions of perceived fairness, and with it some effect on the willingness to cooperate. Yet this is only one part of the equation, and surveillance itself is not found to affect police legitimacy: a core issue would turn on the perceived even-handedness of these procedures with respect to minority groups (Tyler and Jackson 2013). In particular we do not know how people's perceptions of fairness are affected by Big Data, where large amounts of information are collected across the spectrum, compared to intelligence efforts that might be perceived as biased insofar as they target some minority communities rather than others. We speculate that, in the context of counterterror policing, the broad collection of data and its sharing across government agencies may raise fewer concerns for residents' assessments of the legitimacy of police institutions than would more targeted data collection efforts that run the risk of being perceived as biased.

This approach may also underlie the newest polling data from Angus Reid. A large majority of survey respondents support Bill C-51 and do not express concern about its effects on privacy. What does emerge reflects the findings of research on procedural justice: though the data suggest that a majority of surveyed Canadians are not concerned about a security/privacy trade-off, a majority of respondents continue to advocate for better operational oversight of law enforcement agencies that will have expanded counterterrorism powers. Indeed, the procedural justice research suggests that ensuring procedural fairness is important for Muslim and non-Muslim respondents alike (Angus Reid Institute 2015).

Yet something we do know is often left out of the conversation. For

Muslim respondents, these procedural justice studies uncover the normative importance of a "community voice in government policy formation," including assessments of the frequency of community meetings and the degree to which government took into account community views about how to address terrorism. This community opportunity to have a voice builds on a consistent earlier finding in the literature on procedural justice; and in the context of counterterrorism, this suggests to us the importance of a greater reliance on community voices and partnerships with community members, as the French have tried to do through the creation of the new prefect who works with Jewish and Muslim communities alike. We often neglect the integration of community voices in our conversations about oversight, which turn instead on measures to design bureaucratic, legal, or political controls. These results suggest the central importance of voice and fairness in the process of policy formation and, even more so, in implementation by law enforcement agencies. University of Chicago law professor Aziz Huq speaks of "cooperative coproduction" as a central element in legitimate and effective policy (Huq 2013). Consistent with this approach, Scotland Yard created its Muslim Contact Unit, which has for some years been working to produce greater trust and engagement with community groups.

Criminological research also suggests other potential spin-off benefits from this approach. We know that in neighbourhoods with a high degree of collective efficacy, in which there are shared expectations that community residents will intervene on behalf of the common good, we also see greater effectiveness of informal social controls, a bulwark against legal cynicism, and enhanced legitimacy of law enforcement agents. Harvard sociologist Robert Sampson (2013) has recently suggested that this community characteristic can perhaps be enabled through increased institutional integration and partnership between the police and neighbourhood organizations. Others suggest that the legitimacy of government institutions such as the police may encourage residents to invest in their communities and social ties (Tyler and Jackson 2013). In the context of counterterrorism policing, we can imagine such voice-based approaches at all stages in the process – from policy formation, to police implementation, and to a civilian-based review mechanism to monitor compliance – across affected community groups.

We are currently engaged in research that builds on criminological evidence to design effective counterterrorism policies. Building on the research results above, we suggest that the question of privacy and information oversight, so dominant in our current debate, can fruitfully be recast to appreciate the complex ecology of information, trust, and community engagement with law enforcement. We would ask instead, in light of what we know, how we can build and strengthen the legitimacy of law enforcement efforts for those communities that seek protection and fair treatment. We identify steps toward this approach in the new French prefectual mandate, which relies on information sharing and communication in an effort to build institutional trust and community-police alignment. As communities become confident that they are being treated fairly, they are more likely to believe in the legitimacy of law enforcement, and in turn to cooperate and voluntarily enhance the efficacy of counterterrorism policing.

REFERENCES

Acosta, Jim, and Kevin Liptak. 2015. "Obama to Strike Inclusive Tone in Countering Extremism Speech – CNN.com." CNN, February 19.

Angus Reid Institute. 2015. *Bill C-51: Strong Support for Proposed Anti-Terror Legislation, but Additional Oversight Wanted Too.* Vancouver: Angus Reid Institute.

Cazeneuve, Bernard, to Patrice Latron, January 12, 2015. http://www.interieur.gouv.fr/content/download/76600/563338/file/2015-01-12-lettre-demission.pdf.

Goldberg, Jeffrey. 2015. "French Prime Minister: If Jews Flee, the Republic Will Be a Failure." *Atlantic,* January 10.

Huq, Aziz Z. 2013. "The Social Production of National Security." *Cornell Law Review* 98:637–710.

Huq, Aziz Z., Tom R. Tyler, and Stephen J. Schulhofer. 2011a. "Mechanisms for Eliciting Cooperation in Counterterrorism Policing: Evidence from the United Kingdom." *Journal of Empirical Legal Studies* 8:728–61.

– 2011b. "Why Does the Public Cooperate with Law Enforcement? The Influence of the Purposes and Targets of Policing." *Psychology, Public Policy, and Law* 17:419–50.

Mackinnon, Mark. 2015. "Neighbour Says Suspects in Paris Shooting Had 'Cache of Arms.'" *Globe and Mail,* January 8.

Sampson, Robert J. 2013. *Great American City: Chicago and the Enduring Neighbourhood Effect.* Chicago: University of Chicago Press.

Tyler, Tom R. 2012. "Toughness vs Fairness: Police Policies and Practices for

Managing the Risk of Terrorism." In *Evidence-Based Counterterrorism Policy*, edited by Cynthia Lum and Leslie W. Kennedy, 353–63. New York: Springer.

Tyler, Tom R., and J. Fagan. 2008. "Why Do People Cooperate with the Police?" *Ohio Journal of Criminal Law* 6:231–75.

Tyler, Tom R., and Jonathan Jackson. 2013. "Future Challenges in the Study of Legitimacy and Criminal Justice." In *Legitimacy and Criminal Justice: An International Exploration*, edited by Justice Tankebe and Alison Liebling, 83–104. Oxford: Oxford University Press.

Tyler, Tom R., Stephen Schulhofer, and Aziz Z. Huq. 2010. "Legitimacy and Deterrence Effects in Counter-Terrorism Policing: A Study of Muslim Americans." *Law & Society Review* 44:365–402.

Postscript: The Paris Attacks as a Turning Point?

STEPHEN J. TOOPE

In organizing the conference on which this book is based, the assumption was that the attacks on *Charlie Hebdo* and a kosher supermarket marked an inflection point in the continuing struggle for security in the face of global terrorism. That assumption was immediately challenged on two fronts. First, one commentator asked why we assumed that anything had changed for the world outside Europe and North America. Perhaps it was only for Western countries that the Paris attacks meant something particular, and only because we were so caught up in an incoherent defence of "free speech." While proclaiming that we were all *Charlie,* the French state went ahead to prosecute a Muslim "comic" whose stock-in-trade is anti-Semitism. How should that be understood in societies where individual free speech is less privileged than in our own, but where the preaching of the West has been insistent in the post–UN Charter era?

Even more provocatively, another conference participant asked why the Paris attacks had drawn such attention when, comparatively, the brutal assault by Anders Breivik in Norway was so much more deadly. Breivik killed 77 people in 2011, most of them teenagers and young adults attending a Norwegian Labour Party youth camp. Although causing widespread revulsion, the gruesome events in Norway were not commonly treated as a turning point for Europe or the world. Yet Breivik was driven by open Islamophobia and a rejection of multiculturalism. Why was this attack not linked to attacks on immigrants in Europe, prompting soul-searching over a new era of right-wing violence? Or as journalist Mark Steel argued in the *Independent,* why were there no calls for Christian clerics to denounce violence, or to apologize for Breivik's actions, yet a different set of expectations seems to be in place when Muslims commit terrorist acts (Steel 2015)?

Although one must admire critical challenges to assumptions, there is good reason to treat the Paris attacks as particular, and worthy of special attention and analysis. It is important to note that in the immediate aftermath of September 11, 2001, the same debate roiled on: had "everything" changed? I was one of those who argued that it had not, that the attacks were in a continuing line of terrorist outrages that had affected many parts of the world (Toope 2002). I was wrong in my analysis – guilty of mixing what I thought should be the case with what was likely to happen. It turned out that the issue was not what al-Qa'eda's capabilities portended, but what the reactions of states around the globe would mean for human rights, for growing expectations around security, and for some states' willingness to resort to war.

It seems to me readily apparent that the Paris attacks represent an important moment in global affairs, recalling the dramatic effects of the events in September 2001, even though the scale of the Paris attacks was much smaller. First, the widespread reaction of horror and the prompting of a renewed discourse on terrorism in Western countries are undeniable. On January 11, four days after the attacks, roughly 2 million people, including more than forty world leaders, rallied in Paris to express solidarity against terrorism. Across France, an estimated 3.7 million people joined demonstrations. Vigils and demonstrations involving millions of people took place across Europe, in the United States, Australia, and here in Canada. A crowd in Trafalgar Square sang the "Marseillaise," a remarkable show for the sometimes-francophobic English. News media were fixated on the attacks for weeks, and media references to Paris are constant in discussions of terrorism associated with seemingly distinct phenomena like Islamic State and the lone-wolf attacks in Ottawa and Sydney.

A second indication of the potential influence of the events in Paris is the fear that they appear to have generated in minority communities, especially Jewish ones, across Europe. In the days after the assaults on *Charlie Hebdo* and the kosher supermarket, many reports circulated of Jews looking to emigrate from France (Connolly 2015). Similar reports surfaced in the United Kingdom, where the home secretary wrote, "I know that many Jewish people in this country are feeling vulnerable and fearful and you're saying that you're anxious for your families, for your children and yourselves. I never thought I would see the day when members of the Jewish community in the United Kingdom would say they were fearful of remaining here in the United Kingdom" (Chorley 2015). Belgian and Italian Jews expressed similar fears (Associated Press 2015).

The third set of dramatic effects associated with the Paris attacks is the renewal of national efforts to further tighten anti-terrorism regimes. Bill C-51 in Canada is a clear example, discussed in many contributions to this volume. Although the pressure to grant ever-expanding powers to security services seems to have been almost constant across the globe since September 11, 2001, the drama of the Paris attacks has heightened the rhetoric and accelerated governmental anti-terrorism initiatives. In the United Kingdom, Prime Minister Cameron has promised new anti-terror legislation that would allow the security services to monitor encrypted communications (*Guardian* 2015). Terror-inspired legislative initiatives are planned or being reinforced across Europe (Euractiv 2015), in Australia (MSN 2015), and in China (Kinetz 2015).

These legal initiatives have prompted justified fear in many Muslim communities around the world. The fact that the new laws are targeted primarily at Islamic extremism has put communities on edge, with worries that expanded governmental powers will put innocent people at risk of arrest and abuse. Attempted reassurance that we must "balance" rights and security ring hollow for people who fear that "we" will feel more secure but "they" will be more threatened in any such "balance."

In a world where media must react instantaneously to dramatic events, and where governments are required to show decisiveness, even in the face of uncertainty, the Paris attacks have prompted swift and forceful reactions – first of solidarity, but then of generalized fear and widespread legislative overreach. The tendency has been to see contemporary terrorist threats as singular phenomena that can be dealt with in isolation from historical, sociological, and cultural factors. Governments must show immediately that they are "strong," but that often means a complete neglect of social and economic context, and a failure of serious analysis.

In this volume, many contributors have demonstrated that it is not possible to understand and effectively deal with the terrorist impulse without relating it to factors beyond the simpleminded assertion that "they hate our values." In Europe, the legacies of colonialism still play out in hugely damaging ways: in patterns of immigration that do not favour economic integration; in low education levels for second-generation immigrants; in the social isolation of some ethnic communities; in repeating patterns of exclusion rooted in colonial-era attitudes of who counts as part of the citizenry; and in profound frustration at the failed promise of a better life. Even when some social and economic integration is achieved, lingering racism can prompt real anger.

None of this is to say that all terrorists are economically deprived. "Root causes" are complicated and diverse. Not all triggers are even within the influence, much less control, of local and national authorities. The increasing power of transnational terrorist organizations to use the Internet to lure adherents and to radicalize them is a serious challenge that cannot simply be wished away. This reality has led to debates over how international law should respond to cross-border terrorist recruitment, financing, and transit. Although most legal responses will take place at the national level, significant efforts are being made to coordinate and to create international regulation when needed. But as in the case of national efforts to fight terrorism, a backlash is emerging because of the difficulty international organizations like the UN have in creating a framework that ensures the protection of individual human rights in the face of socio-political demands for effective action.

A continuing debate rages over the question how reactions to the threat of terror, specifically radical Islamic terror, actually feed the phenomenon. If there is any consensus reflected in these pages, it is that the biggest threat to "our" way of life may be from the inability of Western nations carefully to calibrate responses to terrorism. But no one suggests that the calibration is easy or that it is simple to extract any shared understanding about what is to be done from the myriad voices calling for action or restraint. Part of the problem is that there is no single phenomenon to be addressed; the approaches of al-Qa'eda and Islamic State are completely different. Their shared motivation to purify Islam is expressed in ways that may require quite different responses.

In these chapters, we read powerful demands that freedom of speech be upheld, moderated by calls for civility in discourse that requires self-restraint, but not self-censorship. Deeply knowledgeable experts insist that we recognize and address the real threats that we face, but are balanced against warnings that we risk losing our own values in a thoughtless and indiscriminate pursuit of security, a security that is often false. Commentators also worry that we risk repeating the excesses of past eras, not having learned from the internment of Japanese Canadians during the Second World War, the false accusations of the McCarthyism in the 1950s, the marginalization of Aboriginal and First Nations peoples, or the torture committed in secret prisons after 9/11.

A particularly hard question is whether or not Western societies are beginning to force upon Muslims an impossible choice: to reject orthodox interpretations of the faith or risk being viewed and treated as politically, and even criminally, suspect. Inversely, we are warned that the media are shaping our thoughts perversely by casting all Muslims as orthodox, failing to recognize the pluralism of belief or the possibility of "secular" Muslims who nonetheless self-identify as part of a religiously inspired tradition. Through both an erasure of Muslim "moderates" in the media or the forcing of a choice to reject orthodoxy, are Western societies destroying the possibility of a "critical middle" in Islam itself, force-feeding greater extremism?

In Canada, the crucible for all of these pressures is the federal legislative process being employed, the government insists, to "strengthen" anti-terrorism laws. Even the writers in this volume who generally share the government's evaluation of the risk Canadians are exposed to from transnational and homegrown terrorism nonetheless worry that the legislation being contemplated is not well considered. There is virtual unanimity that the Canadian security services are not subject to appropriate civilian oversight, especially as they are accorded increasingly intrusive powers. We in Canada have strikingly less supervision of intelligence services than any of our closest information-sharing partners: the United States, the United Kingdom, Australia, and New Zealand.

Many commentators also warn that the broad and loose language in the proposed ban on speech promoting terrorism could inadvertently catch entirely innocent people. The new ability granted the judiciary to pre-authorize the "disruption" of possible terrorist threats is also widely drawn, and probably violates the Canadian Charter of Rights and Freedoms. So too the extraordinarily broad mandate given to security agencies to gain access to the data of individual Canadians from any part of government and to share it widely, even with foreign intelligence agencies. The repeated assurances that Canadians will be protected through existing privacy legislation turns out, upon examination, to be completely illusory.

All in all, the legislation that we are told will "protect" us seems to be so badly drafted, so expansive in scope, and so open to abuse that one must wonder how a responsible political leadership could bring it forward. The answer seems to be two-fold. First, it is a reaction to the attacks in Paris, Ottawa, and Sydney that may be authentic, but it is based in fear and is too quick and unreflective – just the sort of bad policy that fear often generates. Second, and less charitably, it capitalizes on a crisis to create political capital by reaffirming the "tough" credentials of a government that claims to be hard-headed in confronting all threats. Threats are real, and governments have a duty to protect citizens. But we must consider carefully the means we choose to combat those threats. Even in times of danger, not all means are acceptable in free and democratic societies. That is what it means to be free and democratic.

Roughly a month and a half after the attacks in Paris, suicide bombers attacked two mosques in Yemen. More than 130 people died. A Yemeni political analyst noted that "Yemenis knew violence, but not this brutal ... There are no norms. It's a very scary moment" (Kalfood and Fahim 2015). The bombers were Sunni, self-proclaimed followers of the Islamic State, and they attacked the Shiite mosques because they considered the worshippers to be heretics. These terrible events remind us that the primary victims of the "purifying" wars taking place throughout the Arab world are Muslims. The fundamental conflict between Sunni and Shiite extremists is almost certainly a long war, perhaps a multi-generational war, akin to the raging battles within Christianity that crossed centuries. The conflict is exacerbated by the overlay of repressive and corrupt regimes that have suppressed all dissent but are inevitably collapsing.

The abject failure of world political leaders to act in the face of massive war crimes and crimes against humanity in Syria has only heightened a sense of hypocrisy and impotence that helps in the radicalization of youth, not only in the Middle East, but in Western countries as well. In considering the news that seven young Montrealers had disappeared from their families, seemingly on the way to volunteer for the Islamic State, a young friend of theirs is quoted as saying that the seven, like so many young adults, wanted to contribute to something meaningful, bigger than themselves: "In this case, it's the chance to defend their faith from the evils of [Syrian leader] al-Assad" (Perreaux and Stevenson 2015).

Those young people from Montreal are deeply misguided and they are dangerous. And anyone who would seek to kill worshippers in a mosque or church or synagogue is worthy of condemnation and severe punishment. Yes, terrorist threats are real and they must be addressed. But collectively, the chapters in this volume remind us that our responses must be measured and balanced. We need to remember that in Western societies we have committed to the fundamental principle of equal citizenship. That does not require uniformity of belief; perhaps ironically, it requires acceptance of diverse beliefs within our shared civic framework.

Though intolerance must be resisted, that does not mean that tolerance is the highest civic virtue. Beyond tolerance, we must strive for genuine inclusion – social, cultural, and perhaps above all, economic. Without broad inclusion we create risks for our society that no security legislation, no amount of surveillance, can address. In the words of the distinguished Quebec professor Gerald Bouchard, "Unless the trend [towards alienation of minorities] is reversed, we will finish by creating ourselves what we wanted to avoid at all costs – a minority that through stereotype and discrimination gives up little by little on integration and ghettoizes itself. Do we not recognize here the rich soil that produces radicalization?"

The events in Paris are an inflection point in global affairs, if only because they present us with a moment to ask ourselves as Canadians and as global citizens how we want to respond. Are we committed to trying to erase our fears through the imposition of greater and greater constraints on our own freedoms? Are we hoping to protect ourselves by drawing fences around certain communities and treating them as dangerous outsiders to our values? Are we imagining that current military actions in Iraq and Syria will be enough to remove the dangers of those who seek religious and social purity? As citizens, we are called upon to make political choices. The horrors of Paris reveal that those choices will be hard, and the consequences of our choices will affect our lives and the lives of generations to come. The hope that flows through the often-gloomy pages of this book is that we can still pause, consider carefully, and choose wisely.

REFERENCES

Associated Press. 2015. "French Terror Attack Deepens Fears among Europe's Jews," January 12.
Chorley, Matt. 2015. "'Without Its Jews, Britain Would Not Be Britain,' Warns Theresa May over Fears of an Exodus in Wake of Anti-Semitic Attacks." *Daily Mail*, January 18.
Connolly, Kevin. 2015. "'Not Safe': French Jews Mull Israel Emigration." BBC News, January 13.
Euractiv.com. 2015. "Anti-Terrorist Measures in EU Go in All Directions,"

January 16, http://www.euractiv.com/sections/global-europe/national-anti-terrorist-measures-eu-go-all-directions-311343.

Guardian. 2015. "David Cameron Pledges Anti-Terror Law for Internet after Paris Attacks," January 12.

Kalfood, Mohammed Ali, and Kareem Fahim. 2015. "Two Suicide Bombings Strike Yemen." *Globe and Mail*, March 21.

Kinetz, Erika. 2015. "China Plays Down US Concerns over Plan for Sweeping Powers to Police Electronic Communications." Associated Press, March 3.

MSN.com. 2015. "New Australian Anti-Terror Laws Vital in Fighting Paris-Style Attacks: Brandis," January 10, http://www.msn.com/en-au/news/australia/new-australian-anti-terror-laws-vital-in-fighting-paris-style-attacks-brandis/ar-AA7Zt9w.

Perreaux, Les, and Verity Stevenson. 2015. "Quebec's Divide." *Globe and Mail*, March 21.

Steel, Mark. 2015. "Charlie Hebdo: Norway's Christians Didn't Have to Apologise for Anders Breivik, and It's the Same for Muslims Now." *Independent*, January 8.

Toope, Stephen J. 2002. "Fallout from 9-11: Will a Security Culture Undermine Human Rights?" *Saskatchewan Law Review* 6 (5): 281.

Contributors

Lisa M. Austin is an Associate Professor in the Faculty of Law at the University of Toronto.

Jutta Brunnée is Metcalf Chair in Environmental Law and a Professor in the Faculty of Law at the University of Toronto.

Simone Chambers is Director of the Centre for Ethics and a Professor in the Department of Political Science at the University of Toronto.

Ronald Deibert is Director of the Canada Centre for Global Security Studies and the Citizen Lab at the Munk School of Global Affairs at the University of Toronto.

Mohammad Fadel is an Associate Professor and Canada Research Chair in the Law and Economics of Islamic Law in the Faculty of Law at the University of Toronto.

Natasha Fatah is a Toronto based journalist and broadcaster.

Craig Forcese is an Associate Professor in the Faculty of Law at the University of Ottawa.

Randall Hansen is Director of the Centre for European, Russian, and Eurasian Studies at the Munk School of Global Affairs and Canada Research Chair in Immigration and Governance in the Department of Political Science at the University of Toronto.

Edward M. Iacobucci is Dean and James M. Tory Professor of Law in the Faculty of Law at the University of Toronto.

Anna C. Korteweg is an Associate Professor in the Department of Sociology at the University of Toronto.

Ron Levi is George Ignatieff Chair of Peace and Conflict Studies, Deputy Director of the Munk School of Global Affairs, and an Associate Professor in the Department of Sociology at the University of Toronto.

Ruth Marshall is an Associate Professor in the Department for the Study of Religion and the Department of Political Science at the University of Toronto.

Ronald W. Pruessen is Director for International Partnerships and Research at the Munk School of Global Affairs and a Professor in the Department of History at the University of Toronto.

Jeffrey G. Reitz is Director of the Ethnic, Immigration, and Pluralism Studies program at the Munk School of Global Affairs and a Professor in the Department of Sociology at the University of Toronto.

Arthur Ripstein is a Professor of Law and Philosophy at the University of Toronto.

Kent Roach is a Professor and Prichard Wilson Chair in Law and Public Policy in the Faculty of Law at the University of Toronto.

David Schneiderman is a Professor in the Faculty of Law and the Department of Political Science at the University of Toronto.

Hugh Segal is Master of Massey College and a former Senator and Chair of the Senate Committee on Anti-Terrorism.

Ayelet Shachar is Canada Research Chair in Citizenship and Multiculturalism and a Professor in the Faculty of Law at the University of Toronto.

Janice Gross Stein is Belzberg Professor of Conflict Management in the Department of Political Science and the Munk School of Global Affairs at the University of Toronto.

Brian Stewart, former senior correspondent of CBC News, is Distinguished Fellow at the Munk School of Global Affairs, University of Toronto.

Stephen J. Toope is Director of the Munk School of Global Affairs at the University of Toronto.

Mark G. Toulouse is Principal of Emmanuel College and a Professor in the Department for the Study of Religion at the University of Toronto.

Wesley Wark is a Professor Emeritus in the Munk School of Global Affairs at the University of Toronto.